The
BEGINNER'S
Guide to
REAL ESTATE
INVESTING

The BEGINNER'S Guide to REAL ESTATE INVESTING

GARY W. ELDRED, Ph.D.

WILEY

John Wiley & Sons, Inc.

Published by John Wiley & Sons, Inc., Hoboken, New Jersey.
Published simultaneously in Canada.

For general information on our other products and services, or technical support, please contact our Customer Care Department within the United States at (800) 762-2974, outside the United States at (317) 572-3993 or fax (317) 572-4002.

Wiley also publishes its books in a variety of electronic formats. Some content that appears in print may not be available in electronic books. For more information about Wiley products, visit our web site at www.Wiley.com.

Library of Congress Cataloging-in-Publication Data:

Eldred, Gary W.
    The beginner's guide to real estate investing / Gary W. Eldred.
       p. cm.
    Includes index.
    ISBN 0–471–64711–X (paper)
    1. Real estate investment. I. Title.

HD1375.E353   2004
332.63'24—dc22   2004040730

Printed in the United States of America.
10   9   8   7   6   5   4

CONTENTS

WHY THIS BOOK?

Why this book? In writing *The Beginner's Guide to Real Estate Investing*, my intent has been to cover all topics that first-time real estate investors need to know—but to do so in less depth than I've included in my previous Wiley titles.

Here you'll find discussions about credit scoring, mortgages, seller financing, negotiation, foreclosures, bargain-hunting, appraisal, valuation, creating value, cash flow analysis, property management, and dozens of other topics. In this book, you'll gain a profit-generating introduction to the complete range of knowledge you'll need to begin building wealth in real estate.

In other words, another title for this book might have been *Real Estate Investing in a Nutshell.* This book is directed toward those readers who want to sample all investment topics in one easy-to-read volume.

In contrast, for those readers and experienced investors who prefer more depth on each of the topics discussed herein, I might suggest that, you instead select from some combination of these titles: *Investing in Real Estate, 4th ed.* (with Andrew McLean), *Make Money with Fixer-Uppers and Renovations, Make Money with Small Income Properties, Make Money with Condominiums and Townhouses, The 106 Mortgage Secrets All Borrowers Must Know—but Lenders Don't Tell, The 106 Common Mistakes Homebuyers Make—and How to Avoid Them, 3rd ed.,* and *The Complete Guide to Second Homes for Vacations, Retirement, and Investment.*

Either way, whether you select this abridged volume or some combination of my other titles, you'll find that I always offer my readers the most detailed and practical guides to investing in real estate that are available. Although I am quite optimistic on your opportunities to build wealth with property, I never mislead my readers into believing that this wealth will come without knowledge, time, and effort.

It's certainly true. You can still get rich in real estate. But you must learn how to analyze properties, neighborhoods, and financial risks and rewards. And that's exactly what my books will help you learn.

I wish you good luck and good fortune.

Gary W. Eldred

The BEGINNER'S Guide to REAL ESTATE INVESTING

PART ONE

Mindset + Knowledge = Wealth

Get Started Now

In this book, I want to motivate and educate you. I want to get you started in real estate. I hope to persuade you that real estate investing can still lead you to a lifetime of wealth and personal fulfillment. No matter what financial goals you set for yourself, no matter how little cash, credit, or income you currently possess, *if you choose to,* you can still build your fortune in real estate.

> **You can still get rich in real estate.**

Just Say No to Excuses

"But wait a minute," you say. "You can't be talking to me. In my area of the country, property prices have climbed sky-high. Besides, I really don't have enough cash, credit, or time to get started. And even if I did, real estate seems too complex. I can't even balance my checkbook."

As I travel throughout the country and talk with would-be beginning investors, I repeatedly hear these types of excuses. But it may surprise you to learn that I've heard these same excuses for nearly 30 years.

Naysayers Thrive in All Times and Places

When times are good, people fret over the deals they've missed. When times are bad, these same folks claim that real estate is no longer a good investment. Either way, they always find some way to color the future bleak (see Box 1.1).

Yet, since the early 1970s I have seen all types of booms and busts. I have seen 18 percent mortgage interest rates. I've lived through the multiple turmoils of double-digit rates of inflation, the disastrous 1986 Tax Reform Act (which killed off the most profitable real estate tax shelter techniques), and the recent market of sky-high prices. Yet I (and nearly all other savvy investors) have figured out how to make money in every one of these market situations and all of the other types of markets in between.

> **You can make money in any type of market.**

Among all the lessons history teaches, none is more certain than the fact that home prices will go up. Regardless of how high you think prices are today, they will be higher 10 years from now and much, much higher 20 or 30 years into the future. Don't make the mistake of believing that "home prices have reached their peak." Before you accept the naysaying of so-called economic experts, take a quick trip through some of their faulty predictions from years gone by:

- The prices of houses seem to have reached a plateau, and there is reasonable expectancy that prices will decline. (*Time,* December 1, 1947)
- Houses cost too much for the mass market. Today's average price is around $8,000—out of reach for two-thirds of all buyers. (*Science Digest,* April 1948)
- If you have bought your house since the War . . . you have made your deal at the top of the market. . . . The days when you couldn't lose on a house purchase are no longer with us. (*House Beautiful,* November 1948)
- The goal of owning a home seems to be getting beyond the reach of more and more Americans. The typical new house today costs about $28,000. (*Business Week,* September 4, 1969)

(continued)

Box 1.1 Those Folks Who Listen to the Naysayers End Up with a Pile of Regrets

(Continued)

- ◆ Be suspicious of the "common wisdom" that tells you to "Buy now . . . because continuing inflation will force home prices and rents higher and higher." (*NEA Journal,* December 1970)
- ◆ The median price of a home today is approaching $50,000. . . . Housing experts predict that in the future price rises won't be that great. (*Nation's Business,* June 1977)
- ◆ The era of easy profits in real estate may be drawing to a close. (*Money,* January 1981)
- ◆ In California . . . for example, it is not unusual to find families of average means buying $100,000 houses. . . . I'm confident prices have passed their peak. (J. E. English and G. E. Cardiff, *The Coming Real Estate Crash,* Warner Books, 1980)
- ◆ The golden age of risk-free run-ups in home prices is gone. (*Money,* March 1985)
- ◆ If you're looking to buy, be careful. Rising home values are not a sure thing anymore. (*Miami Herald,* October 25, 1985)
- ◆ Most economists agree . . . [a home] will become little more than a roof and a tax deduction, certainly not the lucrative investment it was through much of the 1980s. (*Money,* April 1986)
- ◆ We're starting to go back to the time when you bought a home not for its potential moneymaking abilities, but rather as a nesting spot. (*Los Angeles Times,* January 31, 1993)
- ◆ Financial planners agree that houses will continue to be a poor investment. (*Kiplinger's Personal Financial Magazine,* November 1993)
- ◆ A home is where the bad investment is. (*San Francisco Examiner,* November 17, 1996)
- ◆ Your house is a roof over your head. It is not an investment. (Karen Ramsey, *Everything You Know About Money Is Wrong,* Reagan Books, 1999)
- ◆ The trends that have produced the housing boom . . . have nearly run their course. This virtually guarantees . . . plummeting home prices and mass foreclosures. . . . (John Rubino, *How to Profit from the Coming Real Estate Bust,* Rodale, 2003)

Box 1.1 *(Continued)*

Build Wealth in Any Market

You've heard it said before, "The only constant is change." And when markets change, that change creates opportunities. Here are just a few examples:

- When prices appreciate fast, you can "fix and flip" for quick profits.
- Appreciating prices also give you the tax-free benefit of cash-out refinances.
- Falling interest rates (even with stable prices) reward you with a refinance that lowers your monthly payments and increases your cash flows.
- Depressed markets provide you with an abundance of foreclosures, motivated sellers, and bargain-priced properties.
- High rates of inflation drive up market interest rates and cut down short-term demand. That's the perfect time to look for seller financing, lease options, and low-interest-rate mortgages that you can take over (assume) from the sellers.
- High rates of inflation also reduce the number of newly constructed houses because builders must pay higher construction costs and higher interest rates. Fewer housing starts clearly signals an excellent time to buy. A slowdown in new housing always foreshadows a jump in prices as growing demand outpaces new supply. (California perfectly illustrates this point—albeit low housing starts in California are now being caused by tight land-use controls, environmental protection, and restrictive growth management policies.)

These moneymaking examples merely touch upon the multitude of strategies you will discover throughout this book, but they illustrate one central message that I have advocated throughout my career and in all of my writings:

Q. When's the best time for you to invest in real estate?
A. Today.

But don't jump to the wrong conclusion. By saying "invest today," I don't mean that you can never go wrong. Rather, I mean that there's never a wrong *time* to invest if you choose the right strategy. And that's what I'm going to show you.

You Must *Believe* It to See It

Given the large rewards that most savvy real estate investors have achieved over the years, I've often wondered why most people fail to invest in real estate. After much thought and talks with hundreds of would-be investors, I've come to this conclusion: Most people simply don't believe in the future and they don't believe in themselves.

> **The time to start really is now.**

As a result, most people don't believe in their ability to actually make big money in real estate. These negative thinkers erect a wall of excuses that blocks their vision. This wall prevents them from seeing the profit potential that lies in front of them. So, will you join the ranks of the naysayers? Or will you open your mind to a promising future?

Imagine the Future

Think about your future. Imagine you're reading the real estate classified ads 10 years from today. What do these ads of tomorrow say?

Are property prices higher or lower than they are today? Are rent levels higher or lower than they are today? If you believe in the continuing growth of the United States, you must believe that just as with every past decade, today's property prices and rent levels will look cheap relative to where they will stand 10 years from now (see Table 1.1).

Reprogram Your Self-Talk

Ask yourself whether you really want to benefit from those future gains. Or would you prefer to merely watch others reap these near-certain

Table 1.1   Historical Growth in Median Home Prices

Year	Price	Year	Price
1970	$23,000	1990	$ 95,500
1975	35,300	1995	113,100
1980	62,200	2000	138,400
1985	75,500	2005	182,000 (est.)

Statistical Abstract of the United States 2003, p. 723

profits? If you do want to succeed—yet you feel blocked by excuses—
then reprogram your self-talk.

What Is Self-Talk?   In his mind-opening book, *What To Say When You
Talk to Yourself* (Pocket Books, 1986, p. 25), Shad Helmstetter writes,

> You will become what you think about most. Your success or
> failure in anything, large or small, will depend on your mental
> programming—what you accept from others, and what you
> say when you talk to yourself.

After years of study, this nationally renowned psychologist has
found that as a matter of habit, most of us swamp our optimism and
hence our motivation to change for the better with negative self-talk.
Think about your own thoughts. Do you accept the
negative as "true" or "the way things really are"? Do
you frequently focus on risks rather than opportunities? Ponder these familiar excuses that you've either said to yourself or heard others say hundreds of
times:

> **You must believe
> it to see it.**

- ◆ I can't remember names.
- ◆ It's just no use.
- ◆ No matter what I do, I just can't keep the weight off.
- ◆ I never have enough time.
- ◆ I'm just too disorganized.
- ◆ I'm no good at math.
- ◆ I'm always running late.

Now think about this: If you program yourself with these types of
negative self-descriptions, will you undertake any serious efforts to
change these or other undesirable traits and habits? Of course not! And
the same thing stands true for those beliefs (self-talk) that can block you
from getting started in real estate. Once again, think about the types of
excuses that I frequently hear:

- ◆ Prices are too high.
- ◆ I can't afford to buy.
- ◆ I missed so many good opportunities.
- ◆ I can't get financing because of my credit problems.

- It's too late to get started now. I should have invested years ago.
- Real estate will take up too much time.
- I don't want to deal with tenants, stopped-up toilets, leaky roofs, or broken furnaces.
- I don't know enough to get started—or even how to get started.
- We don't have any extra cash. We're spending more than we make.

> **Use self-talk to discover and develop your real potential.**

You may or may not identify with any of these specific excuses. But unless you discipline your self-talk far better than most people, you undoubtedly have at least a few areas where your false beliefs keep you from taking positive action.

As to real estate investing, I urge you to reprogram your negative self-talk and limiting beliefs with mind-opening questions such as these:

- What are six ways I can save more and spend less?
- Where are the best neighborhoods to find bargain-priced properties?
- How might I persuade the sellers to accept owner financing?
- Who do I know with money that I could partner with?
- How can I boost my credit score?
- How can I improve this property to enhance its value by the largest amount?

Ideally (at least concerning real estate investing), you must erase your negative self-talk tapes. Then rerecord positive self-talk. Instead of bringing yourself down with talk or beliefs that create undesirable habits, attitudes, and outcomes, focus on the behavior and belief patterns that will lead you where you want to go. Ask yourself questions that lead to opportunities and problem-solving.

Why Questions?   To solve any problem, first ask a question. Questions and the habit of asking them lead you to discover possibilities. People (usually underachievers) who merely settle for preprogrammed conclusions won't ask questions. Because they believe they already know the answers, they unwittingly overlook the choices and the possibilities the world is offering them. You must always realize that if you don't like the program you're living, you're free to switch the channel.

> **Questions help you achieve your goals.**

Lifelong Job? The *Wall Street Journal* (September 23, 2003, p. D2) published a recent survey by AARP (formerly known as the American Association of Retired Persons). The *Journal* reporter writes,

According to a new study, many American workers are planning to push their retirement age well into their 70s, or in some cases, their 80s . . . largely because of deep cracks in their nest eggs. . . . These findings quantify a significant shift in thinking that is resulting largely because of the stock market downturn and historically low interest rates on the more conservative investments. . . . The need for money was named as the primary motivation by workers who plan to stay on the job . . .

When I read the results of surveys such as this, two thoughts come to mind:

1. Why didn't more of these now-disappointed workers invest more money in real estate instead of stocks?
2. And more important, why don't they at least get started now? Starting late most assuredly beats never starting at all.

To know that most of these folks are now rushing into low-yielding certificates of deposit, annuities, and government bonds once again reinforces my message here. They're choosing low yields because they hold false beliefs about real estate investing. No rational person could possibly choose lifelong employment and meager returns on so-called safe investments such as annuities, bonds, and CDs if they really believed (and understood) the possibilities that presently exist in real estate.

> **No one needs to accept low yields.**

Two More False Beliefs In his popular book *The Four Pillars of Investing* (McGraw-Hill, 2003), William Bernstein repeats two more widely held myths of modern investing. You've heard them before. But they're false.

1. ***"No guts, no glory."*** Bernstein claims that if you want to increase your potential rewards from investing, you must learn to accept more risk. Bernstein writes, "Whether you invest in

stocks, bonds, or for that matter real estate, you are rewarded mainly for your exposure to one thing—risk."

2. *"The market is smarter than you are."* Here, Bernstein merely repeats the "efficient market" theory of modern finance. In an efficient market, all asset prices supposedly reflect their true market value. According to Bernstein, you can never find bargain-priced investments.

As they pertain to real estate, both of Bernstein's so-called pillars of investing are perfectly silly. When you invest in real estate, you gain these two profit-generating benefits:

1. *In real estate, you are not merely being rewarded for taking risk.* You are rewarded for applying your intelligence and market savvy. You are rewarded for providing a target market (tenants or buyers) a property that offers better value than competing properties.
2. *You can beat the market.* When you put into action the steps and techniques described in this book, you will discover and create opportunities that the majority of property owners (along with those naysayers who shout from the sidelines) consistently miss.

Nevertheless, these widespread false beliefs can actually work to boost your investment returns. Because financial planners and economists (who typically have no meaningful experience with real estate investing) give such faulty advice, their advice keeps investor competition for properties far below the level that would otherwise exist.

> **The false beliefs of others boost your opportunities.**

In other words, as long as most potential investors believe that to earn big returns in real estate they must take big risks, they will continue to stand on the sidelines. They will leave more opportunities for you.

Summing Up Self-Talk and False Beliefs   No doubt, today's real estate market will challenge you. But if you keep your eyes on the prize and your mind filled with possibilities, you will discover multiple ways to build real estate wealth (see Chapter 2). As the dynamic speaker, Les

> **It's possible, and it's worth it!**

Brown, says in his motivation video, *It's Possible,* the road may not be easy, but it's worth it!

Set Goals Now

What's a realistic dream? It's a goal with a deadline. To get started now, act now to reset your priorities.

Most of us squander our time and our money pursuing transient pleasures. A new car, a trip to Europe, $10 lunches, TV football weekends—we waste our precious talents and resources. As a result, we suffer long-lasting regrets. But if you do today what others won't do, tomorrow you'll be able to live in the enviable style that most people will never be able to experience.

Set goals now. Precisely what goals depend on where you are today and what you wish to achieve.

As a starting point, nearly all successful investors agree that if you truly want to build wealth, you will set these stringent goals:

1. Dramatically cut your spending and increase your cash savings.
2. Shape up your credit profile.
3. Closely read the real estate classifieds in your local paper.
4. Diligently telephone sellers and go out and look at properties.
5. Join a real estate investment club.
6. Read at least five more books on real estate within the next three months. Also read at least three books by "personal coaches" such as Tony Robbins, Wayne Dyer, Les Brown, Shad Helmstetter, and Maxwell Maltz.
7. Commit to making your first real estate investment within the next three months.

Spend Less, Save More

When Jack Holden was asked how his family got started investing in real estate, here's how he responded. "We scraped, borrowed, and leveraged from every resource we had to muster the funds we needed. . . . For seed money we cashed in saving bonds and borrowed from our insurance policies. . . . The entire family went on an austerity plan to cut back our food, travel, and entertainment expenses. Today we're thankful we made those early sacrifices." Thankful, yes, and also wealthy. Because of their disciplined spending, saving, and investing, the Holdens (an otherwise average family) built a real estate net worth of $4.7 million that includes not only their home equity of $600,000, but also a variety of rental houses and small apartment buildings.

Like most people who make big money in property, the Holdens didn't start out with cash. As Jack Holden says, his family scrimped, saved, leveraged, and borrowed every way they could.

> **Commit to building wealth before you get the money to invest.**

So what's the lesson that you can learn? To build wealth in real estate, don't wait until you get the cash or credit and then decide to invest. No! First, commit yourself to investing, then figure out how to come up with the money. You can keep "wishing and a-hoping" to invest *someday.* Or you can now decide to own property and immediately begin to shape up your finances and create a plan to invest.

Want some ideas to start your own austerity plan, raise cash, and strengthen your credit? Try these suggestions.

> **Set today's priorities according to what you want to achieve within five years.**

Never Say Budget No one likes to budget. It sounds too much like work. Instead, think priorities. Think reward. The quality of your life improves as you allocate your money according to your highest values. If you truly want to own investment real estate, put your money where it can yield the smartest returns. For example . . .

Stop Paying Rent If you don't yet own your own home, rent is probably your biggest money waster. Can you figure out how to eliminate or reduce your rent payments? Can you switch to a lower-cost apartment? Can you house-share? Can you find a house-sitting job for the next 3 to 12 months? Can you move back with your parents or stay rent-free with relatives or friends? Bank your rent money for 6 to 12 months, and for the rest of your life you need never pay rent again.

Cut Your Food Bills in Half Eliminate eating out. Brown-bag your lunches. Buy unbranded foods in bulk. Prepare your food in large quantities and freeze portions in meal-sized servings. Forget those $2 to $3 microwave lunches and dinners. Locate a remainder and closeout grocery like Save-a-Lot, Big Lots, or Drug Emporium. Or maybe you can shop the food warehouses that have opened in most cities. Food prices in discount stores sometimes run 20 to 50 percent less than big-name supermarkets. Collect and use as many coupons as you can find. When you find bargain-priced items you regularly use, buy them by the case.

Cut Your Credit Cards in Half   Credit card spending is just too easy. Put yourself on a strict diet of cash. Nothing holds back spending more than having to count out real cash. Besides, credit card bills will zap strength from your borrowing power. Even worse, by the time you've finished paying off your credit card balances at 18 percent interest, you will pay back $2 for every dollar you originally charged—and that's in after-tax, take-home dollars. Once you consider that you only take home 60 to 80 percent of what you earn, you'll see that you may have to earn $3 to pay back each dollar you charge to your credit cards.

> Credit card spending kills wealth building.

Don't Put the Car Before the Investment Property   If you own a car that's worth nearly as much as a down payment on an investment property, sell that car. Get rid of those big cash-draining car payments. If your car is mostly paid for, there's a good part of the money you need to move up to investment property. If you're thinking about buying a more expensive car, stop! Until you can afford to pay cash for a new car, drive the least expensive, dependable pre-owned car you can find. For too many Americans, their car is the enemy of their investment program.

Buy Your Clothes in Thrift Shops   In her newspaper column, *Dress for Less,* Candy Barrie writes, "I'm a big fan of these [consignment and thrift] shops for the fashion bargains you can find there. . . . Get on down and you'll discover we're not just talking about 20, 30, or 40 percent discounts. Sometimes you can get your clothes for 90 to 95 percent off retail."

You can save thousands on clothing expenses. Just follow Candy's advice: Check all the recycled, discount, and closeout clothing stores in your area (or a nearby big city). Whatever your tastes and price range, you'll find that you can slash your total clothing costs by 50 percent or more. I regularly shop at a small, local store where the owner provides excellent service and advice along with well-known name brands such as L.L. Bean, Eddie Bauer, and Lands' End, at prices 40 to 70 percent off retail.

Don't Buy New Furniture or Appliances As with their cars and clothing, most would-be investors spend too much, too soon for furniture and appliances. Even worse, instead of paying cash, they charge it. They chain themselves to several years of payments at high interest rates. Increasingly, they are hooked into those "no payments, no interest for six months" types of promotions that make credit purchases almost too easy to pass up. Do yourself a favor: resist this temptation to spend and borrow.

Whenever you buy cars, furniture, or appliances, let someone else suffer the depreciation. Pay for the usefulness of the product. The less money you waste on depreciating assets, the quicker you can start building wealth through real estate investments.

Shape Up Your Credit Profile

Go to www.myfico.com and print copies of your credit reports and credit scores. Examine your reports for errors. If you find errors, start the paperwork now. Correcting credit errors can require weeks—and sometimes months.

If your debt load is too high or your payment record too slow, commit now to positive change. Reduce your balances. Pay all accounts before their due date. Fortunately, when the myfico computer program calculates your credit score, the credit scorers will give your recent and righteous credit experience more weight than your past undisciplined credit habits. (You'll find many more tips on credit scoring in Chapter 3.)

Closely Read the Real Estate Classifieds

When you read the real estate classifieds closely, you'll get a good feel for the relative prices and rent levels that prevail among and within the various neighborhoods and communities in your area. In addition, you'll spot easy buying techniques such as lease option, owner finance, and contract-for-deed. Notice how frequently these techniques show up in the ads.

Telephone Sellers (Agents) and Look at Properties

At this preliminary stage, you're not necessarily looking to buy—you're looking to learn the market. Randomly view properties. Note desirable and undesirable features. Drive through and explore neighborhoods and communities that are new to you. Discover how much "for sale" and "for rent" inventory is sitting on the market. Watch trends in property selling prices, apartment vacancy rates, and rent concessions.

Join a Real Estate Investment Club

Nearly every community offers beginning investors the opportunity to join a locally operated apartment owners' association or real estate investment club. In addition, in most midsized and large cities, real estate and lending pros often offer free (or low-cost) seminars on investing and financing.

Attend these investment group meetings. Talk with others who have learned the secrets of investing from years of experience. Review and ponder the lessons they've learned and the trends they're noticing. Then, always verify what you hear with facts. Some realty pros observe carefully and possess sharp insights. Others merely love to bluster with ill-formed opinions—especially to an eager listener. Perfect your ability to distinguish the sage from the braggart.

Read More

The bookshelves in my offices are loaded from top to bottom with hundreds of books on real estate. Yet I still buy and read nearly every new book in the field. Likewise your search for knowledge, your search to improve your investing techniques and profitability, should never cease. Knowledge not only guides you toward building wealth, it conquers fear.

Read Local Papers   Besides reading books on real estate, read the real estate and community sections of your local newspapers and business journals. From these articles you'll learn about emerging neighborhoods, new property developments, zoning and regulatory issues, price and vacancy trends, business growth, and foreclosure filings. Savvy investors stay on top of local property-related events and adapt their investment strategy to profit from ever-present change.

Read in the Field of Self-Improvement   To follow a path of constant improvement, regularly read books in the self-help/motivational field. I like the work of Tony Robbins, Wayne Dyer, Les Brown, and Shad Helmstetter. But within the broad field of self-help I include books on health, fitness, time management, and dealing with people. If you prefer, *listen* to books. You can find nearly all self-enhancement topics on cassette tapes and compact disks. Rather than waste time when you're driving, put those hours to productive use.

And don't forget, browse the collection of books, CDs, and tapes at your public library. To change your life—financially and personally—persistently use books and tapes to improve your habits, your thinking, your self-talk, and your performance. Your greatest power remains the power to choose the life you want.

Commit to Invest within Three Months

How many times have you heard people lament? "You know, we've been thinking about getting started in real estate investing for years. But I don't know. We just never seemed to get around to it. Gosh, would we be set now if we had only done what we were thinking."

Over the years, I've heard laments like this thousands of times. For some reason, people love to lament and regret—yet they still fail to act. Please, when you find yourself regretting or procrastinating, escape from these traps. Act now! (See Box 1.2.)

Action cures regret. Action prevents future regret. Action creates the wealth you want. Regret mires you in a past that cannot change. Set your most important goals now. Commit to making your first real estate investment within the next 90 days. Mark it on your calendar. You will find that once you get started, your progress will accelerate. Not only will experience teach you better than books, but experience will help make your reading pay much larger dividends.

> **Action cures fear and regret.**

Now, let's get started. You are going to learn how to profit from real estate in multiple ways.

Someday I should write a list
Of all the deals that I have missed;
Bonanzas that were in my grip—
I watched them through my fingers slip;
The windfalls which I should have
   bought
Were lost because I overthought
I thought of this, I thought of that,
I could have sworn I smelled a rat,
And while I thought things over twice,
Another grabbed them at the price.
It seems I always hesitate,
Then make up my mind much too late.
A very cautious man am I
And that is why I wait to buy.

When tracks rose high on Sixth
   and Third,
The price asked was, I felt absurd;
Those apartment blocks—black
   with soot—
Were priced a thirty bucks a-foot!
I wouldn't even make a bid,
But others did—yes, others did!
When Tucson was cheap desert land,
I could have had a heap of sand;
When Phoenix was the place to buy,
I thought the climate was too dry;
"Invest in Dallas—that's the spot!"
My sixth sense warned me I should not.
A very prudent man am I
And that is why I wait to buy.

How Nassau and how Suffolk grew!
North Jersey! Staten Island, too!
When others culled those
   sprawling farms
And welcomed deals with open arms . . .
A corner here, ten acres there,
Compounding values year by year,
I chose to think and as I thought,
They bought the deals I should have
   bought.
The golden chances I had then
Are lost and will not come again.
Today I cannot be enticed
For everything's so overpriced.
The deals of yesteryear are dead;
The market's soft—and so's my head.

Last night I had a fearful dream,
I know I wakened with a scream:
Some Indians approached my bed—
For trinkets on the barrelhead
(In dollar bills worth twenty-four
And nothing less and nothing more)
They'd sell Manhattan Isle to me.
The most I'd go was twenty-three.
The redmen scowled: "Not on a bet!"
And sold to Peter Minuit.

At times a teardrop drowns my eye
For deals I had, but did not buy;
And now life's saddest words I pen—
"IF ONLY I'D INVESTED THEN!"

—Anonymous

Box 1.2   Investor's Lament

CHAPTER 2

Multiple Paths to Building Wealth

Now you're going to see why real estate investing offers you greater opportunities to build wealth than any other type of investment. With real estate, you can make money in dozens of different ways. For starters, here are 16 potential paths to profit:

- Appreciation in market values
- Inflation
- Cash flows
- Mortgage payoff
- Buy below market
- Create property value
- Create site value
- Create neighborhood value
- Condominium conversions
- Improved management
- More-profitable market strategy
- Tax shelter
- Discounted notes and tax deeds
- Real estate stocks (REITs, home builders, mortgage lenders)

Appreciation in Market Values

Over periods of 5 to 10 years, nearly all types of properties gain in value because population, jobs, incomes, and wealth (buying power) grow faster than the amount of new construction. Over the long term, more people with more money consistently push real estate prices up.

"Okay," you retort, "but that was then and this is now. Surely prices can't continue to increase as they have in the past?" I answer, "They can and they will." To see the future, just weigh together these dominant trends:

1. *Population growth.* During the next 20 years, the population of the United States will increase by 40 million people.
2. *Incomes.* During the next 20 years, employees, entrepreneurs, professionals, and business owners will see their incomes rise by over 50 percent.
3. *Vacation homes.* During the next 20 years, at least 10 million more Americans (and foreign nationals) will choose to buy vacation homes within the United States.
4. *Echo boomers.* During the next 20 years, more than 60 million echo boomers (children and grandchildren of the baby boomers) will enter the housing market to buy homes.
5. *Restrictions on development.* During the next 20 years, zoning, environmental laws, building regulations, and land shortages will continue to restrict development in those areas where most people want to live.
6. *Construction costs.* During the next 20 years, the costs to construct houses (and other types of buildings) will follow their past trend line upward.
7. *Immigrants and minorities.* Currently only 40 percent of our fastest growing immigrant and minority groups (Hispanics, blacks, Asians) own their own homes. In contrast, more than 75 percent of whites live in homes they own. With government programs and lender outreach efforts in full swing, during the next 20 years people in these minority and immigrant groups will continue to buy homes in record numbers. Federal, state, and local governments in cooperation with private lenders will be working hard to close the home ownership gap.
8. *Investors.* During the next 20 years, more than 60 million baby boomers will need a retirement income. They will increasingly turn to investment real estate to meet this need. Demand for property as an investment will continue to explode—as it has during the past 5 years.

You don't need advanced knowledge of economics and demographics to recognize the fact that every major social trend is pushing real estate prices upward.

Inflation

Each year and every year the Federal Reserve system increases the money supply. As more money chases after a slowly increasing supply of properties, property prices go up—even *without* an overall favorable change in the underlying forces of supply and demand (market appreciation). The Federal Reserve specifically designs its monetary policies to create a modest (1.5 to 3.0 percent) annual gain in the Consumer Price Index (CPI).

> **Even without market appreciation, inflation will push real estate prices up.**

Sometimes, though, the Fed loses control of inflationary price increases (late 1940s, the entire 1970s, early to mid 1980s). During those superheated, inflationary times, real estate prices will often experience inflationary gains of 6 to 12 percent a year. Buy now and then cheer for inflation.

Interest Rates and Inflation

Journalists repeatedly perpetuate the myth that our so-called "current *historically low* mortgage interest rates" have caused the recent price run-ups in housing.

In reality, today's 30-year mortgage interest rates of 5 to 7 percent only seem low relative to those mortgage rates of 8 to 16 percent that we experienced throughout much of the 1970s and 1980s. During most of our country's 225-plus years of history, mortgage interest rates typically have ranged between 3 and 6 percent. So, today's rates actually stand toward the high-average end of history—not the historically low. But, still, you might ask, what happens to real estate prices if interest rates do go up?

> **Today's mortgage interest rates sit above their long-term average—not below.**

Higher Interest Rates Are Caused by Higher Inflation

Long-term interest rates climbed dramatically during the 1970s and 1980s because the Consumer Price Index (inflation) jumped from the somewhat mild annual levels of 2.5 to 4.0 percent of the early to mid

1960s all the way up to 13 percent in 1982. And for the record, you might note that during those 16 years of increasing inflation and sky-rocketing interest rates (from 1970's 6.0 percent to 1981's 16 percent), most property values nearly tripled.

Although higher inflation drives up interest rates, inflation also drives up rent levels and construction costs. Even better for investors who own real estate, when inflation heats up, the smart money flees financial assets (stocks and bonds) in favor of hard assets (real estate, gold, collectibles). As a result, property prices are pushed even higher as stock and bond prices stagnate or decline.

For example, in 1964, the stock market's Dow Jones Industrial Average peaked at close to 1,000. In 1981, it sat at less than 800—20 percent below its high mark of 17 years earlier. During this same 17-year period of higher interest rates and inflation, the nationwide median house price zoomed from $25,000 to nearly $75,000.

> **During periods of high interest rates, real estate strongly outperforms stocks and bonds.**

History proves that over lengthy periods, higher interest rates *do not* hurt property values. Quite the contrary, higher interest rates (which merely reflect high inflation) propel property prices to new record heights.

Higher Interest Rates? Lower Interest Rates? You Gain Either Way

Say you buy today and secure a long-term mortgage interest rate of 6.5 percent. If interest rates go down, you can refinance and take advantage of lower payments (more on this topic later).

Yet, if inflation again goes wild and interest rates head up to 8, 10, 12 percent or higher, you'll gain as inflation pushes the price of your property up and slices the real dollar (inflation-adjusted) amount of your mortgage balance. You borrow dollars when their purchasing power is strong. You pay them back when their buying power has fallen. You gain. Your lender loses. Unlike mortgage lenders in many countries, lenders in the United States must carry the adverse risks created by both higher interest rates *and* lower interest rates. When rates go down, you can refinance. When rates go up due to inflation, you can collect higher rents and pay your loan off in cheap

> **You profit regardless of whether interest rates head up or down.**

dollars. Regardless of which direction interest rates move, real estate investors (mortgage borrowers) reap the gains for themselves.

Cycling through History

Nothing I've written denies the hard fact of real estate cycles. Every real estate investor knows that rent levels and property prices seldom move upward at an even, steady pace. In some years, prices bolt ahead. In others, they merely crawl. And every now and then, short-term events (excessive job loss, temporary overbuilding) can send property prices lower. But rather than spell doom, these cycles can be used by savvy investors to enhance their profits.

Personally, I love down markets because they make buying much easier. More important, throughout this book, I will show you how to profit in any type of real estate market. You simply adapt your strategy and techniques to whatever new market conditions are emerging. Savvy real estate investors ignore the media chatter about bubbles and peaks, hard times, and depressed markets. Instead, they work the available opportunities—no matter what type of market they face.

> **Use the down cycle to pick up properties at depressed prices.**

Cash Flows

Most real estate produces cash flows from rent collections. Even though today's cash flows (in many high-priced parts of the country) currently throw off *unleveraged* returns of just 4 to 8 percent a year, those cash flows are sure to increase over time. When blended together, inflation and market demand can push rents up an average of 3 to 5 percent a year. Within 15 years, today's rent level of $1,000 a month can increase to $1,500 to $1,800 per month (or possibly more).

You also will be able to boost your cash flows during periods when interest rates decline. Say that, due to a refinance at a lower interest rate, the mortgage payment on your investment property falls from $2,000 per month to $1,700 per month. That refinance just put another $300 a month of cash flow into your pocket.

Mortgage Payoff (Amortization)

Imagine for a moment that inflation ends and market demand (property appreciation) stalls. You collect only enough rents from your property to pay your operating expenses and mortgage payments. With stagnant rent collections and property values, have you made a poor investment? Not at all.

As you pay off your mortgage balance, your equity in the property continues to grow—even without an increase in your property's value.

Your Equity Grows Tenfold

Assume, for example, you buy a $100,000 property with a $10,000 down payment. After 30 years, you own that property (still valued at $100,000) free and clear. Even without positive cash flows or price increases, you've multiplied your original investment of $10,000 ten times over. In terms of compound interest, that gain from amortization (paying off the mortgage with rent collections) alone equals an annual rate of return of 8 percent.

> **You don't need price increases to make money in real estate.**

Amortization Alone Often Beats Other Investments

You might not think 8 percent sounds like much of a return. But it's certainly better than bonds, annuities, certificates of deposit, and even stocks (during many decades of our economic history). Indeed, the famous stock market bull, Wharton professor Jeremy Siegel, forecasts average stock returns over the next 10 to 20 years of just 6 to 8 percent a year. Why? Because stocks today remain highly overvalued relative to historical norms.

> **Earn 8–12 percent a year just by paying off your mortgage with rent collections.**

Remember, too, I've assumed here that your 8 percent property returns result *only* from mortgage payoff, whereas the returns from the other investments cited refer to *total* returns (dividends or interest *and* asset appreciation).

As an aside, note that had your rent collections permitted you to pay off your mortgage loan in 20 years instead of 30 years, your return from paying off your property's mortgage would climb to an annual rate of 12 percent.

Buy Below Market Value

In real estate you can make money the moment you buy a property. Unlike most other investments, you can buy real estate for less than its market value. Distressed owners, owners who want to sell fast and hassle-free, lenders who own foreclosures (called REOs), and poorly informed sellers frequently part with their properties at prices (or terms) that immediately put dollars into your net worth.

> **Bargain prices help you build wealth fast.**

Some investors flip properties they buy at a bargain price to generate quick cash. Others hold for the long term and use the bargain price (or terms) to boost their long-term profits. Either way, bargain prices fill your bank accounts with money.

Create Value with Property Improvements

Most investors (and homeowners) fail to strategically improve their properties to maximize values. As a result, entrepreneurial investors—an investor like you who can spot opportunities for improvements—can dramatically and quickly boost the values of the properties you buy. Plus, when you choose to operate entrepreneurially, you also gain because your properties bring in higher rents.

Multiple Ways to Improve

When we talk about property improvement, most owners look only for profit-making cosmetic changes: Lay some new carpet, paint the walls, clean up the yard, and put new tile floors in the kitchen and bathrooms.

As you will see, though, in Chapters 13 and 14, you can (and should) go far beyond cosmetics. As a truly creative entrepreneurial investor, you will develop a total fix-up and renovation plan that may involve kitchen and bath remodeling, reconfiguring a floor plan, adding skylights or ceiling height, and attic or basement conversions.

As an entrepreneurial investor, you will survey competing properties, look for unsatisfied tenant (buyer) wants, and then strategically design a plan of improvement to create the *wow* factor. With *wow* factors in place, you will not only add to the value of your building, you will attract topflight tenants and collect higher rents.

> **Create value with**
> ***wow* factors.**

Don't Overlook Site Enhancement

As part of your total property improvement plan, you will also focus on potential value improvements that you can create with the site. Maybe you can create a view to a newly beautified backyard, add parking spaces, eliminate a drainage problem, or even slice off part of the lot to construct another residence.

In high-priced areas of the country, site value can easily account for more than 50 percent of a property's total value. When you find better ways to use the property's site, you immediately boost the property's value. Walkways, fencing, landscaping, driveways, storage, and redevelopment may all offer promise for profit. As an alert, entrepreneurial owner, you will think through a dozen or more potential ways to enhance site value.

Improve the Neighbors and Neighborhood

"Buy in the best neighborhood you can afford. The best neighborhoods always appreciate the fastest." So says one of the oldest clichés in real estate. But, in fact, it's the turnaround neighborhoods that can often shoot up in value the most. Throughout the United States, many once downtrodden and shunned neighborhoods have experienced gentrification.

> **Look for up-and-coming neighborhoods.**

Although some investors wait for these neighborhoods to show strong signs of renewal, other investors jump in early while prices are still rock-bottom cheap. They find neighborhoods that show potential. Then they work with other property owners, neighborhood residents, local government, and not-for-profits to create community revitalization.

Either way, you can profit big. Even during those periods when average property prices and rent levels merely edge up (level off or turn down), some neighborhoods remain prime candidates for rapid price escalation. Turnaround neighborhoods clearly give you the chance to realize every investor's dream, "Buy low, sell high."

Convert the Use

From time to time some real estate markets get overbuilt with apartments, office buildings, shopping centers, gas stations, or other types of property. When such overbuilding occurs, alert investors go bargain hunting. Although some bargain hunters hold for the long term, others go for the quick profits by converting properties from one use to another.

For example, New York City currently suffers from a glut of office space and diminishing office building rents. In contrast, housing prices and apartment rents continue to rise in response to New York's perpetual shortage of homes and apartments. So, what route to profits are some New York real estate investors taking? You guessed it. They're buying office buildings on the cheap and converting this excess office space into apartments and condominiums.

Dynamic Markets Precipitate Change

When I-70 came through my hometown, slow-to-adapt motel owners along the previously heavily traveled route U.S. 40 went broke. Alert real estate investors, though, spotted opportunity. They bought the defunct motels at rock-bottom prices and then profitably converted them into efficiency apartments for the growing number of single persons within the city's population.

In our dynamic economy, the need for real estate continues to grow. But the need for specific property uses ebbs and flows. When oversupply or tough times hit some types of property uses, that situation spells profit possibilities for those investors who can figure out a better way to use now obsolete (or unprofitable) buildings.

> **Stay alert for the chance to profit from conversions.**

Neighborhood Changes

For the past two decades, many close-in neighborhoods with obsolete factories and warehouses have experienced a renaissance as real estate investors bought cheap, old industrial buildings and converted them to loft apartment buildings. New York City's Soho District, San Francisco's South of Market (SOMA) area, and Chicago's near north neighborhood stand out as prime examples of this ongoing trend.

> **Watch for neighborhoods where uses are changing.**

Likewise, as commercial areas sometimes encroach into residential neighborhoods, smart property investors have successfully sought zoning changes and then converted large houses into professional offices aimed at those ever-expanding legions of lawyers, accountants, dentists, real estate brokers, and insurance agents.

Condos into Apartments

In the early 1990s, I worked with an investment group that bought controlling interest in defunct condominium projects. After the Texas bust of the late 1980s, large blocks of condo units were selling for as little as $15,000 per unit.

Yet, as apartment rentals these condo units would easily bring $350 to $425 a month. Given these sinking condo prices and relatively high rent levels, more than a few condo projects were essentially converted into apartment buildings. Then, when condo prices revived in the late 1990s, our investment group was able to reconvert and sell off individual apartments at $40,000 to $60,000 per unit.

Apartments into Condos

More recently, rapidly escalating condo prices, rising vacancy rates in apartment projects, and softening rents have encouraged increasing numbers of investors to buy apartment buildings and convert them into condominium developments. Similarly, facing soft office markets, some investors are converting office buildings into *commercial* condominiums. Large numbers of doctors, lawyers, and accountants (or even other investors) are signing up to buy them.

> **Ride the condo cycle to earn big profits.**

Always remember that as various property prices and rent levels change, the opportunity to convert from one use to another can yield solid gold profits. (More on this topic in Chapter 14.)

Manage and Market Your Properties More Profitably

As you might suspect, most small-time investors mismanage their rental properties. Why? Because they get lazy. They fail to keep up with changes in the market. They fail to make desirable improvements to their properties. They fail to develop a sound strategy of target marketing.

> **Effective management yields easy profits.**

All in all, such widespread failures mean that you can almost certainly boost the profits from any property by simply managing and marketing it more effectively. And as a bonus, managing more effectively requires you to put in less time and effort.

Protect Your Profits from the IRS (Tax Shelter)

To build wealth, you must protect your earnings from the greedy hand of government. Fortunately, the income tax laws permit owners of property to escape taxation in at least four important ways:

- ◆ Serial home selling
- ◆ Section 1031 exchanges
- ◆ Depreciation
- ◆ Retirement planning

Serial Home Sellers

Growing numbers of Americans are profiting from investing in their homes *tax free*. Here's how it works.

Generally, when you own an investment property, you will pay a capital gains tax on your resale profits at the time you sell. However, when you sell your personal residence, your gains come to you tax-free up to $250,000 ($500,000 for couples). As long as you have lived in the property for two of the previous five years, you need not even report this profit to the IRS.

Even better, you can repeat this purchase and sale every two years. Ideally, you find a home with strong fix-up and renovation potential. Buy it. Create value. Resell and reinvest your tax-free profits in additional properties. Continue this process until you achieve your desired level of wealth (or until you tire of moving).

> **Serial renovators earn big tax-free profits.**

For singles or couples without children, serial home ownership can prove to be an outstanding method of generating relatively quick, tax-free profits. Or if you do have kids, get them involved. Put them to work. They'll learn some valuable lessons about real estate renovating and investing.

Section 1031 Exchanges

In addition to buying and selling a series of personal residences tax free, you can also sell your investment properties tax free. All you need to do is follow the rules as set forth in Section 1031 of the Internal Revenue Code. Specialist realty pros can easily set up the necessary paperwork to pull off these tax-free "exchanges." I put *exchange* in quotations because it's really a misnomer. You do not actually have to trade your property with another owner. You simply sell one property and buy another one within a period of several months.

Depreciation

In most businesses, the IRS taxes your net cash annual income. But when you own rental properties, you can shelter (protect) much of your cash flow from taxes by using a noncash tax deduction called depreciation.

> **Depreciation gives you tax-free income.**

Say your apartment building (exclusive of land value) is worth $500,000. Your pretax cash income from that property equals $20,000 per year. But you don't pay taxes on that $20,000 of income. You only pay taxes on $1,950 ($20,000 of income less $18,150 for allowable depreciation).

What happens to that $18,150 deduction for depreciation if, say, your rental property yields only $10,000 a year in pretax cash income? In that situation, you may be able to write off (deduct) that $8,150 ($18,150 depreciation less $10,000 property income) of unused "loss" from the taxable amounts you earn from your other taxable income (wages, business profits, interest, dividends).

Tax-Deferred Retirement Plans

Do you own an IRA retirement plan? If so, you may be able to invest all or part of it in real estate.

Unfortunately, most people believe that they can only invest these retirement funds in corporate America's stocks, bonds, mutual funds, or money market accounts. Wrong! Patrick Rice fully explains these real estate investing techniques in his book, *IRA Wealth: Revolutionary IRA Strategies for Real Estate Investment* (Garden City Park, N.Y., Square One, 2003, p. 3). Here's what Rice says:

> After the sharp decline of the stock market, many of us could only stand by and watch as our retirement savings lost their accumulated value. Few [investors] knew that there was an alternative which offered both safety and growth. That alternative is real estate. . . . Contrary to what you may have believed, it is possible and perfectly legal to hold real estate in an IRA account—and to enjoy unprecedented returns.

If you have built up funds in a tax-favored retirement fund, I urge you to talk with a financial pro or read Rice's book. Quite likely, you will find it wise to diversify at least a portion of your IRA monies into real estate. IRA funds invested in real estate build up tax free within that account just the same as would stocks, bonds, and CDs.

Taxes: Summing Up

The tax laws remain too complex for me to itemize and detail in this beginning book on investing in real estate. Nevertheless, please appreciate the fact that, to a large degree, you can protect your real estate profits from the IRS.

To really learn how to avoid taxes on real estate, I recommend these two books:

- ◆ *Aggressive Tax Avoidance for Real Estate Investors*, John T. Reed (available at www.johntreed.com)
- ◆ *Real Estate Investors Tax Guide*, Vernon Hoven (Dearborn, 2003)

Throughout this book, I will focus on showing you how to make money in real estate. In complement, Reed and Hoven show you how to pocket these profits without losing a good-sized portion to the government.

Discounted Notes, Tax Liens, Tax Deeds, and Realty Stocks

Want to make money in real estate without managing tenants or lifting a paintbrush? Then consider the high-return business of buying (and perhaps selling) discounted notes and mortgages.

The Basics of Discounted Notes

Quite often, sellers of houses and investment properties carry back (owner finance) some or all of their buyers' purchase price. Buyers then make monthly payments directly to the sellers.

After some period of time passes, a seller may decide that he or she wants cash instead of those monthly payments. To get this cash, the seller (note holder) sells the note to another investor—usually for an amount somewhat less than the balance on the note owed by the buyers of the original noteholder's property.

> **Buy $100 bills for $80—or less.**

For example, assume I sell you a property and carry back a mortgage note for $25,000. After a few years of payments, the remaining balance on this note drops to, say, $21,500. I now want cash. To entice an investor to buy this note from me, I would likely agree to sell it for $17,500.

You might wonder, "Why sell a $21,500 mortgage for just $17,500?" Because that's the way this market works. In most cases, noteholders who wish to sell must accept a discount.

How much discount? It all depends on a number of factors. Just realize that tens of thousands of investors throughout the United States are making outstanding returns in this field. If you choose to, you can too. (For a good description of this technique, see *The Stefanachik Method,* Morrow, 1994.)

Tax Liens and Tax Deeds

When homeowners or real estate investors fail to pay their property taxes, local governments place a tax lien against the property. If the taxes remain unpaid, the government will eventually sell the property via a tax deed. The "free and clear" infomercials of Ed Beck promise to show investors how they can make money buying up these tax liens and tax deeds.

Although not quite so easy and risk-free as Beck's infomercial makes it sound, once you learn your area's rules and procedures, you can earn tens of thousands of dollars a year by buying these government-issued certificates.

Stocks of REITs and Homebuilders

I strongly encourage you to directly own and manage real estate. By involving yourself directly in the real estate market, you will outearn passive investors in stocks by a long shot. Nevertheless, as one more real estate investing alternative, you can buy the stocks issued by real estate investment trusts (REITs) and large homebuilders such as Toll Brothers, K&B, Lennar, and WPP. REITs are companies that own and manage large properties such as office buildings, shopping centers, warehouses, and apartment complexes.

> **Real estate stocks add both diversity and yield to your stock portfolio.**

Long after the general stock market downturn of early 2000, the stocks of REITs and homebuilders continued to register positive total returns of 10 to 25 percent a year. Also, unlike the stocks of most companies, REIT stocks typically pay cash dividends of 6 to 9 percent a year.

Any investor who wants to build wealth in stocks should definitely own shares in at least several REITs and homebuilders. These companies not only offer good returns, they will reduce the overall risk of your investment portfolio. Real estate stocks diversify your holdings of stocks and bonds.

PART TWO

How to Raise the Money

CHAPTER 3

Strengthen Your Credit Power

If you're like many beginning real estate investors, you may lack substantial sums for a down payment. You may suffer from credit blemishes. Or maybe both of these shortcomings trouble you. So, if you want to convince a lender (or property seller) to shower a huge pile of cash on you—a total stranger—then think about your personal profile the same way a lender (seller) does:

◆ Consistency
◆ Character
◆ Credit

By far, the most important of these three Cs is Credit. With strong credit—even without much cash or income—you will find it easy to buy investment real estate. Yet credit's not the only thing that counts. If you lack a platinum-power credit score, you can still dress yourself up for success. Emphasize your consistent ability to perform and your sterling character.

Consistency: Fast Track or Flake

Have you job-hopped or job-flopped? Have you lived in more places than you can remember? Did you jump through six majors before you finished community college? Do you suffer bouts of binge spending and borrowing? Does your background look more like a tossed salad that's been thrown against a wall than the impeccable dinner presentation of an expensive French restaurant? If so, you've got some explaining to do.

Loan representatives, loan underwriters, and sellers who offer financing want to make sense of your life as it's displayed on your mortgage application.[1] They want to evaluate where you've been and where you're headed.

For you to satisfy their penchant for consistency, figure a theme or angle that ties your loose ends together. Give the lender confidence that six months after you've closed your loan, you won't abandon the property to join a Hare Krishna colony or move to Soho and fulfill your dream of becoming a romance novelist. The lender wants to envision your steady path toward job promotions and career advancement. In borderline cases, a good story can make the difference.

> **Tell the lender a life story that makes sense.**

All in all, you want to persuade the lender, seller, or both that the path you're traveling is leading you toward success.

Character Counts

The famous banker, J. P. Morgan, declared, "I wouldn't loan money to a man I did not trust on all the bonds of Christendom." Don't you feel the same way? Well, so does your lender (seller). You've got to convince the lender (seller) that you'll honor your obligations and commitments. Your credit score provides one indicator. But, when desirable or necessary, bolster the impression this score creates with other types of written information:

1. ***Employer.*** If your lender requires a completed VOE form (verification of employment), ask your supervisor to enclose a letter that commends your dependability, integrity, and responsibility at work.

---

1. Throughout much of this chapter's discussion, I will use the term "lender" to include sellers who offer their buyers owner financing (called OWC).

2. *Credit blemishes.* Explain how misplaced bills, your vacation, a move of residence, or other non-character-indicting reasons account for these lapses that you deeply regret. Even better, discuss the new bill-paying systems that you have now put in place to prevent future lapses.

3. *Credit wreck.* Explain a serious problem as a once-in-a-lifetime, beyond-your-control event that you coped with as honorably as possible. If your lapses really were due to irresponsibility, emphasize that "you've learned your lesson the hard way" and now live well within your means. Put together objective evidence to support your "new you" claims.

4. *Personal references.* In the old days of mortgage lending, younger borrowers were awarded loans merely on the basis of family character and reputation.[2] "Why I've known Luke Jr.'s family for 30 years," the loan rep says. "They're great people. Loan approved." Now, in our big-city, automated world, personal references to lenders seldom count for much. Still, if you've established good rapport with people who could prove influential, it wouldn't hurt to enlist their help.

> **If your credit score is low, document your good character.**

When desirable, accent the fact that you're a good credit risk by showing alternative documentation. Otherwise, the lender will infer your dependability only from the shading provided by your formal record of credit and consistency. When adverse facts color too dark a picture, try to add some brighter highlights to the mix. Think. What evidence can you come up with to bolster your credit profile?

What loans or merchant accounts have you repaid on time that don't show up in your credit file? Will your current and past landlords vouch for you? Have you consistently paid your utilities and phone bills promptly? Often, lenders will accept any or all of this alternative evidence to bolster your reliability and good character.

---

2. In fact, many loan applications used to include spaces for personal references similar to those found on job applications.

Credit Scores Count Most

With a very strong credit score, lenders will lay aside their magnifying glass. With strong credit you will need to worry far less about high qual-

> **Learn how to raise your credit score.**

ifying ratios, low down payments, self-employment (difficult to determine income), piles of verifications, inconsistent life patterns, or character flaws. As a strong credit borrower you will win the lowest interest rate, the best terms, and the fastest approval. You need never suffer the claw marks of predatory (hard money) lenders.

In contrast, if you do need to improve your credit score, here's the knowledge you will need to gain that platinum-power borrowing status.

What Is Credit Scoring?

Through credit scoring, lenders try to minimize individual human judgment in the mortgage lending decision. Credit scoring data with auto loans, department store accounts, and credit cards proves that computer statistical programs can distinguish among platinum, gold, copper, lead, and plastic borrowers far better than back-office loan clerks or front-office loan reps.

To create these credit scoring programs, math whizzes study the credit profiles, borrowing habits, and payback records of hundreds of thousands of people. Then they search for statistically significant correlations that tend to rate borrowers along a continuum from "walks on water" (say, 800 or higher) to "let's pray they drown" (say, 500 or lower). Supposedly, credit scores may range from 350 to 900, but more than 75 percent of Americans fall within the range of 600 to 800.

Credit Scoring Spreads Its Influence

If you've received a preapproved credit card in the mail, or obtained instant credit at Sears, Home Depot, or Best Buy, you've been run through a credit scoring program. That's why the store could make the credit decision so quickly with only minimal information from you (Social Security number, name, address). Even insurance companies (especially auto and homeowners) are now turning to credit scores to decide whether to

> **Employers and insurers also judge you by your credit score.**

insure you, and if so, at what price. Employers, too, have started running credit scores on job applicants and, in some cases, current employees.

We are approaching the time when people will no longer say, "You are what you eat." Instead, they'll remark, "You are your credit score." With that world fast approaching, you must do all you can to strengthen your score. And if your score now shines out in platinum territory, learn to do what's necessary to keep it there. In the United States of tomorrow, Mensa will become old hat. You will gather far more prestige and practical benefit when you're eligible to join the FICO 800 club.

> **Your perfect credit record doesn't mean you'll receive a perfect credit score.**

Your Credit Score Doesn't Necessary Represent Your Credit Strength

Contrary to what many loan reps (and others) believe, your credit score doesn't necessarily represent your credit strength. You may never have paid a bill late in your life and still earn a credit score of less than 660.

Credit Scoring Doesn't Rate You Personally The credit scorers select certain characteristics that you share with others who have (or have not) paid their bills as scheduled. Then, based on these selected characteristics, the scorer's mathematical formula assigns you a number. Supposedly, this assessment accurately gauges the risks you present to the lender. But it doesn't. Why? Because you are a unique individual. Although you share some similarities with this computer sample of debtors, you also differ in many ways of which the credit scoring programs have no knowledge. These unaccounted-for differences may give you far more (or far less) borrowing credibility than your credit score indicates.

You can easily see the parallel here with SAT scores and other college admission tests. If you fail to register a top score, you can kiss Stanford goodbye—unless, that is, you write a superlative admissions essay and beef up your application with science fair awards and club presidencies.

You're Not Just a Number Remember Bob Seger's classic hit, "Feel Like a Number"? When you apply for mortgage credit, don't let the lender make you feel like a number. Yes, do all that you can to boost your credit score. But never let a lender (or seller) confuse the total *you* with your credit score.[3] By the same token, never assume that your astute loan rep and underwriter will intuitively recognize your worthwhile qualities. Just as the aspiring Stanford applicant must document why she deserves admission, you, too, must persuasively document why the lender (seller) can trust you to pay back that $250,000 you're trying to finance.

Discover Your Credit Scores

To discover your credit scores, go to www.myfico.com. There you can see (for a fee) all of your credit reports (Trans Union, Experian, Equifax). Each report will also include an associated credit score.

The three scores provided for you may not vary much from each other. But sometimes they do. That's because Equifax, Experian, and TU don't share credit data with each other. Different credit data yield different credit scores. Big differences in credit bureau data may yield big differences in each of the credit scores they assign you.

Want to Save Money?

If you don't want to spend the money to obtain credit information, you've got several other choices:

1. ***Mortgage loan sites.*** Some mortgage websites will provide you a free, no obligation credit score that simulates, but doesn't precisely mirror, the Equifax-FICO score (trade-named Beacon). However, I have found that these free simulated scores do not provide consistent results, nor do their scores accurately mimic your FICO scores. Because most mortgage lenders use FICO scores, simulated FICO figures provide little useful information.

2. ***Consumerinfo.com.*** This website operated by Experian will give you a free credit report, but it also will automatically en-

---

3. Unless, maybe, your credit score makes you look better than you deserve.

roll you in a $79.95 credit-monitoring service. Cancel this service within 30 days and you owe nothing.

3. *Free reports.* Various states require credit bureaus to provide reports for free (or at nominal cost). Also, under federal law you may receive free reports from each of the credit repositories if (1) you're unemployed and looking for work, (2) you're on welfare, or (3) you've been turned down for credit during the past 30 days.

4. *General commentary.* For the latest (usually critical) commentary about credit scoring and credit reporting, go to www.creditscoring.com and www.creditaccuracy.com. Also, the Federal Trade Commission maintains consumer information on all types of credit issues at www.ftc.gov.

How You Can Improve Your Credit Score

Credit scorers place your credit data into their computer programs and out pops a number. But they won't tell you precisely how they calculated that figure. However, after you've paid your fee at myfico.com, the website info will give you some pointers on how to improve your Beacon®-FICO® score. To learn how much your score actually does improve (if any) over the next 12 months, you will need to pay another fee. For that cost, you get four more periodic Beacon®-FICO® reports.

Unfortunately, the information provided by FICO still doesn't go far enough. It's more like, "try this (really, pay us) to see what happens." You really can't tell ahead of time the specific score boost that suggested changes might bring about. Nevertheless, piecing together clues from myfico.com and several helpful loan reps, here are some good tips on how to raise your credit scores:

1. *Number of open credit accounts.* You can have too few or too many. The optimum number probably ranges between four and six. One highly paid, credit perfect (no lates) executive I know scored 640. After closing the 6 newest of her 12 credit card accounts, her score went to 780. (But it took six months before her score climbed up to that level.)

2. *Balances.* Open accounts with balances reduce your score more than open accounts per se.

3. ***Balances/limits.*** Numerous accounts with balances sitting close to the limit will bring down your score.

4. ***Credit inquiries.*** Whenever someone checks your credit file, it counts against your score. However, multiple checks within, say, two weeks may not hurt as much as if it appears that you're merely shopping different lenders for one loan. Your personal inquiries don't affect your score.

5. ***Payment record.*** Obviously, late payments hurt your score. But, supposedly FICO doesn't distinguish between late mortgage payments and late payments on your Visa or student loan. (Mortgage lenders, though, most certainly do care. Always pay your mortgage or rent first.)

6. ***Recency counts.*** Late payments two years ago don't hurt as much as two months ago.

7. ***Black marks.*** Multiple lates on multiple accounts, collections, unpaid judgments, and tax liens devastate your score.

8. ***Kiss of death.*** Go straight to credit scoring purgatory if you're within two years of a past bankruptcy discharge or a foreclosure sale. Chapter 13 bankruptcy plans and credit counseling debt management plans also count heavily and negatively.

Myfico.com also shows that some categories weigh more than others:

◆ Age of credit (15 percent)
◆ Mix of credit (10 percent)
◆ Amount of balances (30 percent)
◆ Payment history (35 percent)
◆ Recent credit inquiries (10 percent)

The above clues shed some light on the credit scoring process, but far too little. Perhaps most importantly, they do show why "perfect credit" in the sense of "no lates" does not necessarily generate the highest FICO score. To improve your score, you must not only pay your bills on time but also manage your credit according to the likes and dislikes of the FICO (or other) credit-scoring programs.

Garbage In, Garbage Out   Computer data researchers everywhere know of GIGO (garbage in, garbage out). Clearly, this saying also applies to credit reporting. Credit scoring computer programs pull in raw data from the files of Equifax, Trans Union, or Experian. If your credit files include errors (as do at least 50 percent of all files), then your credit scores also will err.

Examine Your Reports Now   Seventy-five percent (or more) of mortgage loan applications require tri-merged credit reports and correspondingly three credit scores per borrower. Because each credit repository holds more than 200 million files and registers billions of computer-generated entries every year, you are unlikely to find three flawless, perfectly matched reports. Thus inconsistencies and mistakes can slow down or derail your mortgage approval.

> **Don't wait until you need credit. Check for errors now.**

What to Look For   You're looking for errors, but what kinds of errors? More than you might think:

1. *Inconsistency.* Evaluate whether your three reports differ significantly from each other. Does each report accurately show your credit accounts along with an appropriate "open" or "closed"?
2. *Late payments.* Make sure that all late payments shown were in fact lates. Also, check the category of lates 30, 60, and 90 days or over. Sometimes creditors overstate the number of days a payment has been late. Watch for rolling lates; you miss a payment, then get back on schedule. Every subsequent payment may show up as late.
3. *Balances.* Verify that the outstanding balances and credit limits don't misstate your true credit position. Remember, when balances push against limits, your credit score goes down.
4. *Disputed claims.* Have you justifiably refused to pay any creditor's bills? Health clubs (and other service contract providers) often continue to bill (and report unpaid) fees for membership that customers canceled long ago.
5. *Credit experience counts.* Do the reports accurately indicate the length of time each account has been opened?
6. *Omissions.* Have you established excellent credit with a credit card, landlord, or retail merchant that does not show up in your credit files? Some creditors withhold excellent

payment records and balance information. Why? If your credit score goes up, that lender's competitors will start mailing you offers to switch to their better terms or higher limits.

7. ***Tax liens.*** This type of claim nearly always must be paid before your mortgage loan closes.

8. ***Judgments.*** Ditto for judgments unless the statute of limitations has passed.

9. ***Collections/write-offs.*** For collections and write-offs, lenders may require that you settle them. Or the lender might calculate your qualifying total debt ratio as if you were paying 5 percent of these delinquent balances each month. If you combine a high current credit score with write-offs more than five years old, the lender may simply ignore them.

10. ***Time limits.*** See if any derogatory information shows up in violation of these legal time limits: credit inquiries (2 years); foreclosure (7 years); lates, collections, write-offs (7 years); judgments and tax liens (usually until statute of limitations runs out). To calculate "time limits," work back from the "date of last activity" on the debt. Also, creditors often sell their bad debts to credit vultures. These outfits may report debts beyond their lawful date of removal. Beware: You can trigger a new time limit by partial payment or settlement. Bankruptcy starts the clock on the date of discharge, not filing. Also, for larger loans, these time limits may not apply.

11. ***Other information.*** Verify all other information such as names, addresses, employment, date of birth, and so on.

12. ***Consistency with application.*** Remember, your loan underwriter will likely verify the data in your credit files with the liabilities and other information you list on your mortgage application. Do they match up?

What to Do Next

Should you discover errors, omissions, or inconsistencies that push down on your credit score, act immediately to correct them. If you wait until a loan rep inquires about these derogatory entries, you could lose your loan and the property you have agreed to buy. Some problems can disappear in a matter of days, but others may take months to clear up.

Contact the Credit Source and the Credit Repository Simultaneously Most credit advisors tell you to notify the credit repository, point out the change you deserve, and formally (in writing) seek compliance with your request. Good advice except for one critical fact: Credit repositories primarily report only the information your creditors give them. Unless the repository has botched the data it's been given (which does happen), the repository must contact the misreporting creditor. If the creditor does not respond within 30 days, the repository must remove the disputed item.

However, if the creditor says, "Sorry, no mistake on our part," the record remains as is. The problem's back in your lap—but now 30 days may have passed by. To head off this potential delay, contact the original source of the information simultaneously and ask to have new, corrected info sent to the repository. Upon request some friendly creditors will even eliminate derogatory remarks if you're a customer the creditor values.

> **Credit bureaus only report the data creditors provide them.**

On the other hand, if you're dealing with a hostile or indifferent creditor, you could face a prolonged battle. In that case, the loan underwriter will either waive the "derog" upon suitable explanation from you; offer you a higher-cost, less-desirable loan; or flat out suspend commitment until you obtain the creditor's correction or release.

To get their mortgage closed on schedule, many borrowers have had to pay disputed claims. Acting early prevents forced settlements on eat-crow terms. So carefully review your credit reports now. Avoid getting into a borrowing situation where you're offering last-minute pleas under deadline conditions.

> **Your spouse or partner's low credit score can squelch your loan approval.**

Multiple Borrowers, Multiple Scores When you and your spouse (or other coborrower) want to buy and finance an investment property, all borrowers will need credit scores (or explanations) that equal or exceed lender minimums. Without meeting this requirement, the low-score borrower must withdraw as a coborrower. The lender will then limit the loan amount to the qualifying capacity of the high-score borrower.

You can work around this problem, though, when you buy an income property. You can bring in another person with strong credit (parent, partner, sibling, friend) to serve as cosignor or coborrower. Be cautious, though. If you don't make the loan payments on time, the lender will report these late payments to the credit repositories (Experian, Equifax, Trans-Union). The derogs will show up in your file. But they will also count against the credit record and credit score of your coborrower or cosignor.

One Borrower, Multiple Credit Scores   Now, here's a question you need to consider. When your credit records show different credit scores, which score will the lender choose to use if one of your scores falls below the lender's cutoff point? To a certain extent, it will depend on the persuasive story you tell about yourself and the reported discrepancies. In other instances, the lender may average the scores or select the middle score. This method discounts your highest score, again underlining the importance of getting all low-scoring files updated and corrected before you apply for your financing.

> **When they differ, the lender may average out your credit scores.**

Your Ex-Spouse Can Ruin Your Credit (and Other Tales of Double-Counting)

Are you divorced, married, or planning to wed? Might you buy a property with a partner or significant other? Then you're going to face the multiple-score, multiple-person problem of credit scoring and mortgage approval.

The Ex-Spouse Dilemma   If a competent lawyer handled your divorce, you should have cut up all joint credit cards and closed all joint accounts. If you and you ex-spouse owned a home with a joint mortgage, one spouse should have bought the other spouse out and refinanced solely in his or her own name. Without these precautions, you're still on the hook for these debts and they will count against you when you apply for property financing. If you haven't yet eliminated this potential debt overload, work out something now.

> **Get your ex-spouse's name off all of your accounts.**

Your Ex-Spouse Can Ruin *Your* Credit   Even worse than debt overload (for purposes of mortgage approval), your ex-spouse's poor repayment habits on joint debts will show up to bruise your credit. These same types of problems can also confront married couples who are separated (either legally or by informal agreement). When ending your personal lives together, abolish all joint credit accounts. Sometimes a lender will permit you to explain away poor credit where the full responsibility actually falls on your ex, but the lender will not overlook joint credit obligations that remain open. When the law imposes legal liability on you for the debt, then as far as the lender's concerned, it's your debt. Or it's your credit line for as long as it remains open or unpaid. The lesson: Get rid of all joint accounts that do not result from a current, trusting, continuing relationship.

Summing Up

For the top 20 to 30 percent of U.S. investors, credit scoring and automated underwriting greatly ease the pain of financing a home or investment property. On the other hand, if you're a borrower without platinum-power credit (say a FICO score below 720), to improve your credit score you must do something more than "pay your bills on time." You must align your credit behavior with FICO (or other credit scoring systems). You (and your coborrowers) will achieve the lowest interest rates, highest loan amounts, best terms, and least hassle only when you play the credit game according to the rules laid down by these new sultans of mortgage credit. The higher you lift your credit score, the greater your borrowing power.

CHAPTER 4

How to Invest Using Little (or None) of Your Own Cash

It's true. You can profit in real estate without much cash—especially if you've strengthened your credit score. But even when you lack platinum-power credit, you've still got a variety of little-or-no-cash-down techniques that you can draw on to get you started as a real estate investor.

Why Low-Cash Deals Magnify Your Returns

Before we go into little-or-no-cash-down techniques, you need to see why deals with small down payments can magnify your returns. Even if you're hoarding a pile of cash, you may still choose to hang onto your money as you benefit from the power of leverage.

The Power of Leverage

Leverage (other people's money, commonly referred to as OPM) means that you buy (or otherwise control) a property that's worth perhaps 10 times as much as your original cash investment. To illustrate, suppose you invest $10,000 in a $100,000 rental property. You finance this investment with a 30-year, $90,000 mortgage at 7.75 percent. After eight years you will have paid down your mortgage balance to $81,585. With 4 percent a year appreciation for eight years, your property's value will

> **Four percent appreciation can give you 20 percent returns.**

have grown to $136,860. When you subtract the balance of $81,585 from the property's appreciated value of $136,860, you'll find that your original $10,000 investment has increased more than fivefold to $55,275 of equity. That result gives you an annual growth in equity of around 24 percent (see Table 4.1). Through the power of leverage, you gained a return six times larger than the 4 percent rate of appreciation. Now you see why real estate investors call leverage the eighth wonder of the world.

> **Investors call leverage the eighth wonder of the world.**

Sometimes leverage can even yield much higher returns. And used foolishly—as you will soon see—leverage can magnify your losses. But, over the long run, the great majority of homebuyers and investors gain tremendously from leverage. That's why even wealthy real estate moguls like Donald Trump and the late Harry Helmsley (past

Table 4.1 With Leverage, Even Low Rates of Appreciation Yield High Returns

Today	
Property purchase price	$100,000
Original mortgage	90,000
Cash invested	10,000

Eight Years Later	
Market value at 4% appreciation	$136,860
Mortgage balance	81,585
Your equity	55,275

Growth in Your Equity

$10,000								$55,275

0	1	2	3	4	5	6	7	8 years

Annual growth rate of equity = 24%. Of course, proportionately increasing the rental income, the down payment, and the purchase price of this property would still yield a 24 percent rate of return. These figures assume that you financed this property with a 7.75 percent mortgage amortized over 30 years.

owner of the Empire State Building) always relied heavily on borrowed money to acquire and finance their property investments.

Leverage Can Also Magnify Your Annual Cash Returns

In addition to multiplying your profits from appreciation, leverage magnifies your annual returns from cash flows. Say you find a seller who is asking $100,000 for a rental property that yields a net operating income (called NOI) of $10,000 a year. If you paid all cash for this property, you would receive a return of 10 percent:

Example 1: $100,000 all-cash purchase

$$\text{ROI (return on investment)} = \frac{\text{Income (NOI)}}{\text{Cash investment}}$$

$$= \frac{\$10,000}{\$100,000}$$

$$= 10\%$$

Now let's say that you also want to compare your all-cash returns to those you would receive using 75 percent and 90 percent financing, respectively. Assume that you can borrow money at 6.5 percent and pay it back over a term of 30 years. Here's how leverage boosts your annual returns from cash flow.

Example 2: $25,000 down payment; $75,000 financed. Yearly mortgage payments equal $6,607 (75 × $7.34 × 12). Net cash flow after mortgage payments (called cash throw-off) equals $3,394 ($10,000 NOI less $6,606).

$$\text{ROI} = \frac{\$3,394}{\$25,000}$$

$$= 13.6\%$$

Example 3: $10,000 down payment; $90,000 financed. Yearly mortgage payments equal $7,927 (90 × $7.34 × 12). Net cash flow after mortgage payments (cash throw-off) equals $2,073 ($10,000 NOI less $7,927).

$$\text{ROI} = \frac{\$2,073}{\$10,000}$$

$$= 20.7\%$$

With the figures in these examples, the highly leveraged financing (10 percent down payment) yields a cash-on-cash rate of return more than double that of a cash purchase. In principle, the more you borrow and the less cash you invest in a property, the more you magnify your cash returns. Of course, these examples merely illustrate the principle of leverage. The examples show how leverage *may* boost your returns. In practice, the properties you find may produce numbers that look better or worse than those returns you see here. Still, the fact that nearly all *wealthy investors* finance their properties with large mortgages proves that leverage works.

> **Even wealthy investors use low-down-payment techniques to increase their leverage.**

Leverage Can Increase Risk

Savvy investors reap the benefits of leverage. Foolish investors can lose their shirts. What makes the difference? Financial discipline and cash reserves.

Financial Discipline   If you can't handle money responsibly, borrowing to the hilt can swamp you with debt. Never try to substitute "nothing down" for financial discipline. It doesn't work that way. As I emphasize in Chapter 1, before you invest in real estate, make sure you're living *below* your means. Learn to carefully manage your everyday spending and borrowing.

> **Never combine high leverage with financial recklessness.**

Don't let the real estate gurus suck you into believing that high leverage alone can make you rich. No! High leverage can help you get started. High leverage can boost your returns. But without financial discipline, high leverage can push you into foreclosure or bankruptcy.

Cash Reserves   Foolish investors always view the future through rose-colored glasses. These investors never anticipate an unexpected streak of vacancies, a roof that needs to be replaced, or a spiked increase in property taxes.

Over the long term, your rent collections and property appreciation will put hundreds of thousands of dollars into your bank accounts. Over the short term, rent shortfalls and unbudgeted expenses can cause

> **Always keep a reserve of cash and credit.**

unprepared investors to miss their mortgage payments and suffer foreclosure, or perhaps force them into a quick sale at a loss (to an opportunistic investor such as you?). To benefit over the long run, you must successfully navigate through the storms you'll encounter along the way. When high seas are trying to drown you, your cash reserves will prove to be your life jacket.

With these words of caution now in view, we next turn to the best type of high-leverage financing currently available.

Minimize Your Down Payment with Owner-Occupant Financing

By far, the easiest, safest, surest, and lowest cost way to borrow all (or nearly all) of the money you need to invest in real estate centers upon owner-occupied mortgage financing. In other words, lenders give their most favored interest rates and terms to investors and homebuyers who live in their properties (for a minimum of 12 months). Numerous high LTV (loan-to-value) owner-occupied loan programs are readily available for single-family homes, condominiums, townhouses, and two- to four-unit apartment buildings.

Owner-Occupants Get the Lowest Down Payments

Many owner-occupied loan programs offer 3 percent, 5 percent, or even 0 percent down payment loans. With sterling credit, some lenders will even loan you 125 percent of a property's purchase price (if you agree to live in the property). In contrast, if you do not plan to live in the property, many mortgage lenders (banks, mortgage bankers, savings institutions) often require investors to put 20 or 30 percent down. However, since the late 1990s, some lenders have allowed investors to finance their rental properties with only a 5 or 10 percent down payment. When property markets soften, though, these liberal lenders will probably shut their easy credit windows and force investors to put more cash into their deals and dance through more hoops.

Besides offering low-down-payment financing, lenders also qualify owner-occupants with less exacting standards. Plus, interest rates for owner-occupants can sit below the rate charged for investor loans. If lenders are charging, say, 5.5 to 6.5 percent for loans to owner-occupants with strong credit, the rate for most creditworthy investor loans will probably range between 6.75 and 7.5 percent. As a beginning real estate investor, you definitely should explore owner-occupied mortgage loans.

Owner-Occupied Buying Strategies

If you don't currently own a home, you can begin building your wealth in income properties very easily. Simply select a low-down-payment loan program that appeals to you (the most popular ones are described later in this chapter). Buy a one- to four-family property, live in it for (at least) one year, then rent out your living unit and repeat the process. Once you get your owner-occupied financing, that loan can remain on a property even after you move out and move a tenant in. Because the second, third, or even fourth homes you buy and move into will still qualify for high-LTV financing, you can quickly accumulate several rental properties as well as your own residence—all without large cash investments.

> **To build wealth fast, use multiple owner-occupant loans.**

Although you will be able to go through this process two, three, maybe four times, you can't execute it indefinitely. At some point, lenders will shut you off from owner-occupied financing because they will catch on to your game plan. Nevertheless, buying houses (or 2–4 unit apartment buildings) and holding on to them as you successively move in and move out makes a great way to accumulate your first several investment properties.

Current Homeowners, Too, Can Use This Method

> **You may already own an investment property—your own home.**

Even if you already own a home, you too should definitely weigh the advantages of using owner-occupied financing to acquire your next several properties. Here's how: Locate a property (condominium, house, 2–4 unit apartment building) that you can buy and move into. Find a good tenant for your current home. Complete the owner-occupied financing on your new property and move into it. If you really like your current home, at the end of one year, rent out your recently acquired investment property and move back into your former residence. Or alternatively, find another "home" to buy and again finance this property with an owner-occupied mortgage.

Why One Year?

To qualify for owner-occupied financing you must tell the lender that you *intend* to live in the property for at least a year. Intent, though, does not mean *guarantee*. You can (for good reason, or no reason) change your mind. The lender will find it difficult to prove that you falsely stated your intent at the time you applied for the loan.

Nevertheless, to succeed in real estate over the short and long term, you must establish, maintain, and nurture your credibility with lenders— and everyone else. Always build your deal making on a foundation of trust. When you sidestep agreements, slip through loopholes, make false promises, or connive in any similar slights, you will water down your credibility. Unless you really do encounter an unexpected turn of events, honor a lender's occupancy requirement. When you establish and nurture your credit and credibility, you will attract money as a magnet attracts iron filings.

> **Never fib to a lender about owner-occupancy.**

Where Can You Find Low-Down-Payment, High-LTV, Owner-Occupied Mortgages?

Everywhere! Look through the yellow section of your telephone book under "mortgages." Then start calling banks, savings institutions, mortgage bankers, mortgage brokers, and credit unions. Also, many mortgage lenders advertise in local daily newspapers.[1] Check, too, with your state, county, or city departments of housing finance. Homebuilders and Realtors also will know various types of low- or nothing-down home finance programs. An hour or two on the telephone will turn up dozens of possibilities.

---

1. For more extensive tips and insights on mortgage lending, see my book, *The 106 Mortgage Secrets that All Borrowers Must Learn—But Lenders Don't Tell* (New York: John Wiley & Sons, 2003).

> **You can find dozens of low- or no-down-payment mortgages.**

Although space here doesn't permit a full discussion of all low- or no-down-payment possibilities, here are a variety of widely available programs.

Don't Overlook FHA

> **FHA does not restrict its loans to low- or moderate-income individuals.**

The Federal Housing Administration (FHA) offers the most well-known low-down-payment home finance plans. Yet, somewhat perversely, many homebuyers believe that FHA limits its loans to people who earn low or moderate incomes. For instance, one of Florida's largest newspapers continues to describe FHA as a program for "low-income homebuyers." Not true. No matter how much you earn, FHA may provide the key to your home financing.

FHA 203(b)

When Realtors and mortgage lenders talk about an FHA loan, they are typically referring to the FHA 203(b) mortgage. With close to 1 million new FHA 203(b) loans made last year alone, this program is the largest single low-down-payment loan available throughout the United States.

You can get into this type of FHA mortgage for just 3 or 5 percent out-of-pocket cash—sometimes a little more, sometimes less. On an $85,000 property you would pay around $3,250. To finance a $125,000 property you'd pay approximately $6,000, and a property priced at $175,000 would require cash of around $8,250.

How Much Will FHA Finance?

FHA sets loan limits for each locale around the country. In high-priced cities such as Los Angeles, San Diego, Washington, D.C., and Boston, the FHA maximum loan currently tops out (for *single-family* houses, condos, and townhomes) at $290,319. In the lowest priced areas of the country, the maximum FHA home loan comes in at $160,176. Because FHA limits vary, consult with a Realtor or mortgage loan advisor in the area where you would like to own. Then compare these limits to property prices to see if FHA 203(b) can work for you. (Note: Much higher FHA limits apply in Hawaii. You can also check the maximum loan amounts for any county in the country at HUD.gov.)

Buy Rental Properties

As another choice, buy a duplex, triplex, or fourplex. As long as you live in one of the units, you still get a low down payment. Here are some examples of maximum FHA loan figures for 2–4 unit properties:

	Lower Cost Areas	Highest Cost Areas
Two units	$205,032	$371,621
Three units	247,824	449,181
Four units	307,992	558,236

> **To get on the fast track to investing, buy a 2–4 unit building.**

If you buy a 2–4 unit property, you won't have to qualify for the loan using just your monthly earnings. The rents that you collect from the property also will count. Because my first investment property was a five-unit apartment house, I strongly favor this approach to getting started.

Other FHA Advantages

Besides offering a low down payment, FHA borrowers enjoy many other advantages:

1. You can roll many of your closing expenses and mortgage insurance premiums into your loan. This cuts the out-of-pocket cash you'll need at closing.
2. You may choose from either fixed-rate or adjustable-rate FHA plans. (FHA adjustable-rate mortgages give you lower annual caps and lower lifetime caps than most other ARM programs.)
3. FHA authorizes banks and other lenders to use higher qualifying ratios and easier underwriting guidelines (see Chapter 5).

After you've shaped up your finances, FHA will do all it can to approve your loan.

4. If interest rates drop (and as long as you have a clean mortgage payment record for the previous 12 months), you can "streamline" refinance your FHA loan at lower interest rates without a new property appraisal and without having to re-qualify.

5. If you can persuade your parents or other close relatives to "gift" you the down payment, you won't need to come up with any closing-table cash from your own pocket. (Undoubtedly, many "gifted" down payments are really loans in disguise.)

6. Unlike most nongovernment loans, FHA mortgages are assumable. Someone who later agrees to buy your home need not apply for a new mortgage. When mortgage interest rates are high, an assumable low-rate FHA mortgage will give your home a great selling advantage.

The Verdict on FHA 203(b)

If you're a cash-short investor who wants to begin acquiring properties, definitely consider the FHA 203(b) finance plan. The

> **Don't choose your financing until you've at least talked to an FHA loan specialist.**

U.S. Department of Housing and Urban Development or HUD (the parent of FHA) is pushing for favorable changes in the 203(b) program. Lower costs, higher limits, and faster closings are three important goals. Both the HUD Secretary and President Bush are trying to make FHA more attractive to a wider number of Americans and legal immigrants.

Discover FHA's Best Kept Secret: The 203(k) Program

Like many renters, Quentlin Henderson of Orlando, Florida, hoped to invest in real estate some day. Yet, with little savings, Quentlin thought he wouldn't realize his hopes for at least three to four years. He never dreamed that within six months he would actually own a completely renovated, three-bedroom, two-bath house of 2,288 square feet—more than two and a half times as large as his previous 900-square-foot apartment.

How did Quentlin manage this feat? He discovered the little known, but increasingly available, FHA 203(k) mortgage loan program. FHA 203(k) allows owner-occupant investors to acquire and improve a rundown property with a low- or no-down-payment loan. "The house needed a new roof, new paint, new carpeting; and a bad pet odor needed to be removed," says Quentlin. "There was no way I could have paid for the house plus the repairs at the same time. And there was no way I could have otherwise afforded a house this size."

Locate an FHA 203(k) Specialist

To use a 203(k) plan, first locate a mortgage loan advisor who understands the current FHA 203(k) purchase and improvement process. In the past, FHA often stuck borrowers in red tape for months without end. But now with recent FHA streamlining and special software, Robert Arrowwood of California Financial Corporation reports that up-to-date, direct endorsement (DE) firms like his can "close 203(k) loans in four to six weeks instead of four to six months." (HUD lists 203(k) specialists on its website at HUD.gov.)

Search for Good Value

After you've located 203(k) advisors who know what they're doing, next search for a property that offers good value for the money. In Quentlin

> **The 203(k) program helps you build instant equity.**

Henderson's case, his Realtor found him a bargain-priced, six-year-old house that was in a sorry state because its former owners had abandoned it as a result of foreclosure. "The good news for people who buy such houses," says Bob Osterman of FHA's Orlando, Florida office, "is that purchase prices are generally low so that after repairs are made, the home's new value often produces instant equity."

Not surprisingly, the term "instant equity" was also used by John Evianiak, a 203(k) investor in Baltimore. "Not only can you buy a house and fix it the way you like," John says, "but you can buy a property for much below its market value, put some money into it, and create instant equity. There were a lot of other houses we checked out. But we were going by the profit margin."

Inspect, Design, Appraise

Once you locate a property that you figure can be bought and rehabbed profitably, you next must come to terms with the owners on price and other conditions of sale. With agreement in hand, the house (or condo or 2–4 unit apartment) is then inspected, a formal plan of repair and renovation is designed, and the home is appraised according to its value *after* your improvements have been completed. The amount of your loan is based upon your purchase price plus your rehab expenses up to around 100 percent of the property's renovated value.

Eligible Properties and Improvements

As long as you plan to pay more than $5,000 in rehab expenses, you can use a 203(k) mortgage to acquire and improve nearly any one- to four-unit property. In terms of specific repairs and renovations, the 203(k) mortgage permits an almost endless list of possibilities. Here are some examples:

- ◆ Install skylights, fireplaces, energy-efficient items, or new appliances (stove, refrigerator, washer, dryer, trash compactor, dishwasher).
- ◆ Finish off an attic or basement.
- ◆ Eliminate pollution or safety hazards (lead paint, asbestos, underground storage tanks).
- ◆ Add living units such as an accessory apartment or two.
- ◆ Recondition or replace plumbing, roof, or HVAC systems.
- ◆ Improve aesthetic appeal (paint, carpet, tile, exterior siding).
- ◆ Install or replace a well or septic system.
- ◆ Landscape and fence the yard.

As you can see, the FHA 203(k) program can really help you increase the value of a property—using little or none of your own cash.

Too Many Vets Pass Up VA Loans

If you're a veteran with eligible active military service, or if you have served at least six years in the reserves, the Department of Veterans Affairs holds your ticket to nothing-down investing. The VA mortgage is truly one of the best benefits offered to those who have worn our country's uniform. Last year alone, a record 600,000 veterans took advantage of this loan program. Here are several of the great benefits you'll get with a VA mortgage.

- ◆ *No down payment.* With a VA loan you can finance up to $240,000 without putting any money down. If you want to buy a higher-priced property, you need only come up with 25 percent of the amount over $240,000. For instance, if the property you want to buy is priced at $300,000, you'll need a down payment of $15,000 (0.25 × $60,000)—or just 5 percent of the purchase price.
- ◆ *Liberal qualifying.* Similar to FHA, VA loans offer liberal qualifying guidelines. Many (but not all) VA lenders will forgive properly explained credit blemishes. The VA loan also permits higher qualifying ratios. I've seen veterans with good compensating factors close loans with a 0.48 total debt ratio. (See Chapter 8.)
- ◆ *Closing costs paid.* Often homebuilders and cooperative sellers will pay all of the veteran's settlement expenses. In fact, builders sometimes advertise that veterans can buy homes in their developments for just $1 total move-in costs.
- ◆ *2–4 unit properties.* As with FHA loans, VA will finance a single-family house or an owner-occupied 2–4 unit property. However, unlike FHA, VA does not raise its lending limits for duplexes, triplexes, and quads.
- ◆ *Assumable.* Like FHA, a non-vet buyer may assume your VA mortgage when you sell your home. Also like FHA, if interest rates fall you can streamline a no-appraisal, no-qualifying refinance.
- ◆ *No mortgage insurance.* But unlike FHA, when you use a VA loan, you won't have to buy mortgage insurance. You will have to pay a one-time "funding fee" ranging between 1.5 to 2.75 percent of the amount you borrow. If you don't want to pay this fee in cash at closing, you can tell the lender to add it to your mortgage loan balance.

> **Be sure your FHA/VA loan rep specializes in these types of loans.**

As with some other types of mortgages, VA loans may require piles of paperwork. You will need to comply with rules that look into job history, property condition, property value (called a CRV), and seller prepaids. That's why you should work with a mortgage loan advisor who is skilled and experienced in the day-to-day job of getting VA loans approved. "The devil is in the details," says loan consultant Abe Padoka. Make sure you work with professionals who know the ins and outs of the VA application and approval process.

Even Fannie and Freddie Accept Little- or Nothing-Down Loans

> **Conventional lenders (nongovernment loans) now offer multiple types of low-down-payment loans.**

In the mid 1990s, both Freddie Mac (see www.homesteps.com) and Fannie Mae (www.fanniemae.com) have committed to making far more little- or nothing-down loan programs available. Since then, in addition to their standard 5 percent down loan product, Fannie and Freddie have pioneered community homebuyer programs, 3 percent down loans, and now even 103 percent LTV loans—meaning qualified borrowers can go through closing with almost no cash out of their own pocket. For a full view of Fannie/Freddie programs, visit these companies' websites.

Tougher Credit Standards and Lower-Cost Private Mortgage Insurers

Fannie Mae and Freddie Mac low-down-payment loans do apply tougher credit standards than either FHA or VA, but their loan limits reach substantially higher. Also, borrowers whose credit scores top 680 (possibly 620) will probably pay less for private mortgage insurance with these loan programs than they would with FHA.

On the other hand, borrowers with FICO scores of less than 620 may find that FHA's mortgage insurance premiums (MIP) now fall below the premiums of the private insurers who guarantee Fannie Mae and Freddie Mac's low-down-payment mortgages (LTVs greater than 80 percent). That's because the private mortgage insurers recently kicked up their costs to give marginal borrowers a real wallop—an increase of nearly $200 per month on a $200,000 mortgage.

Fannie Mae/Freddie Mac Loan Limits

Unlike FHA loans, the maximum amount you can borrow under Freddie Mac and Fannie Mae programs does not vary by area of the country—except for Alaska, Hawaii, Guam, and the Virgin Islands, where loan limits are 50 percent higher than the continental United States. Generally, Freddie and Fannie loan limits are high enough to finance good properties in decent neighborhoods. Freddie Mac and Fannie Mae programs will lend up to the following amounts (adjusted upward each year):

Maximum Loan Limits (Continental United States)

Type of Residence	Loan Limits
One-family	$333,700
Two-family	427,150
Three-family	516,300
Four-family	641,650

As you can see, a Fannie or Freddie low-down-payment loan can get you a property valued in excess of $650,000. Remember, too, all you need to do is move into the property for a minimum of 12 months. What a great way to buy a fourplex—yet still benefit with high leverage and the lowest mortgage interest rates available.

Summing Up

Whether you currently rent or own, if you're cash-short, I urge you to seriously consider the advantages of financing your next investment property with a low- or no-down-payment owner-occupied loan. In fact, even if the amount of your bank balance climbs up to six figures or more, remember the great (potential) benefits of high leverage. Whatever your financial situation, before you invest, carefully weigh the advantages of owner-occupied financing.

But if you can't or don't want to go for this type of easy financing, take heart. You've still got many other low- or no-cash possibilities. For those techniques, we now turn to Chapter 5.

Forget the Banks, Seek Out Seller Financing

Robert Bruss, the nationally syndicated columnist, real estate attorney, and investor, was recently asked, "Where's the best place to get a mortgage? At a bank, savings and loan, or credit union?" He answered, "None of these is the best. The best source of financing is the seller." If you can persuade the sellers to help with your financing, you'll probably get many of the following benefits:

1. ***Little (or nothing) down.*** Although some sellers do insist on a 20 or 30 percent down payment, most owners who offer OWC (owner-will-carry) financing will accept 10 percent down (or less).
2. ***Lower credit standards.*** Although banks have made qualifying easier, they're still tougher than most sellers.
3. ***No qualifying income.*** As we discuss in Chapter 8, many sellers expect you to pay their monthly payments from the income the property produces rather than use their own earnings. As long as your rent collections look like they're enough to cover all of your expenses, the seller won't usually ask for your W-2s or income tax returns (as will a bank).
4. ***Flexibility.*** Price, interest rate, monthly payments, and other terms are set by mutual agreement. You and the sellers can put together a financing package in any way that works for both of you.

5. *Lower closing costs.* Sellers seldom require points, origination fees, and loan application costs. Unlike lending institutions, sellers don't have to cover office overhead.

6. *Less paperwork.* Although sellers may ask for your credit scores, they won't require a stack of forms, documents, and verifications.

7. *Quicker sale.* Seller financing can help sellers get their property sold more quickly. Plus, for properties that require extensive repairs or renovations, seller financing can make the difference between a sale and no sale.

The types of seller-assisted financing that you might use to buy a property are as varied as your imagination. But be aware, not all owners who will accept (OWC) financing advertise that fact. Indeed, Robert Bruss says, "I've bought many properties with seller financing. But I can't recall a single one that was advertised 'seller financing.' Until they saw my offer, none of the sellers had informed their agent that they would help finance the sale."

> **Even sellers who do not advertise OWC will often accept it.**

Although many sellers do advertise, Bruss is right. Regardless of whether sellers state their intention to carry back financing, keep the possibility in mind. You won't know for sure until you've written up an offer.

For numerous examples of seller-assisted financing that I've reprinted from the pages of recent newspapers, see Box 5.1. Look through your local papers. More than likely you'll find many similar types of ads. And even if you don't, never fear to make seller financing a part of your offer.

Sellers Can Nearly Always Beat the Banks at Their Own Game, But You Must Do More than Ask

Here are the differences: Mortgage lenders operate by bureaucratic rules. Sellers are free to listen to any deal you suggest that provides them worthwhile benefits. Lenders may require qualifications, paperwork, documents, and verifications piled higher and deeper. Sellers can agree to as few documents and qualifying standards as reasonable in a specific situation. Lenders pay huge costs for fancy buildings, office overhead,

Box 5.1   A Sampling of Ads with Seller-Assisted Financing

> **OWC offers you flexibility and often lower costs.**

loan rep commissions, and executive perks. Sellers incur none of these expenses. In addition to interest, lenders may charge you thousands of dollars in origination fees, closing costs, and mortgage insurance. Sellers expect payment only for interest and maybe a few out-of-pocket costs.

How to Get the Sellers Interested

If you simply pop the question to sellers out of the blue and ask them to carry back financing, many will answer with a quick no. So, always put your proposal in writing as part of your offer to buy the property. Don't necessarily expect oral concessions on this issue right away. (Prior to

> **Use OWC feeler questions.**

writing an offer, I do frequently pose feeler questions such as, "Have you given any thought to offering financing with the property?") Most important, before you write an offer, learn the seller's needs and selling motives:

1. Do they want or need a quick sale?
2. Do they seriously need cash?
3. Would a safe 6 to 8 percent return seem attractive to them?
4. If the property is currently owned by investors, what kind of capital gains tax liability will these sellers incur from an all-cash sale? Would an IRS-approved installment sale save the sellers taxes?
5. What do the sellers plan to do with the proceeds of sale?
6. What other pressures of time, money, family, or work bear on the sale?

These questions merely suggest lines of inquiry. Basically, you should tactfully learn as much about the sellers as you can. Then draft your written offer to play into their most pressing needs.

Explain point-by-point how your offer alleviates their principal concerns without giving rise to new ones. Are you a credible buyer? Does the proposal create too much risk? A skilled Realtor may be able to help you achieve this result. Remember, a confused mind always says no. Eliminate seller doubts with clear and compelling reasons.

What Type of Seller Financing?

Although we often speak of "seller financing," the term really doesn't refer to just a single technique. In fact, as you gain experience, you'll find that the wide flexibility of seller-finance techniques gives OWC considerable advantage over bank financing. Here are several of the most popular ways that sellers can cooperate and participate in the financing arrangement:

◆ Mortgage or trust deed	◆ Lease purchase
◆ Contract-for-deed	◆ Mortgage assumption
◆ Lease option	◆ "Subject to" purchase
◆ Master lease	◆ Wraparound

Mortgage (Trust Deed)

Generally speaking, when you finance your property with a bank, the bank will loan you money (which is immediately turned over to the sellers), and you will sign a mortgage (or depending on the state where you are buying property, the lender may use a deed of trust). By signing this document, you pledge the property as security for your loan. If you fail to make your payments, the lender can follow a legal procedure to auction off the property at a public foreclosure (trustee) sale.

Seller Mortgages (Trust Deeds)

Essentially, seller mortgages work the same as bank mortgages—except that no money (aside from your down payment, if any) changes hands. Instead, the sellers deed you their property in exchange for your pledge to pay the sellers over time through periodic installments (usually monthly payments).

But like a bank, if you don't pay as agreed, the sellers can file a foreclosure lawsuit against you. If the sellers prove that you've failed to pay (and you offer no persuasive legal defenses), your property will be sold to the highest bidder at a public auction. You (and quite likely the sellers) will lose money. As a rule, foreclosure sales seldom bring in enough money to make everyone whole.

Persuade the sellers with credibility and benefits.

Because OWC sellers can lose money if you don't pay, most property owners initially prefer to cash out at the time of sale. They simply don't want to take the risk that you will default. Therefore, especially in low-down (or nothing-down) deals, you must persuade the sellers using two separate reasons:

Emphasize Your Credibility and Reliability

Even though few sellers will put your credit and finances under a magnifying glass (as will a bank), they still want you to assure them that they can count on you to make your payments on time, every time. You must persuade sellers of your credibility and reliability.

To achieve this goal, marshal as much convincing evidence as you can. Emphasize your consistency, character, and when favorable, your credit scores (see Chapter 3). In addition, if you've built up a significant net worth, accumulated cash reserves, or maybe you earn a good income from a secure job, play up any or all of these positives.

Stress Seller Benefits   To make OWC financing attractive to the sellers, also stress the benefits that the sellers will receive. I have found many sellers who fear to carry back OWC financing because they don't want the worries. But after I persuade them of my credibility *and* the advantages they can reap, more often than not, they accept my offer.

What do the sellers get out of the deal? As noted earlier, I have found that sellers are willing to carry back financing for some combination of these six reasons:

1. *No bank financing available.* A property may not qualify for bank financing. The property might suffer from poor condition; be located in a less-desirable neighborhood; or stand functionally out-of-date (rooming house, apartment units with shared bathrooms, irregular floor plan). Also, many lending institutions won't write mortgages on condominiums or townhouses where more than 30 or 40 percent of the units in the complex are occupied by renters instead of owners.
2. *Quick sale.* One of the best ways for an owner to sell a property quickly is to accept easy terms of financing. Do the sellers want to move on with their lives? Then follow the adage, "a buyer at hand is worth two 'maybes' six months into the future." Emphasize the here and now.

3. ***Higher price.*** Property owners who accept easy financing can often sell at a higher price than they otherwise could expect to receive.
4. ***High interest on savings.*** Sellers who plan to deposit the cash they receive from a sale in certificates of deposit or money market accounts can get a higher return on their money by financing a buyer's purchase of their property. A 6 to 8 percent return from a real estate installment sale certainly beats a 2 to 5 percent return from a certificate of deposit.
5. ***Low closing costs.*** With OWC financing, sellers (and buyers) pay far less in closing costs. You avoid much of the expense that a mortgage lender would charge.
6. ***Tax savings.*** When the seller is an investor, an installment sale of a property produces a smaller income tax bite than does a cash sale. Installment sales permit sellers to spread their taxes on depreciation recapture and capital gains over the entire term of the mortgage.

As we look to the future, I expect the aging of the U.S. population will bring about more seller-financed transactions. Why? Because savings accounts offer too little interest. Stocks offer too much perceived risk. As a result, increasing numbers of seniors will prefer the larger returns and small risks of seller financing.

Who Handles the Legal Work?

In a few states, chiefly in the northeast, lawyers get themselves involved in most property purchases—with or without seller financing. In the great majority of states, most sellers and buyers set up an escrow account with a title insurance company. Experienced personnel at the title company then take care of all the paperwork. I have used this approach many times and have never run into any difficulties because of it.

Typically, a title company can handle the OWC paperwork.

Nevertheless, as a beginning investor, you may want to discuss the details of your deal with a knowledgeable and trustworthy real estate attorney. True, I sometimes find that lawyers create more problems and expenses than they're worth. And I know many real estate investors who feel the same way. Still, when necessary, we do use them.[1]

Try a Contract-for-Deed

Among the most famous lines in American silent film history (in *The Perils of Pauline*) is Oil Can Harry's repeated warnings to Pauline, "If you don't give me the deed to your ranch, I'm going to tie you to the railroad tracks." Oil Can Harry knew that if Pauline signed over the deed to her

ranch, that deed would transfer the property's title to Harry. Although Oil Can Harry's no-money-down approach to property ownership was somewhat unorthodox (not to mention illegal), typically, whenever someone buys real estate, they receive a deed at the time of purchase. With the deed comes ownership (albeit often subject to a mortgage).

> Some types of
> OWC delay the
> transfer of deed.

In some purchases, though, buyers don't receive a deed at the time of sale. Instead, they buy a property on the installment plan. In this type of purchase, buyers usually pay the sellers a small down payment and promise to continue paying monthly installments. In return, the sellers give the buyers possession. But unlike with a mortgage, the sellers don't deliver the deed at "closing." Rather, they contractually promise to deliver a deed to the buyers only after they have completed their scheduled payments.

This type of OWC agreement is known by various names such as *contract-for-deed, installment sale,* or *land contract.* For beginning investors, a land contract can be an excellent way to buy property. I know from experience.

Why Sellers Are Willing

When I turned age 21, I wanted to acquire real estate as quickly as possible. At the time I was an undergraduate college student. I had little cash,

---

1. For more on taking advice from lawyers, real estate agents, friends, and family, see my book, *The 106 Common Mistakes Homebuyers Make—And How to Avoid Them, 3rd ed.* (New York: John Wiley & Sons, 2002), pp. 216–220.

no full-time job, and no significant credit record. My immediate chances for getting a bank to write a mortgage for me were zero. But this fact didn't deter me. I searched for owners who would sell their properties to me on an installment contract. By the time I completed my Ph.D., I had bought around 30 houses and small apartment units. The cash flow from these properties paid many of my college expenses (and yes, for my Cessna and Jaguar XK-E[2]).

My sellers accepted this type of OWC financing for most (or all) of the reasons I listed. But the contract-for-deed then offered sellers one more important advantage. If I failed to make my monthly payments, the sellers could repossess the financed property—almost as easily as a bank can repossess a car.

Today, though, many states have made it tougher for sellers to repossess properties. Now, courts sometimes force contract-for-deed sellers to file a foreclosure lawsuit. Buyers gain more protection, but fewer sellers are willing to put up with this extra hassle. So (in the tough states), the land contract has lost much of its popularity to the lease option (discussed later).

Follow These Guidelines

When you and the property you buy meet the qualifying standards of a lending institution, great. You can weigh the relative costs and benefits of each type of financing. On the other hand, if bank financing is not available, always try to negotiate a contract-for-deed (or seller-held mortgage). Buying from a seller on the installment plan beats not investing at all. If you're a cash-short buyer, you can win with this strategy in the following way: Buy a rundown property with an installment contract. Then create value through improvements. Next, refinance based on the now higher value of the property and pay off the sellers and put title in your own name.

If you do finance a property with a contract-for-deed (or other type of OWC), follow these guidelines:

    1. ***Buy the property, not the financing.*** Don't let easy credit draw you into the purchase of an overpriced property. When

---

2. When I was younger, I did waste too much money on expensive toys—a mistake I no longer make.

circumstances warrant, you might in good judgment pay a price slightly higher than market value. But you would not pay $8,000 for any old car from Easy Ed's "buy here, pay here" used car lot just because Easy Ed will sell it to you with nothing down and low monthly payments. This same principle applies to investment properties. Beware of the real estate gurus who urge you to entice the seller with the proposition, "You name the price; I'll name the terms." Verify value through an appraisal or other professional opinion. Don't agree to overpay.

2. *Beware of hidden defects.* A property that seems priced right might suffer hidden defects. Take care to obtain experienced and knowledgeable estimates for any repairs or renovations that you plan. Never "ballpark" or casually figure the costs necessary to bring a property up to the condition you want it. Get professional property inspections and cost estimates before you invest.

3. *Contract terms are governed by law.* A contract-for-deed places you and the seller in a relationship that is governed not only by the contract language, but also by state laws and court decisions. Under an installment sale, your rights and responsibilities differ from those you acquire when you finance a property with a mortgage or trust deed.

> **Don't let a lawyer derail you without first considering benefits as well as risks.**

Before you sign an installment-sale agreement, consult a real estate attorney who can tell you the details of land contract law in your state. Be aware. Many lawyers warn against buying a property on the installment plan because such contracts pose more risk than a mortgage agreement. These lawyers look at risks without considering benefits and opportunities. (Using similar logic, such lawyers would advise against marriage because you might suffer the pain of divorce.)

Get a lawyer who understands both rewards and risks. Then negotiate a contract-for-deed that can work for you and the sellers. Over the years, millions of Americans (especially low-to-moderate-income Americans) have successfully bought houses and small rental properties on the land contract installment plan. I was one of them.

Assume a Low-Interest-Rate Mortgage

Although technically not a form of seller financing per se, some sellers do offer you the opportunity to take over their current mortgage. This process is called "assuming the sellers' financing." Seller assumables may offer distinct advantages over new financing:

- ◆ Lower interest rate
- ◆ Easier qualifying
- ◆ Low closing costs
- ◆ Little or nothing down

Return to the Past with an Assumable Loan

When market interest rates climb back up, you don't have to pay those higher rates. Instead, shop for a property with a low-interest-rate assumable loan. Say it's three years into the future and you want to buy a property. But market interest rates are again hovering around 9 percent. You fondly recall those bygone days when 30-year fixed rate loans set below 6 percent. If you could only climb into a time machine. You can. Here's how.

When you assume a mortgage, you roll back the clock and take over the mortgage of the seller at the same rate the seller is paying— even if that rate sits well below current market rates. Years ago, nearly all sellers could transfer their low-rate mortgages to their buyers. By the early 1980s, however, most lenders had changed their mortgage contracts to include the "due on sale" clause (the notorious paragraph 17). This clause prohibits routine assumptions and upon sale (or long-term lease) requires sellers to pay off their mortgage balance.

As a result, too many people today erroneously believe that *all* assumption possibilities have died. To further the problem, loan reps seldom tell borrowers about assumptions because assumptions originate directly between sellers and their buyers. You cannot walk into a lender's office and say, "I'd like one of those low-rate, assumable mortgages that's going to save me tens of thousands of dollars." No, before you can assume a real estate loan, you must locate a seller who has one.

> **Many assumable mortgages still exist.**

Which Sellers Can Offer Assumable Financing?

Generally, sellers who have financed their properties with FHA, VA, or most types of adjustable-rate mortgages can offer an assumption to their buyers. Realtor Roger Rodell describes his experience with assumables during a past period of high mortgage rates.

Roger Rodell's Experience with Assumables   Roger has said, "I'm promoting low-interest assumable FHA/VA mortgages. True, buyers do have to qualify to assume these loans. And some of the lenders I deal with aren't too eager to push through loan assumptions for a few hundred dollars in transfer fees (compared to the several thousand dollars they earn for new loan originations). But the lower rates and monthly payments make qualifying easier and the cash savings for buyers are tremendous. If a fairly priced home with a low-interest-rate assumable hits the market, I tell my buyers to go for it. Don't try to pull the sellers down. When there's a pile of $1,000 bills sitting in front of you, don't get greedy and demand an even better deal."

> **Loan assumptions can save you big dollars.**

Cut Your Interest Costs by Thousands   "I've worked out the numbers," Roger continues. "Over a period of 5 years on a $100,000 loan, as compared to a 9 percent new mortgage, a 7 percent assumable will save you $8,400 in interest. Over 10 years, the savings are nearly $17,000; and over 25 years, you'll keep an extra $42,000. And those numbers don't include the $2,000 to $4,000 that an assumable might save you in points, origination fees, appraisal, and closing costs. Now, you can see why I refer to a good low-interest assumable as a pile of $1,000 bills."

Short-Term Strategies

Under some situations, you might even gain by assuming a mortgage that carries a higher-than-market interest rate. Say current rates are at 6.5 percent and you're negotiating with a seller whose assumable mortgage has a rate of 7.5 percent. Not worth assuming? Don't jump to that conclusion. Assumptions usually cost less in terms of time, effort, and cash-to-close than new mortgage originations. So, this 7.5 percent loan assumption could prove profitable if, say,

1. You plan to own the property for only a year or two.
2. Inflation has dropped to almost zero, and interest rates are sure to fall further. You want to time your new mortgage to coincide with the lower rates that you foresee.
3. You plan to improve the property to increase its value. Then, you'd like to get a new loan based on the higher property value that you have created.
4. Your borrower profile displays some warts. New financing at the lowest rates available could prove iffy. In contrast, qualifying for the assumption probably will not require the same exacting standards. One year or two years of perfect payments could set you up to then qualify for a new loan as an "A" borrower.

How to Find Assumables   Right now, millions of outstanding FHA and VA loans (fixed-rate and adjustable) permit assumptions. Plus, most conventional (Fannie Mae/Freddie Mac) and portfolio lenders will allow sellers to transfer their adjustable-rate mortgage (ARM) loans to buyers.

> **You can assume (as an owner-occupant) any FHA/VA mortgage.**

To find these loans requires you to ask sellers and investigate. Frequently, sellers or their realty agents either don't know or don't publicize mortgage assumptions. On the other hand, when interest rates do shoot up, the search for assumables becomes intense. Savvy sellers and agents then tout their assumables to favorably differentiate their properties from others that require buyers to obtain more costly new financing.

Lower-Rate Assumable ARMs   Nearly all adjustable-rate mortgages include lifetime rate caps. No matter how high market interest rates climb, ARM borrowers know that their loan rate will max out at 8, 9, 10, or 12 percent (or possibly higher). Therefore, in periods of very high mortgage rates, you may find ARMs that are maxed out (or close to maxed out), yet still sit below the going rates for new 30-year, fixed-rate mortgages. In that case, you're sitting pretty. Your (assumable) ARM rate can't go up (much), but it can go down.

> **ARMs also offer assumable possibilities.**

Search for Sellers with Low-Equity Assumables

You've already seen that in periods of higher interest rates, you can slash your interest costs by assuming a mortgage that carries a below current-market interest rate. In addition, assumables can help you buy with little or nothing down. Just locate a seller who has bought (or refinanced) recently with a low-down, high-LTV assumable mortgage. Within the past three or four years, FHA and VA have originated millions of low- and nothing-down home finance plans.

> **Assumables give you another low-down-payment possibility.**

Due to the fact that the original loan balances often add in closing costs and fees, most of these buyers (now sellers) have built up little equity in their homes. In many instances, you can assume for less than 10 percent cash out-of-pocket. In those cases where sellers do own substantial equity, you might ask for a seller second or arrange a second mortgage through a mortgage lender.

"Assume" a Nonassumable Mortgage

Nearly all *non*-FHA/VA long-term fixed-rate mortgages include the once infamous paragraph 17 (the "due on sale" clause). This clause reads (in part) as follows:

> ¶ 17. If all or any part of the [mortgaged] property or an interest therein is sold or transferred by the Borrower *without Lender's prior written consent . . . Lender may, at Lender's option, declare* all the sums secured by this Mortgage to be immediately *due and payable.*[3]

Very few people understand the precise wording of this clause, but that wording carries significant implications.

---

3. This clause now often shows up as paragraph 18. It might carry another number in some other mortgage contracts.

What This Clause Does and Does Not Say

Notice that nothing in this paragraph prevents owners from selling you their property *without* first paying off their mortgage. This clause only gives lenders the right to call the mortgage due and payable if such a transfer occurs without "Lender's prior written consent."

You Can Assume a "Nonassumable" Mortgage

Nothing prevents you and a seller from asking a lender to give its written consent. Why would the lender agree to accept your request? Here are several reasons:

1. The sellers have fallen behind in their payments and you agree to bring the mortgage current.
2. The interest rate on the mortgage equals or exceeds the current market rate. Lenders hate "portfolio runoff" of their market or above-market rate loans.
3. You, the sellers, or both parties give the lender substantial amounts of other business (loans, CDs, savings and checking accounts).
4. You (or the sellers) promise to move much of your banking business to the lender.

Will these or any other reasons you can think of persuade the lender to grant its consent? Sometimes yes, sometimes no. But it doesn't cost to ask. When the situation warrants, lenders do oblige.

Unfortunately, most people ask the wrong question and get the wrong answer. When looking at a property, they query the seller or agent, "Is the financing assumable?" If the mortgage includes a due-on-sale clause, the sellers or real estate agent will routinely answer, "No, the mortgage is not assumable." Wrong answer. The correct answer is, "Yes, it's assumable with the lender's consent. If you would like to try to assume it, we can make the lender an offer."

Buying Subject to: "Assuming" without Consent

Again I emphasize that the wording of the "due on sale" paragraph does not stop owners from selling a mortgaged property to anyone

> **Sellers willing, you can buy any property with "subject to" financing.**

they choose to. Nor in such sales does the clause *require* the sellers or the buyers to pay off the loan. This clause merely gives the lender the right (or option) to call the loan due.

Therefore, sometimes when buyers and sellers believe that a lender won't grant an assumption, they complete the sale anyway and never inform the lender that the property has a new owner. The buyer then continues to make the payments to the lender on the same terms and interest rate that applied to the sellers. Contrary to what some people say, this "subject to" technique is neither illegal, immoral, or fattening. It does not even violate the mortgage contract.

How I Have Used a "Subject To" I have used "subject to" financing with a number of property purchases. In 1981, for example, market mortgage rates were at 16 percent. I bought a property "subject to" that carried a mortgage rate of 10 percent. Because this property was a "flipper," I only owned it 18 months. But even during that short period, the "subject to" mortgage arrangement saved me $17,000 in interest, points, and closing costs.

Beginners Beware Several current authors and real estate get-rich-quick gurus are now peddling the "subject to" technique to the uninformed and inexperienced. Only instead of advising it for saving money on interest, they're pushing it to the credit-impaired as a means to buy a property without lying prostrate before a lender. Here's my advice: Beginners beware! Although this technique can prove appealing in some situations—short-term holding periods, high interest mortgage environment, credit impaired—don't blindly fall for the sweet talk of the gurus. "Subject to" financing holds risks for sellers and buyers. If you don't pay the lender on time, the lender chalks up late payments in the seller's credit record. If the lender calls the loan due, someone must either pay up or refinance the property.

> **Never use "subject to" financing without weighing your risks.**

Will Lenders Really Call the Loan? Some real estate gurus say, "Don't worry. Here's a bag of tricks. Use these tricks and the lender won't find out about the property transfer. Surely what the lender can't see won't hurt you. No problem. Just keep the lender in the dark."

Do these tricks work? Maybe, maybe not. After suffering through the tumultuous 1980s and early 1990s, lenders have become far more savvy. Some time within a year or two after a sale, the lender will probably learn that the previous owner (and original borrower) has sold you the mortgaged property.

"No worry," the gurus say. "Even if the lender discovers the transfer, chances are the lender won't call the loan due. Most lenders follow a 'don't ask, don't tell' policy. But they're not going to advertise their forbearance. As long as your mortgage payments keep flowing in on time and the property taxes and insurance get paid, your risks are small."

On this point (for now at least) the gurus may be right. That's because today interest rates on most "subject to" mortgages equal or exceed current market rates. When rates spike up, though, I suspect that lenders will send out the enforcers. Stay prepared.

Use "subject to" financing to solve a *short-term* need. But, over the longer term, you'll probably need to come up with another source of financing.

CHAPTER 6

Five More Techniques to Finance Your Investments

You find a property that you would like to buy, but the seller (or lender) won't let you use a mortgage assumption or "subject to" purchase. Instead, the seller proposes a *wraparound* mortgage. Especially in times of high interest rates, a wraparound mortgage can provide a win-win solution for buyers and sellers.

Wraparounds Benefit Buyers and Sellers

Wraparound financing yields big savings for buyers at the same time that it puts profits into the pocket of the seller. Only the lender gets short-changed. Here's how a wraparound works to overcome higher market interest rates:

Financial Facts

Asking price	$200,000
Mortgage balance	$100,000
Interest rate	6%
Term remaining (years)	20
Monthly payment	$716
Market interest rate	9%

You offer to buy the property for $200,000. If the seller agrees to finance $180,000 at 7.5 percent fully amortized over 20 years, your payment (P&I) equals $1,450 per month.[1] The underlying $100,000 mortgage remains in place, and its monthly payments will be paid by the seller. To complete the purchase, you sign a land contract, mortgage, or trust deed with the seller.

Each month the seller collects $1,450 from you and pays the bank a monthly mortgage payment of $716 for a net in the seller's pocket of $734 ($1,450 less $716). Because the seller has actually financed only $80,000 ($180,000 less the 100,000 still owed to the bank), he achieves an attractive rate of return on his loan of 11.1 percent.

$$\text{Seller ROI} = \frac{\$8,808}{\$80,000}$$
$$= 11.1\%$$

> **You gain a lower interest rate. The seller gains a high return.**

Yet, you, too, gain. Had you financed $180,000 with a bank at the market rate of 9 percent amortized over 20 years, your payment would total $1,619 per month instead of the $1,450 that you'll pay to the seller. The actual spread between the current market interest rate, the seller's old bank rate, and the interest rate you pay the seller will depend on the motives and negotiating power of you and the seller. But this example shows how a wraparound can benefit both parties—true win-win financing.[2]

Lease Options

Would you like to own a property? Yet, for reasons of blemished credit, self-employment (especially those with off-the-books income or tax-

---

1. You also pay for the property insurance, property taxes, maintenance, and upkeep.

2. If the lender can enforce a due-on-sale clause, this technique does bring about that risk. In that situation a wraparound works better as a short-term financing strategy. If the lender calls, there may be no long term.

minimized income), unstable income (commissions, tips), or lack of cash, do you believe that you can't currently qualify for a mortgage from a lending institution? Then the lease option (a lease with an option to purchase) might solve your dilemma. Properly structured, the lease option will permit you to acquire ownership rights in a property. At the same time, it also gives you time to improve your financial profile (at least from the perspective of a mortgage lender).

Here's How It Works

As the name implies, the lease option combines two contracts into one: a lease and an option to buy. Under the lease, you sign a rental agreement that covers the usual rental terms and conditions (see Chapter 17) such as:

- Monthly rental rate
- Term of lease
- Responsibilities for repair, maintenance, and upkeep
- Sublet and assignment
- Pets, smoking, cleanliness
- Permissible property uses
- House rules (noise, parking, number of occupants)

The option part of the contract gives you the right to buy the property at some future date. As a minimum, the option should include (1) the amount of your option payment, (2) your purchase price for the property, (3) the date on which the purchase option expires, (4) right of assignment, and (5) the amount of the rent credits that will count toward the purchase price of the house.

Benefits to Tenant-Buyers (an Eager Market)

In recent years, the benefits of lease options to tenant-buyers have been extolled by the respected, nationally syndicated real estate columnist Robert Bruss as well as by most books written for first-time homebuyers. For example, in my book, *Yes! You Can Own the Home You Want* (New York: John Wiley & Sons, 1995, p. 59), I tell hopeful homebuyers,

There's simply no question that lease options can bring home ownership closer to reality for many renters in at least six ways:

1. ***Easier qualifying.*** Qualifying for a lease option may be no more difficult than qualifying for a lease (sometimes easier). Generally, your credit and employment record need meet only minimum standards. Most property owners will not place your financial life under a magnifying glass as would a mortgage lender.

2. ***Low initial investment.*** Your initial investment to get into a lease option agreement can be as little as one month's rent and a security deposit of a similar amount. At the outside, move-in cash rarely exceeds $5,000 to $10,000, although I did see a home lease optioned at a price of $1.5 million which asked for $50,000 up front.

3. ***Forced savings.*** The lease option contract typically forces you to save for the down payment required when you exercise your option to buy. Often, lease options charge above-market rental rates and then credit perhaps 50 percent of your rent toward the down payment. The exact amount is negotiable. And once you have committed yourself to buying, you should find it easier to cut other spending and place more money toward your "house account."

4. ***Firm selling price.*** Your option should set a firm selling price for the home, or it should include a formula (perhaps a slight inflation-adjustment factor) that can be used to calculate a firm price. Shop carefully, negotiate wisely, and when you exercise your option in one to three years (or whenever), your home's market value could exceed its option price. If your home has appreciated (or you've created value through improvements—see below), you may be able to borrow nearly all the money you need to close the sale.

5. ***100 percent financing possible.*** You also can reduce the amount of cash investment you will need to close your purchase in another way: Lease-option a property that you can profitably improve through repairs, renovation, or cosmetics. After increasing the home's value, you may be able to borrow nearly all the money you need to exercise your option to buy the property.

   For example, assume that your lease option purchase price is $75,000. Say by the end of one year, your rent credits equal $2,500. You now owe the sellers $72,500.

Through repairs, fix-up work, and redecorating, you have increased the property's value by $10,000. Your home should now be worth around $85,000. If you have paid your bills on time during the previous year, you should be able to locate a lender who will finance your purchase with the full $72,500 you need to pay off the sellers. Or, as another possibility, you could sell the property, pay the sellers $72,500 and use your remaining $12,500 in cash proceeds from the sale to buy another property.

6. ***Reestablish credit.*** A lease option also can help you buy when you need time to build or reestablish a solid credit record. Judy and Paul Davis wanted to buy a home before prices or interest rates in their area rose above their reach. But the Davises needed time to clear up credit problems created by too much borrowing and Judy's layoff. The lease option proved to be the possibility that helped the Davises achieve their goal of home ownership.

Experience shows that when prospective tenants and homebuyers think through this list of benefits, they become a ready market for lease options.

Benefits to Investors

Although the lease option might help you buy a property, it can also prove to be a good way for you to rent out your investment property. You can structure lease options in many ways. This type of agreement can typically benefit you as an investor in at least three ways: (1) lower risk, (2) higher rents, and (3) guaranteed profits.

Lower Risk   As a rule, tenants who shop for a lease option will take better care of your property than would average renters. Because your lease-option tenants intend one day to own the house, they will treat it more like homeowners than tenants. Also, they know that to qualify for a mortgage they will need a near-perfect record of rent payments. (If your tenant-buyers don't know that fact, make sure you impress it into their consciousness.) As a minimum, lease-option tenants expect to pay up front first and last month's rent, a security deposit, and, more than likely, an option fee

> **Lease-option tenants take better care of properties.**

of $1,000 to $5,000 (possibly more). Taken together, all of these factors spell lower risk for you the property investor.

Higher Rents   Lease-option tenants will agree to pay higher than market rents because they know you will apply a part of that monthly rent to the home's purchase price. The tenants view these "rent credits"—actually they should be called purchase price credits—as forced savings that will contribute toward a lender's required down payment.

> **Lease-option tenants typically pay higher rents.**

From your immediate standpoint, the higher rent payments increase your monthly cash flow and boost your cash-on-cash return. In high-priced areas where newly bought rental properties awaken a hungry alligator, the increased rent from a lease-option rental may turn a negative cash flow into a positive.

Guaranteed Profits   Experienced investors know that (on average) fewer than 50 percent of lease-option tenants take advantage of their right to buy their leased home. Sometimes they change their mind. Sometimes their finances fail to improve as much as they hoped. Sometimes their personal circumstances shift (separation, divorce, job relocation, additional children).

> **Lease-option tenants often forfeit their option payments and rent credits.**

Whatever the reason, the tenants forfeit (at least in part) their rent credits, option fee, and any fix-up work they have performed around the house. As a sympathetic person, you may feel badly for the tenants. But as an investor, their loss means your gain. Because your tenants did not follow through with their purchase, you end up with more profit than you would have earned under a traditional rental agreement.

Even if the tenants do buy, you still win, because in setting your option price, you built in a good profit margin over the price you originally paid for the property. The lease-option technique works especially well in those transactions where you have bought at a bargain price. You net more than you would have gained from a straight sale of the property because you didn't have to pay high marketing costs or agent's commissions.

For investors, the lease option makes for truly a win-win agreement. You win when your tenants buy, and you win when the tenants don't buy and forfeit their rights in the property.

How to Find Lease-Option Buyers and Sellers

To drive the best bargain on a lease option as a buyer/lessee, don't limit your search to sellers who advertise lease options. These sellers are trying to retail their properties. It will be tougher for you to find a bargain here. Instead, look for motivated for-sale-by-owner (FSBO) sellers in the "Homes for Sale" classified ads. Or, you might also try property owners who are running "House for Rent" ads. Often, the best lease-option sellers will not have considered the idea until you suggest it.

When you search for tenant-buyers, generally you will be able to choose from three different classified newspaper ad categories: (1) homes for sale, (2) homes for rent, and (3) the specific category "lease option" that some newspapers include. Unfortunately, no one can say which ad category will work best in your market. Experiment with each of these choices. To learn which one is pulling the best responses, ask your callers to tell you in which category they saw the ad. Don't simply assume that any single category listing will draw the largest number of qualified callers.

A Creative Beginning with Lease Options (for Investors)

To start building wealth fast without investing much money up front, try the lease-option approach of Suzanne Brangham. Although Suzanne stumbled into her investment career quite fortuitously, you can follow her path more purposely. From her book, *Housewise* (New York: Harper-Collins, 1987, p. 39), here's Suzanne's story:

> While searching for the ideal career, I was also looking for a place to live. I located a lovely but dilapidated apartment house. The building was making a painful transition from rentals to condominiums. Units were for sale or rent. But sales were practically nonexistent.
>
> With my head held high, preliminary plans and a budget tucked under my arm, I decided to make the manager an offer he couldn't refuse.
>
> I told him that in lieu of paying the $800-a-month rent that was being asked for a 2-bedroom, 2-bath unit, I would renovate the entire apartment. I would agree to spend $9,600 for

labor and materials, the equivalent of a full year of rent payments. Along with a 12-month lease, I also requested an option to buy the unit at its $45,000 asking price.

Three months later, Suzanne was on her way. She then bought her renovated condo unit at her lease-option price of $40,000. Then, simultaneously, sold the unit to a buyer for $85,000. After accounting for renovation expenses, closing costs, and Realtor's commission, she netted $23,000. Suzanne no longer had a home, but she had found a career.

> **A $40,000 condo lease option led to a multimillion-dollar net worth.**

Twenty years, 23 homes, and 71 properties later, Suzanne had become not just independently wealthy, but a nationally recognized author, speaker, and entrepreneur. In her excellent book, *Housewise,* she tells about her renovation experiences and the career she found by chance. As I've said, it's a great book for anyone who would like to learn hundreds of profit-making ideas that can be applied to buying and renovating fixers.[3]

The Lease-Option Sandwich

The lease-option sandwich truly magnifies your profit potential. Instead of buying a property outright, you find *motivated* sellers who are willing to lease-option their property to you at both a bargain rental rate and a bargain price. Typically, such sellers were not advertising their property as a lease option. They generally are trying to sell it. In fact, they may not even have thought of the lease-option idea until you put a proposal in front of them.

Control without Cash

Ideally, through this lease option you gain control of the property for two to five years. Your cash-out-of-pocket totals less than you probably would have paid in closing costs had you immediately bought and financed the property with a new mortgage.

---

3. See also my own book on this topic: *Make Money with Fixer-Uppers and Renovations* (New York: John Wiley & Sons, 2003).

> **The lease-option sandwich maximizes your leverage.**

Next, you spend some money on spruce-up expenses (if desirable) and readvertise the property as a lease option. You find tenant-buyers and sign them up on a lease option with you as the lessor. Your tenant-buyers agree to pay you a higher monthly rental and a higher option price than you've negotiated for yourself in your role as lessee with the property owners. You profit from the markup in price and option money.

Your rate of return skyrockets because you gain control of a property with almost no cash investment. The up-front money you've collected from your tenant-buyers more than covers the amount you paid as option money to the property owners. Essentially, you're buying wholesale and selling retail—without actually having to pay for your inventory.

Does the Lease-Option Sandwich Really Work?

Theoretically, it can work. (Just make sure you protect yourself fully in the lease-option contracts you sign.) Robert Allen and James Lumley, for example, two well-known real estate investors and book authors, claim to have used this technique successfully to generate big profits with little or no cash.

Personally, I wouldn't try it. For my taste, giving someone an option to buy a property that I don't yet own seems fraught with dangers. Nevertheless, *in theory* this technique can yield high returns. So, if you're interested in biting into a lease-option sandwich, read Lumley's *5 Magic Paths to Making a Fortune in Real Estate* (New York: John Wiley & Sons, 2000). Also, Peter Conti and David Finkel advocate this technique in their book *Making Big Money Investing in Real Estate* (Chicago: Dearborn, 2002).

Lease-Purchase Agreements

As a practical matter, the lease-*purchase* agreement works about the same as a lease option. However, instead of gaining the right to either accept or reject a property, the lease-purchaser *commits to buying it*. As an investor, you can often persuade reluctant sellers to accept your lease-purchase offer, even though they may shy away from a lease option. The lease-purchase offer seems much more definite because you are saying that you will buy the property—you would just like to defer closing until some future date (say, six months to five years more or less) that works for you and the sellers.

"Seems" More Definite

I say "seems" more definite because there is a loophole. You can (and should) write an escape clause into your purchase offer called "liquidated damages." With a liquidated damages clause, the sellers could not sue you to go through with your purchase (specific performance) if you chose to back out. Nor could they sue you for money damages that they may have suffered due to your failure to buy. Instead, the liquidated damage clause simply permits your sellers to pocket your earnest money deposit.

> **Always use a liquidated damage clause in your purchase offers.**

In effect, your earnest money really acts like an option payment. No matter what the purchase contract appears to say, in reality you have not firmly committed to buy.

Amount of the Earnest Money Deposit

The real firmness of either a lease-option or a lease-purchase contract lies in the amount of the up-front money the seller receives—regardless of whether it's called an "option" fee or an "earnest money" deposit. If you want to really show a seller that you intend to complete a lease-option or a lease-purchase transaction, put a larger amount of cash on the table. By the same token, if you truly do want to "keep your options open," negotiate the smallest "walkaway" fee that you can, even if it means conceding elsewhere in the agreement.

Contingency Clauses

You also can escape from your obligation to buy a property through the use of contingency clauses. If the contingency (property condition, ability to obtain financing, lawyer approval, sale of another property, etc.) isn't met, you can walk away from a purchase and at the same time rightfully demand the return of your earnest money or option fee. Contingencies, option fees, and earnest money deposits are further discussed in Chapter 16.

Master-Lease an Apartment Building

To make money in real estate, you need to control a property. The most common way to obtain this control is through ownership. Some investors, though, don't buy their multiunit properties—at least not right away. Instead, they master-lease them. As we just discussed, buyers and sellers typically use a lease-option agreement to convey condominiums and single-family homes. But to acquire (without purchase) apartment buildings, you would use a master lease.

A Turnaround Property

Say you locate a 12-unit apartment building that is poorly managed and needs upgrading. You might offer to buy the property. But you really don't have the financial power to arrange new financing, and the owner doesn't want to sell the property using a land contract or purchase-money mortgage.

Currently, the property barely produces enough cash flow to pay expenses, property taxes, and mortgage payments. The owner wants to turn this money pit into a money-maker, but lacks the will to invest time, effort, money, and talent.

> **You control the property without putting in much cash.**

The solution: master-lease the entire building and guarantee the owner a steady no-hassle monthly income. In return, you obtain the right to upgrade the building and manage the property to increase its net operating income (NOI).

Generally, a master lease gives you possession of the property for a period of 3 to 15 years and an option to buy at a prearranged price. During the period of your lease, you would pocket the difference between what you pay to operate the property, including lease payments to the owner, and the amounts you collect from the individual tenants who live in each of the apartments. This technique resembles the lease-option sandwich that we discussed earlier, only it applies to multiple-unit buildings as opposed to single-family houses. Here's how the before-and-after numbers might look:

Before (Owner Management)

Gross potential income at $500 per unit	$72,000
Vacancy losses at 15%	10,800
Effective gross income	$61,200
Expenses	
Utilities	14,400
Maintenance	8,360
Advertising	2,770
Insurance	3,110
Property taxes	6,888
Miscellaneous (evictions, attorney fees, bad debts, vandalism, pest control, bookkeeping, etc.)	5,000
Total expenses	40,528
Net operating income	20,672
Mortgage payments	19,791
Before-tax cash flow (cash throw-off)	$881

After (Your Management)

Gross potential income at $575 per unit	$82,800
Vacancy losses at 4%	3,312
Effective gross income	$79,488
Expenses	
Utilities	2,230
Maintenance and upkeep	13,200
Advertising	670
Insurance	2,630
Property taxes	7,300
Miscellaneous (evictions, attorney fees, bad debts, vandalism, pest control, bookkeeping, etc.)	2,500
Total expenses	28,530
Net operating income	50,958
Leasehold payments to owner (master lessor)	25,000
Before-tax cash flow (master lessee)	$25,958

How to Achieve Your Turnaround

How can you achieve such a spectacular turnaround? (1) Upgrade the property and implement a thorough maintenance program; (2) your more attractive property and more attentive management will attract and retain high-quality tenants; (3) meter the apartment units individually to reduce utilities; (4) raise rents to reflect the more appealing condition of the property and the more pleasant ambiance created by the new higher-quality, neighbor-considerate, rule-abiding tenants; (5) shop for lower-cost property and liability insurance coverage; and (6) reduce turnover and encourage word-of-mouth tenant referrals to eliminate most advertising expenses.

> **Property turnarounds increase cash flows and boost the property's value.**

Not only did this turnaround increase the property's net income (NOI), but, correspondingly, the higher NOI, lower risk, and more attractive apartments lifted the value of the building. This means that when you exercise your option to buy, you will be able to arrange 100 percent financing to pay off the owner, yet still give the lender a 70 to 80 percent loan-to-value ratio as measured against the property's new higher value.

Sell Your Lease-Option Rights

Instead of going through with your purchase of master-leased property, you might sell your leasehold and option rights to another investor. Given the much higher NOI that you've created, you can assign your rights at a very good price markup. In effect, an investor would pay for the right to earn $25,958 per year (plus future rent increases) for the remaining term of the master lease. He would also gain the right to buy the property at a now bargain price.

As you can see from this example, a master lease with option to buy can create significant profit opportunities for investor-entrepreneurs who are willing to turn a poorly managed, run-down apartment building into an attractive, effectively operated residence for high-quality tenants.

CHAPTER 7

How to Come Up with the Money to Close

You've now learned several dozen ways that you can acquire investment properties with little- or nothing-down financing. Yet, even 100 percent loans typically require at least some cash to close.

Plus, you may find a great mortgage assumption or "subject to" deal where the seller needs (wants?) to cash out the substantial equity that he has accumulated in his property. So, for most of your investments, you will need to bring some cash to the closing table.

Here are 23 ways that you can use to come up with all or part of this money.

Cash Out Some of Your Current Home's Equity

> **A low-cost home equity loan makes an excellent source of cash to expand your real estate wealth.**

If you've owned a home for a number of years, you've no doubt built up tens (perhaps hundreds) of thousands of dollars in equity. Through either a home equity loan or a cash-out refinance, you can raise money at quite favorable rates. In fact, I know of some high-equity homeowners who are refinancing their homes with larger mortgages and then using the net proceeds for cash bids on fix-up properties at discount prices.

If your home has proved to be a good investment, now's the time to leverage up. Put some of that equity into buying and renovating properties. You might even consider downsizing. Move (at least temporarily) into a smaller abode. To raise even more cash and credit power for investing in real estate, you could—Heaven forbid—even go back to renting for a while.

Don't tie up large chunks of capital in your house when you could use that money to accelerate your wealth building.

Bring in Partners

Who do you know that would like to earn the profits that real estate can provide, but lacks the time or inclination to take an active role? Such investing partners can provide cash to the deal and they also may enhance your credibility and borrowing power.

> **Right now, millions of people with money would like to invest in real estate.**

Although space here doesn't permit a full discussion of the legal, tax, and practical issues that partnerships can entail, I will urge you to look into this approach to raising cash for investment. I have brought in a partner on a number of my property investments. All have worked out well for both me and the partners.

Attract Money with a Business Plan

Later, after you gain experience and credibility, you will be able to raise money based on your reputation and achievements. When you're just getting started, though, I recommend that you write out a business plan for two reasons:

> **Partners can provide the money. You provide the talent, time, and business plan.**

1. *Think it through.* Writing out a plan forces you to think through your investment project and goals from start to finish. As you write, you clarify. You see glitches (and perhaps opportunities) that more casual analysis frequently misses.

2. *Credibility.* Which of these approaches would most per-
    suade you to invest in a property? Someone simply asks,
    "Hey, how would you like to invest $20,000 in a real estate
    deal I'm putting together?" Or she says, "Here's a copy of my
    business plan for a real estate investment that I'm acquiring.
    As you can see from this market and financial analysis, a
    $20,000 investment will pay you back $30,000 within six
    months."

To write this plan, you would highlight the market and property data
that we discuss later. To further boost your credibility and forthright-
ness, you should also pinpoint risk factors and how you're prepared to
deal with them. For example,

♦ What if interest rates go up?
♦ What if your repair and improvement costs exceed the estimate?
♦ What if the rent raises or value-enhancing improvements take
  longer than planned?
♦ What if rental or sales prices begin to soften?

> **Don't overpromise. Anticipate risks.**

All smart investors realize that no one can perfectly predict the future. You can, though, anticipate problems. Then take steps beforehand to alleviate, reduce, or eliminate them. "What if" scenarios should stimulate you to build safeguards into your plans and prepare alternative exit strategies.

Seek Favored Partners

> **Choose a person with character first, money second.**

Because even the most promising partnerships (that is, marriages) can break down into contentiousness, choose your real estate partners carefully. Deal only with someone who's reasonable, easy to get along with, and lives by a personal code of integrity and fairness. If plans go awry as they sometimes do, you want a partner who will sit down and look at reasonable and fair ways to resolve the cause of the detour and cooperatively steer the investment back on track.

You do not want a partner who insists that you sign a 10-page, fine-print partnership agreement that has been drafted by his or her lawyer. The more you let the lawyers intercede into your agreement, the more likely you and your partner will come to discord. Of course, here I'm talking about small deals—not multimillion-dollar agreements, when like it or not, the lawyers will probably actively participate in the partnership negotiations.

Most lawyers would like you to believe that a good partnership requires an "airtight" partnership agreement that nails down precisely each partner's rights and responsibilities. Wrong! A good partnership requires good people as partners. If, for small deals, you (or your partner) think that you need a 10-page, fine-print document of legal jargon to set the terms of your agreement, that partnership is headed for trouble.

> **No fine-print contract can substitute for your partner's character.**

In your eagerness to do a deal, never jump for the money until you're perfectly confident that your investor will make a great partner. No contract can ever substitute for the character of the people involved.

Second Mortgages

Say that you've found a great property, a motivated seller, and a low-interest-rate assumable (or "subject to") mortgage. You face only one problem. The existing mortgage has a balance of $190,000, the owner wants a price of $225,000. You can only come up with $20,000 in cash. How can you cover the $15,000 gap? Use a second mortgage.

> **Seller seconds reduce the amount of cash you need to close.**

A holder of a second mortgage simply stands in back of the claims of the first mortgage holder. Upon foreclosure, the sales proceeds go first to pay the highest priority liens. Then, if any money is left, lower-priority claims like a second mortgage are paid. On any given property, a second mortgage lender faces more risk than does the first lender.

> **All types of lenders grant second mortgages.**

To arrange second-mortgage financing, ask the seller to carry back a loan for $15,000 of your purchase price. If the seller won't or can't oblige you with this second mortgage, turn to a bank or private mortgage company to provide the money. In the world of investment real estate (and increasingly, too, in the world of homebuying), cash-short buyers use second mortgages to help close the gap between the amount of the first mortgage financing and the purchase price of the property.

Personal Savings

How much cash can you raise from your personal savings and investments? If your answer comes in at anything under five figures (not counting decimals!), you need to work through some fiscal fitness exercises. For a philosophy that leads to sensible spending and wealth building see *The Millionaire Next Door* by Thomas Stanley and William Danko (Atlanta: Longstreet, 1996). Their PWAs (prodigious wealth accumulators) rarely conspicuously flaunt their wealth. Virtually every financial expert agrees that before you can invest profitably, you must learn to spend *well below* your means. Save, save, save.

Sell Unnecessary Assets

Other than your house, can you sell, trade, or downsize any assets? Do you own cars, boats, jet skis, or expensive furniture? What about that no-longer-pursued stamp or coin collection? I recently talked with one of my readers who wanted to invest in properties but said she lacked cash.

> **Nearly everyone owns assets that they could sell to raise investment cash.**

"What would you recommend?" she asked. When I queried her about assets that she could draw on, she admitted that she and her husband owned a vacation property at Lake Tahoe with $150,000 of equity.

Do you see the problem here? All of us love our possessions. We don't want to give them up. But ask yourself whether those assets are truly worth the price you pay to own them. Several years back, I owned a Porsche 911. Obviously, that's a car that I

> **Learn to live with less so you can eventually enjoy far more.**

> **Build wealth to achieve financial freedom—not costly possessions.**

loved to drive. But when I calculated my out-of-pocket costs of ownership plus the money I could earn by investing the cash that I had tied up in the car, the decision to sell became a no-brainer.

Your decision to sell wasteful assets becomes even more important when you're shelling out money for monthly payments. Possessions you finance not only eat up your cash, they also drag down your credit score and borrowing power. Get rid of those unnecessary assets now. The returns you earn over time will permit you to later replace them many times over. (Also, as I have noted, you may find that cutting back on your costly toys and material possessions actually leads you to a higher quality of life.)

Down-Payment Assistance

From Oakland, California, to Atlanta, Georgia, from Boston to Miami, from Chicago to Houston, city and county governments and not-for-profit housing organizations have been providing down-payment assistance to persons who have not owned a home during the past three years. Typically, these grants range from $1,500 to $5,000, but I've seen them go as high as $15,000. See, for example, the front-page *Wall Street Journal* article "Buyers Get Free Down Payments on Homes" (December 10, 2002).

> **Local governments give buyers down-payment money.**

To learn what is offered in your area, telephone your city or county department of housing finance or community development. Often these programs fit right in with your efforts to buy and renovate fixers because they may be targeted toward neighborhoods to prime them for revitalization. The same government and not-for-profit agencies may also provide low-cost money to cover rehab and renovation expenses.

Easy Money—Hard Terms

On those occasions when you exhaust all other sources of cash and financing, you've got a possibility that I hesitate to mention, but will do so

> **Be careful. "Easy-money" lenders play rough if you don't pay on time.**

only in the cause of thoroughness. In some limited situations, you may want to turn to an easy-money lender. Within the real estate industry, such lenders actually work under the label of "private money" or "hard money." I call them easy-money lenders because they will loan you money to buy, improve, or refinance almost any type of property as long as you can fog a mirror.

Predatory Lending

In fact, some easy-money lenders intentionally loan money to people who stand very little chance of paying it back. Why? Because these lenders *want to foreclose* the property. Such lenders profit from this tactic for three reasons:

1. *Low loan-to-value ratio (LTV).* Easy-money lenders only make loans where the property value greatly exceeds the amount borrowed.
2. *Immediate collection.* Unlike reputable mortgage lenders, these easy-money folks don't know the concept of forbearance. Miss a payment and they will sic the lawyers on you as soon as legally possible.
3. *High late fees and penalties.* Not only do these predatory lenders go after the delinquent amount owed on the mortgage, they make sure that you pay dearly for your failure to make your payments as scheduled.

Both the state and federal governments have initiated an enforcement campaign against illegal predatory lending practices. Two such

> **Be wary of predatory lenders.**

lenders (Citigroup and Household Lending) recently paid a total of $700 million to settle charges of bilking tens of thousands of their mortgage customers. Although easy-money lenders do make borrowing easier for the credit-impaired, such lenders also expect to receive a huge (and perhaps illegal or unconscionable) profit from these hard-money loans.

Why Would You Want to Deal with This Type of "Easy Money" Lender?

> **Hard money might serve a short-term profit opportunity.**

Lenders who specialize in easy money with hard terms appeal to three types of borrowers: (1) the poorly educated who don't really understand the terms and costs of the loan, (2) those who need money so desperately that they'll sign away their future for immediate relief from some financial difficulty, and (3) optimistic real estate investors who care nothing about the hard terms of the easy money because they imagine high profits from their venture. Assuming that you're not a type 1 or 2 borrower, I will focus on a type 3 situation.

The Optimistic Entrepreneur   Say you find a desperate (that is, motivated) property owner who is willing to sell you his $300,000 "as-is" property for $220,000 if you can come up with the cash within 10 days. You know that after putting in $25,000 for repairs and sweat equity, you could sell the house for at least $335,000. You want to grab this deal before someone else beats you to it. But how can you raise $220,000 on such short notice?

> **Hard term-lenders specialize in fast-cash deals.**

The answer: An easy-money-hard-terms lender. What will this loan cost you? Can't say for sure because the private mortgage industry includes thousands of small players as well as some of the major mortgage lenders like Citigroup (which runs its hard-money operations through no-name subsidiaries). Each player sets its own costs, terms, and loan-to-value ratios. The structure of the deals also varies over time. Sometimes too much money is chasing too few borrowers. At other times, too many borrowers are chasing after too little money.

With all of these caveats in view, Table 7.1 shows how your deal in this situation might look.

Table 7.1 You Might Profit Using Hard Money

Source	Cash to You	Cash You Pay
Amount borrowed	$220,000	
Interest at 15% p.a. (6 months)		$ 16,500
Settlement costs		9,000
Mortgage broker fee at 5%		11,000
Mortgage payback		$220,000
Total	$220,000	$256,500
Net cost of funds for 6 months		$36,500
Your Expected Profit		
Sales price of renovated property		$335,000
Marketing costs at 6%		20,100
Cost of funds		36,500
Acquisition cost of property		220,000
Costs of improvements		$ 25,000
Profit (before tax)		$ 78,500

Are these numbers realistic? Yes. Do they reflect a norm? No. As I said, easy-money lenders remain idiosyncratic. Each deal is negotiated according to the particulars of the loan, the property, the lender, and the borrower. No Freddie Mac or Fannie Mae dictates rules. Plus, this deal showed a great buy on the property, which is possible but not typical.

Nevertheless, this example does indicate that, on occasion, you can earn a good profit—even after paying the high costs of a hard-terms lender. Before you enter into such a loan agreement, though, take off your rose-colored glasses. Sharpen your pencil. Critically work through the numbers. Remember to include a liberal amount for the oops factor. If the profit still outweighs costs and risks, maybe you should go for it.

> **Before you sign up for hard money, take off your rose-colored glasses.**

Where to Find This Easy Money The classified ad section of most city newspapers includes a category entitled, "Loans," "Financing," or perhaps "Money to Lend." More often than not, these advertisers represent easy-money-hard-terms lenders. Also, look in your telephone book listings under mortgages and mortgage brokers. You're looking for listings that use language such as "credit problems okay," "non

Box 7.1   Sample Ads for Hard Money Lenders

conforming," "secured," "fast closing," "investor loans," "rehab acquisitions,"
"we buy mortgages and land contracts," or "no income verification." Box
7.1 shows a sampling of "easy-money" ads from the *New York Times* and a
local newspaper.

Use Credit Cards

Although it's one of the more risky techniques of creative financing, some
investors take advantage of every credit card offer they receive in the mail.
Then when they need quick cash to close a deal, they raise $5,000,
$10,000, or even $50,000 from cash advances. Investors have been known
to pay all cash for a property with the entire sum
raised from credit cards.

> **Remember,
> though, too many
> credit cards lower
> your credit score.**

Naturally, neither you nor anyone else should use
cash advances for long-term financing. On occasion,
though, you might find plastic a good source to cover
short-term needs. You may, for example, find a "steal"
that you can renovate and immediately flip (resell) at a
great profit.

Personal Loans

In the days before credit card cash advances (which today are the most popular type of personal loan), personal loans were called signature loans. As you build your wealth through growing real estate equity, you'll find that many lenders will gladly grant you signature loans for $10,000, $25,000, or even $100,000, if your credit record and net worth can support repayment. You can use the money from these signature loans to buy even more real estate. (Signature loans typically charge much lower fees and interest rates than do credit card cash advances.)

Although some mortgage lenders set rules against using personal loans for property down payments, a seller who finances your purchase will seldom investigate the source of your down-payment money.

Sweat Equity (Creating Value through Renovations)

To enhance value through improvements and renovations, buy a fix-up property with 100 percent financing. Say you find a property that should sell (in tip-top condition) for around $300,000. Yet, because of its sorry state of repair as well as an eager seller, you can buy this property for $160,000 with short-term no-money-down owner financing. You then contribute your labor and buy $10,000 in materials with your credit card (or signature loan).

Once you complete your work and bring the property up to its $300,000 market value, you arrange a 70 percent LTV mortgage with a lender. Then with the loan proceeds of $210,000, you pay off the seller and your credit card account. Voilà—you not only have achieved 100 percent financing for your acquisition price and expenses, you've created $130,000 of instant equity (wealth).

> **Sweat equity builds instant wealth.**

Eliminate Your Down Payment with Pledged Collateral

If you don't have enough money for a big down payment and you can't (or don't want to) buy mortgage insurance or obtain a second mortgage, you've got another possibility. It's called pledged collateral. "We don't care where the collateral comes from," says Elmer Frank of First American Savings, "As long as we feel secure, we'll consider the loan. We've taken stocks, bonds, mortgages, retirement accounts, and once a Mercedes 300 SL Gullwing. We did, though, refuse to accept a racehorse."

Pledged Retirement Accounts

In terms of popularity, Elmer Frank adds, "Retirement accounts have become one of the most frequent sources of pledged collateral for our first-time home buyers. We don't even require that the account belong to the buyers. We'll accept funds from any close family member. On no-down-payment mortgages, we usually like to see 30 percent, but for good customers, we've gone as low as 20 percent."

> **The account you pledge need not be your own.**

"In other words," Elmer continues, "we'll give homebuyers or investors a no-down-payment, 100 percent loan, if, say, those buyers (or close relatives) move enough of their 401(k) funds to our bank to offset 20 or 30 percent of the home's purchase price. Last week, we closed a loan for a young couple in their 30s who bought a $165,000 property. Between them, they earn $70,000 a year; but they had little savings because they've been rapidly paying off their student loans. We financed their full purchase price without private mortgage insurance and the wife's mother deposited $45,000 of her 401(k) monies with us."

Other Types of Pledged Collateral

Retirement funds aren't the only source of pledged collateral you can use to offset your lack of a down payment. As Elmer Frank points out, his bank (like some other lenders) will accept nearly any type of asset (savings account, stocks, bonds, perhaps even a valuable antique automobile). If you or your parents have built up a large equity in their home, many lenders will accept that equity as pledged collateral.

If your parents (or other close relatives) would refinance their home (or other real estate), you might be able to use a blanket mortgage to buy a home with no down payment. Say your parents owe $130,000 on their home now valued at $510,000. You want to buy a property priced around $185,000. Many mortgage lenders would loan you and your parents $315,000 so your parents could pay off their old mortgage balance of $130,000 and you could buy the property you want at a price of $185,000 ($130,000 + $185,000 = $315,000).

The lender would then record a blanket mortgage for $215,000 to cover both properties that together have a value of $695,000 ($510,000 + $185,000). You and your parents would share responsibility for making the monthly payments. You would have bought your property with no cash down and without having to pay mortgage insurance.

Student Loans

As I have mentioned, I bought my first investment properties while I was still in college. While my friends were using their college loans to pay for their rent, food, clothing, tuition, and books, I used my student loan money to acquire real estate. While my friends were stacking up debt, I was building wealth.

Do you have access to any easy money like student loans? If so, there's the cash you need to close your first investment. Student loans work great because not only do you get a low interest rate, often you don't have to start paying them back until after you've been out of school for a year. Remember, too, I sought out seller financing—and the sellers (unlike banks) didn't ask where I was getting my down payment.

Use More Creative Finance

In addition to the techniques just discussed, here are several other more creative ways to fund your cash to close:

- ◆ *Agree to swap services or products.* Does the seller need some service or expertise that you can render? Inventory your skills (law, medicine, dentistry, writing, advertising, carpentry, accounting, landscaping, architectural, etc.). Include all talents and expertise of your profession, trade, and avocation. How about products? Say you own a radio station or newspaper. Trade off advertising time or space for a down payment. Anything you can produce, deliver, or sell wholesale (at cost) might work.

♦ ***Borrow (or reduce) the real estate commission.*** Although most brokers and sales agents generally hate this technique, on occasion buyers and sellers ask the agents involved in a transaction to defer payment until some later date. Also some agents actually prefer to have their commissions in the deal. In doing so, they avoid income taxes on these fees, while at the same time they build wealth through their interest earnings or by receiving a "piece of the action" (future profits from the later sale of the property).

♦ ***Simultaneously sell off part of the property.*** Does the property include an extra lot, a mobile home, timber, oil, gas, or air or mineral rights? If so, find a buyer who will pay you cash for such rights. In turn, this money will help you close the deal.

♦ ***Prepaid rents and tenant security deposits.*** When you buy an income property, you are entitled to the existing tenants' security deposits and prepaid rents. Say you close on June 2. The seller of a fourplex is holding $4,000 in damage deposits and $3,800 in tenant rent money prepaid for the month of June. Together, the deposits and prepaid rents amount to $7,800. In most transactions, you can use these monies (credits at closing) to reduce your cash-to-close.

♦ ***Create paper.*** You've asked the seller to accept owner financing with 10 percent down. She balks. She believes the deal puts her at risk. Alleviate her fears and bolster her security. Offer her a lien against your car or a second (or third) mortgage on another property you own. Specify that when your principal paydown and the property's appreciation lift your equity to 20 percent (LTV of 80 percent), she will remove the security lien she holds against your other property.

♦ ***Lease-option sandwich.*** Don't forget the lease-option sandwich (Chapter 6). If you can pull it off, your lease-option buyers supply you with all (or nearly all) of the cash you will need to take over control of the property from the sellers.

CHAPTER 8

Here's How to Qualify

Up to this point, you've learned several dozen ways to raise the money you will need to invest in real estate. Some of these techniques require you to pass under a lender's microscope. Others do not.

In the main, I've written this chapter to help you anticipate and prepare for those instances when you must go through a mortgage lender's formal qualifying process.

This chapter will also help you deal successfully with potential investment partners, real estate agents, and OWC sellers. Even though these folks won't scrutinize your finances as closely as a mortgage lender, they will still want to see evidence that they can count on you to live up to your promises.

Be Wary of Prequalifying (and Preapproval)

Most supposed experts in mortgage finance give this advice: "Before you even begin to shop for a property, meet with a lender to get prequalified for a loan.[1] With prequalification you'll learn *exactly* how much property you can afford. You won't waste time looking at properties outside your price range."

---

1. Some say "preapproved." But that advice, too, fails to address the critical points raised here.

Superficially, this advice makes sense. Why try to order filet mignon on a hamburger budget? Yet, at a deeper level, realize that this advice to prequalify does not necessarily promote your needs. You may be able to borrow far more than a prequalification (or preapproval) suggests.

Why Prequalifying Sometimes Underqualifies

In theory, prequalifying (preapproval) for a loan seems to make sense. If you look at properties you can't afford (unless you're just curious), you waste your time and it may psych you up for a big letdown. But here's the rub: No 10-minute computer-qualifying exercise can measure you for a loan program as a tailor might measure you for a new suit.

> **Preapproval programs are too simplistic.**

No simple qualifying formula can even begin to accurately tell you "how much mortgage you can afford," or more important, "how much property you should buy." Plugging your current credit and finances into a prequalification or preapproval computer program pushes aside the real questions you should be asking:

1. What are your goals to build wealth?
2. How do your budget constraints differ (positively or negatively) from those assumptions embedded in the prequalification program?
3. Are your current spending, saving, and investing habits consistent with your life priorities?
4. How long do you plan to own the property?
5. What steps can you take to improve your credit record or credit scores?
6. What steps can you take to improve your qualifying ratios?
7. What percentage of your wealth do you want to hold in real estate investments?
8. What types of real estate financing (other than those loan programs offered by the lender you're talking with) might best promote your goals for cost savings or wealth building?
9. What types of real estate financing (other than those loan programs offered by the lender you're talking with) might best enhance your affordability?

10. What type of property (fixer, foreclosure, duplex, fourplex, multiunit apartment building, single-family house, condo, etc.) might best fit into your financial goals?

Although a relative few highly professional loan representatives will help you accurately address important financial and life-planning issues such as those listed above, most will not. The majority of loan reps lack the time, the intellectual acumen, and the practical knowledge necessary to guide you to your best investment and borrowing decisions. Never forget: Loan reps, like car salespeople, want you to buy the products they are selling. Would you expect unbiased auto advice from the sales agent at the Buick dealer? No? Then why would you expect unbiased advice from the loan rep at the Old Faithful Mortgage Company?

> **Loan reps want you to buy what they are selling.**

Where You Stand versus Where You Want to Go

Most mortgage lenders emphasize where you stand financially today. You must look into your personal future. Most lenders emphasize your ability and willingness to pay your mortgage as evidenced only by their approval formula. You need not accept this narrow view. You must decide for yourself. Should I buy more (or less) property than the standard formulas suggest? And correspondingly, should I borrow more (or less) than this lender's guidelines recommend?

> **You determine how much property you can afford.**

You Can Make Your Qualifying Ratios Look Better

If you buy anything up to a four-unit property (condo, single-family house, duplex, triplex, quad) and finance it through a mortgage lender, you will probably need to pass through the lender's qualifying standards. A majority of lenders will assess your borrowing power through the use of two qualifying ratios: (1) the housing cost (front) ratio, and (2) the total debt (back) ratio. These ratios will apply regardless of whether you apply for owner-occupied financing or investor financing.

Run-of-the-mill loan reps will merely plug your financial data into their computer automated underwriting (AU) program. Savvy loan reps will do a "first-review" and then, if desirable, suggest ways that you can improve your financial profile.

> **Always search for ways to improve your qualifying ratios.**

Calculating the Ratios

With the advent of automated underwriting (AU) by computer, many loan reps and loan underwriters no longer calculate housing ratios directly. In fact, some newer reps wouldn't know what to do with a loan ratio even if you showed it to them. Nevertheless, qualifying ratios matter a great deal, only now the math is hidden in the automated underwriting program.

But make no mistake. If you understand and improve your qualifying ratios, you will raise the odds for loan approval and increase the amount the lender will loan you. Strong ratios may also help you slice your interest rate and your mortgage insurance premiums (if any). Both the housing cost ratio and the total debt ratio give lenders a way to measure whether your income looks like it's large and dependable enough to safely cover your mortgage payments, monthly debts, and other living expenses.

> **Low ratios may decrease your interest rate and down payment.**

Housing Cost (Front) Ratio   You can easily figure your housing cost (front) ratio with this formula:

$$\text{Housing cost ratio} = \frac{(P \& I) + (T \& I) + (MI) + (HOA)}{\text{Monthly gross income}}$$

where: P&I represents principal and interest (the basic monthly mortgage payment).

T&I represents the amount you must pay monthly for property taxes and homeowners insurance.

MI represents the monthly mortgage insurance premium you may have to pay if you put less than 20 percent down.

HOA represents the monthly amount you may have to pay to a condominium or subdivision homeowners association.

To keep things simple, let's say that your household income (including anticipated rent collections) equals $7,000 a month. To buy the property you want, you need a loan of $235,000. You decide to go for a 30-year, fixed-rate loan at 7 percent interest. This loan will cost you $1,563 per month (235 × $6.65; see Table 8.1). Property taxes and homeowners insurance on this property will total $400 per month. No mortgage insurance applies, but you must pay the homeowners association $125 per month to maintain the community swimming pool, tennis courts, and clubhouse. Here's how to compute your housing cost ratio for this example:

$$\text{Housing cost ratio} = \frac{\$1563 + 400 + 125}{\$7000}$$

$$= \frac{\$2088}{\$7000}$$

$$= 0.298 \text{ or } 29.8\%$$

Because the lender your talking with has set a housing cost guideline ratio of 28 percent, your numbers look like they might work. So we next turn to the total debt ratio.

Total Debt Ratio   The total debt ratio begins with your housing costs and then adds in monthly payments for all of your monthly payments (other mortgages, credit cards, student loans, auto loans, etc.). At present, say your BMW hits you for a payment of $650 a month, the Taurus another $280. Your credit card and department store account balances total $8,000 and require a minimum payment of 5 percent of the outstanding balance per month ($400). Here are the figures:

$$\text{Total debt ratio} = \frac{\text{Housing costs} + \text{installment debt} + \text{revolving debt}}{\text{Monthly gross income}}$$

$$= \frac{\$2088 + 650 + 250 + 400}{\$7000}$$

$$= \frac{\$3388}{\$7000}$$

$$= 0.484 \text{ or } 48.4\%$$

With this loan program, the lender would like to see a total debt ratio no greater than 36 percent. Whoops. Looks like you've blown through the

Table 8.1   Monthly Payment Required per $1,000 of Original Mortgage Balance

Interest (%)	Monthly Payment	Interest (%)	Monthly Payment
2.5	$3.95	7.5	$6.99
3.0	4.21	8.0	7.34
3.5	4.49	8.5	7.69
4.0	4.77	9.0	8.05
4.5	5.07	9.5	8.41
5.0	5.37	10.0	8.77
5.5	5.67	10.5	9.15
6.0	5.99	11.0	9.52
6.5	6.32	11.5	9.90
7.0	6.63	12.0	10.29

Note: Term = 30 years.

limits. But does this mean you won't get the loan—or maybe you'll have to settle for a lesser amount? Not necessarily.

If your credit score (see Chapter 3) is high enough, your loan may still get approved. If that doesn't work, maybe you can increase your qualifying income, reduce your monthly debt, or provide compensating factors.

You Can Lift Your Qualifying Income

In the previous example, we *assumed* that your income totaled $7,000 per month. In the real world, figuring your income presents a somewhat greater challenge (and opportunity). For to calculate *qualifying* income—that specific income amount entered into the denominator of your qualifying ratios—lenders evaluate a range of actual and potential income from sources such as:

- Salary
- Hourly wages
- Overtime
- Bonuses
- Commissions
- Scheduled raises
- Alimony

- Social Security
- Unemployment insurance
- Self-employment
- Moonlighting/part-time job
- Tips
- Disability insurance
- Stock dividends

◆ Welfare/ADC
◆ Pension
◆ Tax-free income
◆ Child support

◆ Interest
◆ Consulting
◆ Rent collections
◆ Annuities

As you look through this list, you can see that for many borrowers, no precise income figure can be calculated. Consider the entries for overtime, bonuses, and commissions. Over a period of months or years, these amounts could vary widely.

Or what about unemployment insurance payments? How could someone who's unemployed (or expects to become unemployed) ever hope to get qualified for a mortgage? Why would income from this source count? Well, I know a savvy loan rep who routinely gets unemployment insurance counted. His borrowers work during summer stock theater for very good wages. Then during the off-season, they regularly collect unemployment. So, their qualifying income includes both their earnings from summer stock acting and their regular checks from the government.

Regularity, Stability, Continuity   Lenders will count any income that you can show as stable, regular, and continuing. Usually, a two-year history with a promising (realistic) future is enough to satisfy the lender. On the other hand, what if during the past five years you've typically earned sales commissions of $4,000 a month, but during the past eight months that income has jumped to $6,000 a month? Here, the loan rep or loan underwriter must make a judgment call—which you can influence. Show the loan rep persuasive evidence why your more recent earnings should weigh more heavily than those lower earnings of years past.

Or think about alimony and child support. You may hold a court order that requires your ex-spouse to pay you $1,500 per month. But your spouse displays a casual indifference to honoring this legal decree. Sometimes you get paid. Sometimes you don't. So, what amount will the lender count as qualifying income? Again, a judgment call that you can influence according to how well you explain away your ex's past irresponsibility and provide assurances of future compliance.

> You can increase your qualifying income.

Anticipated Earnings   Sometimes you can persuade a lender to accept anticipated earnings that may lack a past or a present. Say your spouse has just taken a new job in Topeka. You previously worked as a teacher, but for family reasons, took leave for the past two years. Once the family gets resettled in your new community, however, you plan to return to full-time teaching. Will the lender count your future earnings? With a good argument and evidence of intent, you probably can get at least part of this potential income included. In fact, Fannie Mae and Freddie Mac both offer dispensation for "trailing spouses."

> **Sometimes you can count future income.**

Recent college graduates (or recent graduates of professional schools such as nursing, law, medicine, business, or engineering) also can secure mortgages without immediate past or present income or employment. A contract for a new job may work to establish your qualifying income.

When Current Income Doesn't Count   For the past 12 years, you worked as a master mechanic at the local Ford dealer. You earned $5,350 a month. Then, six months ago, you got hooked on Shaklee products. You quit your job at Ford and became a Shaklee sales distributor. Business was slow at first, but during the past three months you've cleared close to $25,000. Will this income qualify? Sorry, your newfound success would not impress most lenders. They would tell you to reapply after proving your Shaklee sales skills for another 18 to 24 months.

Maximize Your Qualifying Income

> **Use your artistic skills. Paint the lender a pleasing picture.**

To secure loan approval and to maximize borrowing power, present your income history, current earnings, and future prospects as optimistically as possible. You must anticipate and effectively respond to any negative signals that may cause the lender to doubt the amount, stability, or continuing nature of your income.

Overcome the Negatives   If your earnings were lower last year only because you went back to school to get your M.B.A. so you could advance in your job, make sure the loan rep knows it. If last year you earned $60,000, but as of September 1 this year you've only taken in $40,000, show the lender that your big earnings season runs from September to December. Provide evidence that typically you earn 40 percent of your commissions during the last three months of the year. So, actually, you're on track to outpace last year's record.

If your income is complicated by self-employment earnings, prepare explanations. For truly complex situations involving important amounts of money, enlist the aid of your accountant. Potential problems, for example, include tax losses offset by positive cash flow, or strong business profits, yet small wage or salary draws from the business (to minimize your personal income taxes). Many run-of-the-mill loan reps can't effectively understand these issues without guidance or persuasive input from you.

> **Self-employment income needs more explanations.**

Put Positives in Writing   Award-winning credit explanations can only sway hearts and minds when you put them on paper. Lenders follow this rule: "If it's not in writing, it doesn't exist." Mortgage underwriters need CYA paperwork piled higher and deeper, just in case a loan auditor investigates the files.

Nearly all lenders today monitor loan quality and data integrity through internal audits. Without the paperwork to justify their loans, the lender could run into trouble with regulators, Fannie Mae, Freddie Mac, HUD, or bank insurers. So if you want a lender to view your past, present, and future income more favorably than it otherwise would, write out and deliver your evidence—before the lender formally reviews your application. (Even when an AU system approves your loan application, a human underwriter must still sign off on a loan commitment. You will be called upon to deliver documents and explanations such as tax returns, W-2s, 1099s, tenant leases, verification of employment, verifications of bank accounts, and statements to explain credit derogatories. Without adequate support, the underwriter can reject a loan. Also, with good supporting evidence, an underwriter can accept what AU has failed to approve.)

> **Write out persuasive explanations.**

Reduce Your Disqualifying Debt

The flip side of income is debt. High monthly payments can either block your loan approval or, at a minimum, reduce the amount you can borrow. From the list below, total your current monthly payments.

- ◆ Car #1   _____
- ◆ Car #2   _____
- ◆ Car #3   _____
- ◆ Motorcycle   _____
- ◆ Jet ski   _____
- ◆ Power boat   _____
- ◆ Furniture   _____
- ◆ Student loan(s)   _____
- ◆ Appliances   _____
- ◆ Credit card #1   _____
- ◆ Credit card #2   _____
- ◆ Credit card #3   _____
- ◆ Credit card #4   _____
- ◆ Medical bills   _____

- ◆ Alimony   _____
- ◆ Child support   _____
- ◆ Merchant account #1   _____
- ◆ Merchant account #2   _____
- ◆ Merchant account #3   _____
- ◆ Judgments/liens   _____
- ◆ Personal loans   _____
- ◆ Mortgage #1   _____
- ◆ Mortgage #2   _____
- ◆ Mortgage #3   _____
- ◆ Other   _____
- ◆ Other   _____
- ◆ Other   _____

Total monthly debt repayments $_____

What to Count, What to Leave Out

To calculate total debt ratio, lenders usually divide your monthly payments into two types: (1) installment debt, which includes loans you're paying off such as autos, boats, medical bills, and student loans, and (2) revolving (or open) accounts which include Visa, Mastercard, Amex Optima, Home Depot, Texaco, and any other credit line that remains open until you or your friendly creditor closes it.

Not All Payments Count   Most lenders ignore payments for *installment* debts that are scheduled to be paid off within 6 to 10 months from the date of your mortgage application. But if the lease on your auto is set to end within a few months, you're out of luck. Those payments still count against you. The lender assumes (unless convinced otherwise) that you will continue to incur this expense when you lease a new car to replace the old one.

You do, though, get a break for qualifying when lenders look at your revolving debt. Even if you regularly pay hundreds of dollars more per month than your minimum payment(s) due, most lenders will only count your payment as 5 percent of your outstanding balances. Or if your minimum payment is less than 5 percent, lenders will count that lower amount instead.

Prepare Far Ahead of Time   Get your debt situation shaped up as soon as you can. Not only will this fiscal fitness program lift your qualifying ratios, it *may* also boost your credit scores. Here are some tips:

1. *Consolidate bills.* One loan consolidation payment of $280 a month will hurt you less than four separate bill payments of $125 each. However, don't close three accounts and run one up close to its credit limit. Credit scoring doesn't like "high" balances relative to credit limits.
2. *Pay down debt.* If your installment debt has only 11 or 12 months to go, prepay two or three payments. That pushes those debts off the table and out of sight—under the rules followed by most lenders.
3. *Pay off debt.* If you can swing it, get rid of as much debt as you can.
4. *Avoid new debt.* No matter how much you are tempted, do not take on no new debt prior to applying for a mortgage. Even if you can easily afford it, you're better off waiting until after you've been through closing.

These tips especially apply if your ratios are pushing against the lender's guideline total debt limits, if your credit score falls below, say, 700, if you're requesting a low-down-payment loan (a loan-to-value ratio of greater than 80 percent), or if you're trying to qualify for a non-owner-occupied investment property.

A pint-sized debt load will help offset any warts in your credit profile.

Use Compensating Factors to Justify Higher Qualifying Ratios

No two borrowers are exactly alike. That's why many lenders will bend their approval guidelines when you give them prudent reasons to do so.

Compensating Factors Make the Difference   Gordon Steinback, an executive who works for the Mortgage Guarantee Insurance Corporation, says his firm "routinely approves borrowers who don't meet standard underwriting criteria." Yet, as Steinback points out, "regrettably, too many borrowers never get beyond the application stage. This

> **List all of the reasons why you will be able to pay your loan on time, every time.**

happens because these borrowers don't meet the AU qualifying standards and are thoughtlessly screened out prematurely by inexperienced loan reps. Experience shows, however, that most would-be borrowers can get approved for a loan if only someone shows them how."

Types of Compensating Factors   What types of compensating factors might lenders consider? Virtually anything positive that reasonably demonstrates you can make your monthly payments responsibly and control your finances. Here are a dozen examples:

- You've been making rent payments that equal or exceed the after-tax cost of your proposed mortgage payments.
- You have a good record of savings. You regularly spend less than you earn and you use credit sparingly.
- You are situated on the fast track in your career or employment. You have a good record of promotions and raises.
- For your age and occupation, you have a high net worth (cash value life insurance, 401(k) retirement funds, stocks, bonds, savings account, other investment real estate).
- You have put aside more than adequate cash reserves to handle unexpected financial setbacks.
- You or your spouse will generate extra income through part-time work, a second job, tips, bonuses, or overtime.
- You carry little or no monthly installment debt. This can work well when your housing cost ratio exceeds its guideline, but your total debt ratio falls within its preferred limits.
- You've been through a homebuying counseling program that helps homebuyers develop a realistic budget. Fannie Mae and Freddie Mac lenders give special deals to first-time buyers who complete these programs. Many only last four hours, and they're well worth the time.
- You're making a down payment of 20 percent or larger.
- Your employer provides excellent benefits: auto, cash reimbursement for a home office, a superior health and dental insurance plan, large contributions to your retirement account.

◆ You earn an above-average income. Budget-conscious people whose earnings exceed $4,000 or $5,000 a month often enjoy the financial flexibility to devote more money to real estate than typical qualifying ratios indicate.

◆ Your nonhousing living expenses are lower than average. You would explain that you can afford higher mortgage payments because: (1) the property is energy efficient; (2) you can walk to work or just drive a short commute; (3) you have no costly vices (smoking, drinking); (4) you spend conservatively: you backpack for vacations, drive an unassuming car, and buy clothes at the outlet stores; (5) you're handy with tools so you can perform your own property maintenance; or (6) your food costs are low because you grow your own garden and enjoy all the fresh and home-canned vegetables you can eat.

Put Your Compensating Factors in Writing   After you've developed a list of reasons why you can afford the mortgage you want, put your reasons in writing. Get supporting letters from your employer, minister, former landlords, clients, customers, or anyone else who can vouch for your good character, creditworthiness, job performance, earnings potential, or personal responsibility. Sometimes, too, it's a good idea to write out a household budget. Deliver all of your evidence to the loan underwriter. With good explanations, you'll break through qualifying guidelines that would deter or delay other ill-prepared investors.

The Application Itself Contains Many Clues to Your Integrity

Most lenders will carefully review your loan application. They search for numerical discrepancies, missing information, gaps in dates, inconsistencies, and anything that smells fishy. "Hmm," the lender muses, "You say you've been out of college only three years. But you show no debts for student loans on your application and you report cash savings of $25,000. Would you mind telling me how you managed that feat?"

Experienced loan reps and underwriters have examined thousands of loan apps. Their eyebrows rise easily. If your life story evokes an air of mystery, don't leave the loan rep in the dark. Provide firm evidence that you're traveling the straight and narrow. Even innocent lapses or discrepancies in your application can spell trouble—if not satisfactorily explained.

No Rigid Borrowing Limits Apply to Commercial Properties

As you've just learned, when you finance a 1–4 unit residential property through a mortgage lender, the lender will run through your total finances to calculate whether your personal income is large enough to cover all of your monthly expenses—including all mortgage payments (existing and those for which you are applying).

> **You may not need qualifying income to finance an apartment building.**

In contrast, most lenders expect commercial properties to pay for themselves. Commercial property includes all office buildings, shopping centers, and apartment properties of five units or more. Ideally, you will be able to use a commercial property's rent collections to cover all of its operating expenses and mortgage payments.

An Eight-Unit Money Maker

I recently discovered an eight-unit property that is up for sale. This apartment building generates $40,800 a year in rents. The seller is asking $245,000.[2] Operating expenses (maintenance, property taxes, insurance, management, yard care, etc.) for the property total about $18,000 per year. After allowing, say, $3,000 per year for vacancy and collection losses, an investor would still net (before mortgage payments) $19,000 a year.

Even if you paid this seller's full asking price of $245,000 and financed 100 percent (no down payment), your annual mortgage payments would total just $16,700 (based on 30 years at 7 percent). Your property would throw off a positive cash flow of $2,750 a year—net of all expenses and debt repayment. Because this property would pay for itself, many lenders (or sellers) would not particularly care how much (or how little) you earned from your job. As long as you show that you are a credible and creditworthy buyer, the amount of your personal earnings would not play a major role in the lending decision.

---

2. I realize these numbers look absurdly low to Californians and residents of other high-cost areas. That's why I encourage you to invest elsewhere if prices where you live stand way out of reach.

No Cash, No Credit, No Experience

When I began buying properties, I was a third-year college student. I possessed no wealth, no credit record, and my only earned income came from a part-time job. Nevertheless, by the time I had completed graduate school, the income from my rental properties exceeded my job income many times over. In fact, I owed $600,000 in real estate-related debt and earned less than $20,000 a year.[3]

Are Such Deals Possible?

Are deals like these still available? Absolutely. They're not as easy to find today—especially in high-priced cities—but the basic principle holds. When you become a commercial investor, your borrowing power will greatly exceed your personal qualifying power. I know a 43-year-old investor who earns $51,350 *a year* ($4,280 a month) from her job, yet *each month* she pays $26,430 in mortgage payments. This investor consistently finances properties solely on the rental revenues she collects.

"Low" Income, Inexperienced Developers

As another example of borrowing way outside the bounds of one's income, consider this project.

I'm currently working with an inexperienced development team (an architect, lawyer, and building contractor) that is building a $40 million mixed-use residential/retail/office project. Other than sweat equity for personal (professional) services and some upfront incidental expenses for planning the project, none of the team members is putting any significant amount of his own money into the development. As to borrowing power to finance construction of the center, the lender (Wachovia Bank) primarily wants to see that the prelease and presale activity for the project provides strong evidence that the center will generate enough revenue to pay back the development loan.

> **Financing new development doesn't require your own money.**

---

3. These figures are presented in current (inflation-adjusted) dollars.

Although this team of developers earns a combined professional income of around $300,000 a year, in the eyes of the lender this earned income will play no significant role in its lending decision. When viewed against a $40 million loan, personal earnings of $300,000 a year don't count for much. The potential revenue from the property will determine the lender's decision to finance (or withdraw) from the project.

> **Wealthy investors rarely make loan payments from their personal incomes.**

Indeed, Donald Trump doesn't personally earn enough in a year to cover even one month's worth of expenses and mortgage payments on all the properties he owns. How does he do it? The same way that you can. He buys, develops, or renovates properties that yield enough income to pay for themselves.

The Debt Coverage Ratio

Your lender will use a debt coverage ratio (DCR) to help figure out whether a multiunit investment property will yield enough net operating income (NOI) to cover the debt service and still leave some margin of safety.[4] Lenders want to satisfy themselves that even if rent collections fall or property expenses increase, you will still be able to make your mortgage payments *without* dipping into your personal funds.

You can calculate the debt coverage ratio according to this formula:

$$\text{Debt coverage income (DCR)} = \frac{\text{Net operating income (NOI)}}{\text{Annual debt service}}$$

An illustration: Let's return to that eight-unit property. Plugging in the relevant numbers, we calculate the debt coverage ratio as

$$\text{DCR} = \frac{\$19,000 \ (\text{NOI})}{\$16,700 \ (\text{mortgage payments})}$$

$$\text{DCR} = 1.137, \ \text{say } 1.14$$

---

4. To investors, the term "debt service" means the same thing as mortgage payments.

> **Lenders want to see enough NOI to create a margin of safety.**

Most mortgage lenders like to see a debt coverage ratio of at least 1.1, and preferably in the range of 1.15 to 1.3. The higher this ratio, the better. The more net income you collect relative to the amount of your mortgage payments, the larger your margin of safety.

Even though you're a beginning investor, I would encourage you to see what types of small income properties are available in your area.[5] You will find that these properties (typically 5 to 24 units) will usually give you more cash flow and higher debt coverage ratios than single-family rental houses. As a result, you may be able to finance a larger loan on a more costly property. That has certainly been my experience.

---

5. You might also profit by reading my book, *Make Money with Small Income Properties* (New York: John Wiley & Sons, 2003).

PART THREE

How to Invest for Maximum Gain

CHAPTER **9**

Twenty-Seven Ways to Find or Create Below-Market Deals

In real estate—unlike the stock market—you not only make money when you sell, you can make money when you buy. In the stock market, you can't buy a stock for less than its market value. In real estate these transactions occur every day. If the shares of General Motors are selling at $47 each, no investor would tell Merrill Lynch to try to find a GM shareholder who will part with 100 shares at $40 each. But if you want to buy a $250,000 house or apartment building for $200,000 to $225,000, it's possible that you can locate a seller who will oblige you.

> **You can buy properties at less than their true value.**

Why Properties Sell for Less (or More) than Their Market Value

To see why you can buy properties for less than they're worth, you need to dig deeply into the meaning of the term "market value." Under market value conditions, a property sale meets these five criteria:

1. Buyers and sellers are typically motivated. Neither is acting under duress.
2. Buyers and sellers are well informed and knowledgeable about the property and the market.

3. The marketing period and sales promotion efforts are sufficient to reasonably inform potential buyers of the property's availability (no forced or rushed sales).

4. There are no special terms of financing (e.g., very low down payment, bargain price, below-market interest rate).

5. No out-of-the-ordinary sales concessions are made by either the seller or the buyer (for instance, sellers are not permitted to stay in the house rent-free for three to six months until their under-construction new house is completed).

As you think through this description of market value, you will realize that owners who are in a hurry to sell may have to accept a price lower than market value. Likewise, an owner-seller (FSBO) who doesn't know how to market and promote a property will not likely receive top dollar. Or, say, the sellers live out of town and don't have accurate information about recent sales prices. Or maybe the sellers don't realize that their property (or the neighborhood) is ripe for profitable improvement. In general, we can place those owners who will sell at a bargain price into eight categories.

Owners in Distress

Every day property owners hit hard times. They are laid off from their jobs, file for divorce, suffer accidents or illness, experience setbacks in their business, and run into a freight train of other problems. Any or all of these calamities can create financial distress. For many of these people, their only way out of a jam is to raise cash. If that means selling their property for "less than it's worth," then that's what they're willing to do. For these people are not just selling a property, they are buying relief.

> **High pressure forces sellers to accept less.**

Under these circumstances, as long as the sellers believe they have gained more from the sale than they've lost, it's a win-win agreement for both parties. If you are willing to help people cope with a predicament—as opposed to taking advantage of them—seek out distressed owners. On occasion, they will give you the bargain price (or favorable terms) you want.

The "Grass-Is-Greener" Sellers

One day Karla Lopez was sitting in her office and in walked the executive vice president of her firm. "Karla," she said, "Aaron Stein in the Denver branch just quit. If you want his district manager's job you can have it. We will pay you $25,000 more a year plus a bonus. But you have to be relocated and on the job within 30 days."

> **Opportunities elsewhere encourage sellers to accept loss.**

"Do I want it?" Karla burst out. "Of course I want it. Hope for a promotion like this is why I've been working 75-hour weeks for these past four years."

Will Karla Insist on Top Dollar?   Think about it. In this situation, does Karla think, "Well, the first thing I must do is put my house up for sale and go for top dollar"? Hardly. More than likely Karla will be willing to strike a deal with the first buyer who gives her any type of offer she can live with. Karla's got her eyes on the greener grass of Denver. Optimistic about her career and facing a time deadline, first and foremost, Karla simply wants to get her home sold as quickly as possible.

Grass-is-greener sellers stand in contrast to the financially distressed. Whereas distressed owners sell on bargain terms or price to relieve themselves of pain, grass-is-greener sellers are willing to accept a less than market-value offer so they can quickly grab better opportunities that lie elsewhere.

Even Pros Give Bargains Sometimes   On one of several occasions where I have been a grass-is-greener seller, not only did I give my buyers a slight break on price but, more important from their perspective, I let them assume my below-market-rate first mortgage and carried back an unsecured note for virtually all of their down payment. On at least a dozen occasions, I've bought from sellers who were eager to pursue better opportunities elsewhere. Each time, I negotiated a good (if not great) price and favorable financing.

If looking for distressed owners doesn't appeal to you, turn your search in the opposite direction: Sellers who want to graze in greener pastures (especially under a time deadline) are frequently the easiest people to work with and the most accommodating in price and terms.

Stage-of-Life Sellers

When shopping for bargains, you also can find good deals among stage-of-life sellers. These sellers are typically people whose lifestyle now conflicts with their property. They may no longer enjoy keeping up a big house or yard, collecting rent, or dealing with tenant complaints. They may eagerly anticipate their move to that condo on the fourteenth green at the Bayshore Country Club. Or perhaps these sellers would rather not go through the trouble of updating and repairing their current property. Whatever their reasons, stage-of-life sellers are motivated to get on with their lives.

> **Sellers who are eager to move to their next stage of life often accept less.**

In addition—and this circumstance makes these sellers good prospects for a bargain price or terms—stage-of-life sellers typically have accumulated large amounts of equity in their properties. Plus, because they're older, they have accumulated savings and don't need cash. Stage-of-life sellers can be flexible. They don't need to squeeze every last penny out of their sale.

Good Prospects for OWC   Given their financial well-being, stage-of-life sellers make excellent candidates for some type of "owner will carry" (OWC) financing. Not only will OWC terms help them sell their property more quickly, but an installment sale can also reduce or postpone the capital gain taxes that a cash sale might otherwise require. As another advantage, OWC financing—even when offered at below-market rates—will bring the sellers a higher return than they could earn in a savings account, certificate of deposit, or money market fund (or perhaps even stocks).

> **Stage-of-life sellers will often give owner financing.**

My Early Strategy   As a college student who wanted to invest in real estate, I sought out stage-of-life owners of rental houses and small apartment buildings. These people were tired of managing their properties. Yet, at the same time, they liked a monthly income and didn't want to settle for the meager interest paid by banks or take on the risks of stocks. They also didn't want to sell their properties outright for cash and get hit with a heavy tax bill for capital gains.

Their solution: Sell on easy OWC terms to an ambitious young person who was willing to accept the work of rental properties in exchange

for an opportunity to start building wealth through investment real estate. This technique remains valid today. Because properly selected, well-
managed rentals will pay for themselves, an investor who is willing to
work may be able to draw on ambition and perseverance instead of a
large down payment, a high credit score, and strong qualifying income.

Seller Ignorance   Some sellers underprice their properties because
they don't know the recent prices at which similar properties have been
selling. I confess that as a seller, I have made this mistake of selling too
low because I was ignorant of the market.

> **Sellers who are
> out of touch with
> the market often
> sell for less.**

In one particular case, I was living in Palo Alto,
California. The rental house I decided to sell was located in Dallas, Texas. A year earlier, the house had
been appraised for $110,000, which at the time of
the appraisal was about right. So I decided to ask
$125,000. I figured that price was high enough to
account for inflation and still leave room for negotiating.

The first weekend the house went on the market, three offers came
in right at the asking price. Immediately, of course, I knew I had under-
priced. What I didn't know but soon learned was that during the year I'd
been away, home prices in that Dallas neighborhood had jumped 30 percent. After learning of my ignorance, I could have rejected all the offers
and raised my price. Or I could have put the buyers into a "bidding war."
But I didn't. I just decided to sell to the person with the cleanest offer
(no contingencies). I was making a good profit; why get greedy?

Cranky Landlords

I love to buy from cranky landlords. These are the type of rental property
owners who still think they're living in feudal times. These owners per-

> **Cranky landlords
> often become
> eager sellers who
> will accept less.**

sistently battle their tenants. They complain, complain, complain. Eventually, they end up hating the
whole idea of investing in real estate. These owners
see landlording as nothing but trouble. They want
out.

At that point, they're nearly always willing to
give in to a lowball offer in exchange for getting rid
of their perpetual headaches.

(Whoa, you say, "Is this what I'm getting myself into? Trouble, headaches, and battles with tenants?" No, not at all. That's because in Chapter 18, you will learn the 12 secrets of successful landlording—actually I even detest the term *landlord*. That title no longer fits the modern, enlightened owner of rental properties.)

Preserve the Lender's Image and Balance Sheet

Banks, government agencies (FHA, VA), and the government-chartered mortgage companies such as Fannie Mae and Freddie Mac often become "don't wanters." When their mortgage borrowers fail to pay back their loans, these mortgage lenders often end up with foreclosures on their books (called REOs, which stands for real estate owned).

Lenders Want to Mitigate Their Losses   Once lenders take back a property in foreclosure, they switch their thinking. They no longer focus on making money. Instead, they want to get rid of these REOs on prices or terms that will cut their losses. (Banks often name their REO departments "Loss Mitigation.")

That's where you come in. Because a pile of foreclosures hurts the lender's image with regulators and depresses its balance sheet with "reserves for bad debts," lenders will frequently give investors good deals to take these properties (or delinquent loans) off of their hands.

Multiple Investor Opportunities   As you will see in Chapter 10, when you learn how the total foreclosure process works in your state—the foreclosure process is governed by state law—you can play and win the foreclosure game with a variety of approaches. For beginning investors who are willing to put in the effort, lender foreclosures offer great opportunities to snare below-market deals.

The Possibility-Impaired

Who are the possibility-impaired? This type of owner confuses his diamond in the rough with a lump of coal. These owners don't see the potential that their property offers. Why? Several reasons explain this infirmity.

- The sellers are out of touch with what features buyers (renters) want.
- The sellers lack the capacity to imagine and create.
- The sellers have lived with the property so long that they have come to accept their property's shortcomings.
- The sellers don't know that the local zoning and building regulations actually permit a higher and more profitable use for the property.

This short list does not even come close to exhausting the reasons people miss the opportunities that lie before them. As the best-selling author, Wayne Dyer, says, "You must believe it to see it." Because the possibility-impaired don't believe their property offers great potential, they never even think to look.[1]

Don't Dilly-Dally with Due Diligence

Although good deals go fast, don't jump in before you've checked to see whether there's water in the pool. Always remember that not all bargain-priced properties represent good deals. You have scored a good deal only if you can sell the property for substantially more than you have put into it. Beware of underestimating fix-up expenses. Beware of hidden defects. Beware of environmental problems (e.g., lead paint, underground oil storage tanks, asbestos, contaminated well water). Beware of pouring so much cash into improvements that you'll have to overshoot the rent level that tenants are willing and able to pay.

Always temper your eagerness to buy a bargain-priced property with a thorough physical, financial, market, and legal analysis. Especially in cases of low- or nothing-down seller financing, many beginning investors grab at a "great" deal without first putting it under a magnifying glass. Act quickly when you must. But the less you know about a property, the greater your risk.

---

1. For detailed ideas on how to create value with your properties, see Chapters 13 and 14 and my book, *Make Money with Fixer-Uppers, Renovations, and Rehabs* (New York: John Wiley & Sons, 2003).

The Disclosure Revolution

Most states now require certain types of sellers to complete a disclosure statement that lists and explains all *known* problems or defects that may plague a property. But even if your state doesn't yet mandate seller disclosure, you still should obtain a disclosure form (most major realty firms keep blank copies on hand) and ask the owners to fill it out. In reviewing a completed disclosure statement, however, keep in mind the following five trouble points:

1. Sellers are not required to disclose facts or conditions of which they are unaware.
2. Disclosure reveals the past. It does not guarantee the future. By completing the statement, sellers do not warrant the condition of the property.
3. Many disclosure questions require somewhat subjective answers. Are playing children a neighborhood "noise" problem? Is a planned street widening an "adverse" condition?
4. Disclosure statements may not require sellers to disclose property defects that are readily observable.
5. Pay close attention to any owner (or agent) statements that begin, "I believe," "I think," "as far as we know," and other similar hedges. Don't accept these answers as conclusive. Follow up with further inquiry or inspection.

> **Insist on disclosure facts— not mere opinions.**

Seller disclosure statements help alert you to potential problems. But even so, independently check out the property to satisfy yourself that you really know what you are buying.

Excluded Income Properties

Many seller disclosure laws apply only to 1–4 unit owner-occupied properties. If you're buying an investor-owned property or an REO, the law may not require the seller to fill out a disclosure statement. If the seller does refuse, offset your additional risk by scaling down the top price you're willing to pay. Also, toughen up your prepurchase inspections.

> **Many states exempt investor properties from their seller disclosure statutes.**

Additionally, when buying income properties, verify rental income and operating expenses. Ask the sellers to sign a statement whereby they swear that the income and expense figures that they have reported to you stand true. Beware of owners who put friends, relatives, and employees into their buildings at inflated rent levels. These tenants don't really pay the rents stated (or if they do, they get kickbacks in cash or other benefits), but their signed leases sure look attractive to unsuspecting buyers.

How to Find Bargain Sellers

Okay, now you're ready to start finding these potential bargain sellers. Here are five broadly defined techniques:

1. Networking
2. Newspapers and other publications
3. Cold calls directly to owners
4. Real estate agents
5. Information highway

Networking

Some time back I was leaving the country for several years and decided to sell my house with a minimum of hassle. Coincidentally, the Ph.D. student club at the university where I was teaching was looking for a faculty member to host the upcoming faculty-student party. Aha, I thought, what better way to expose my house to more than 100 people? So I volunteered. The week following the party, I received two offers and accepted one of them.

The buyers got a good price and excellent financing. I avoided the hassle of putting the property on the market and did not have to pay a real estate commission. Everyone involved was satisfied.

This personal example shows the power of networking. What's surprising, though, is that so few buyers and sellers consciously try to dis-

> **Whether buying or selling, tell everyone you know.**

cover each other through informal contacts among friends, family, relatives, coworkers, church groups, clubs, business associates, customers, parent-teacher groups, and other types of acquaintances. So don't keep your search a secret. Tell everyone you know. Describe what you're looking for. Why search alone when you can enlist hundreds of others?

Newspapers and Other Publications

When most people look for real estate, they browse the real estate classifieds with a highlighter, call owners or Realtors, get basic information, and, when something sounds promising, set up an appointment. While this method can work reasonably well, it also can fail for two reasons: (1) if a property isn't advertised, you won't learn about it, and (2) if the ad for a property you might be interested in is not written effectively, you may pass it by without serious notice.

Try Running Your Own Ads   To at least partially overcome these drawbacks, run your own advertisement in the "wanted to buy" column. When you describe the type of property and terms that you're looking for, you invite serious sellers to contact you. When I began buying real estate, I used this technique to locate about 30 percent of the properties I bought.

As another way to use the newspaper, read through the "houses for rent," "condos for rent," and "apartments for rent" ads. Not only will this research help you gauge rent levels, often you'll see properties advertised as "lease-option" or "for rent or sale." These kinds of ads generally indicate a flexible seller.

Look Beyond the Classifieds   To search for potential bargain sellers in the newspaper, go beyond the classified real estate ads. Locate names of potential sellers from public notices: births, divorces, deaths, bankruptcies, foreclosures, or marriages. Each of these events can trigger the need to quickly sell real estate. If you contact these owners (or their heirs) before they have listed with a sales agent, you stand a fair chance of buying at a bargain price. (In addition, you might subscribe to the "default" or "foreclosure" lists and newsletters published in your area.)

Cold Calls Directly to Owners

To learn successful cold-calling, follow the techniques of Realtors. Most successful real estate agents develop listing farms. A listing farm represents a neighborhood or other geographic area that an agent consistently cultivates to find sellers who will list their properties for sale with that agent. Agents who cold-call typically telephone property owners with names gathered from a crisscross directory, walk the neighborhood, talk to residents, circulate flyers by mail or doorknob hangers, and take part in neighborhood or community-sponsored events. By cultivating a farm, an agent hopes to become well known in the area. An agent positions himself or herself to be the first person property owners think of when they contemplate a sale.

Take a lesson out of the real estate agent's playbook. Cultivate a farm in the neighborhoods or communities where you would like to buy. Circulate a flyer, for example, that reads:

> Before you list your home for sale, please call me. I am looking to buy a property in this neighborhood directly from the owners. Let's see if we can sit down together and work out an agreement that will benefit both of us.

> **Cultivate your farm.**

When property owners learn how they can save time, effort, and money selling direct, they may be willing to offer you a favorable price or terms.

Vacant Houses and Out-of-the-Area Owners   Your farm area will include some properties (vacant or tenant-occupied) that are owned by people who do not live in the neighborhood. These owners may not see your flyers, nor will they be listed in a crisscross directory. To learn how to reach these potential sellers, ask neighbors of nearby properties or talk directly with the tenants who live in the property.

> **Often out-of-area owners are sleeping sellers.**

If this research doesn't reveal the owners' names and addresses, you can next contact the county property tax assessor's office. There you can learn where and to whom the property tax statements are mailed. It's not unusual to find that out-of-the-area property owners are actually "sleeping sellers." That is, they would like to sell, but haven't awoken to that fact. With luck and perseverance, you could become their alarm clock.

Expired (or About to Expire) Listings   For any of a number of reasons, many properties listed with real estate agents do not sell during their original listing period. When this situation occurs, the listing agent will try to get the owners to relist with his or her firm. And quite likely, agents from other brokerage firms also will approach the sellers. However, here's what you can do to cut them off at the pass and perhaps arrange a bargain purchase.

When you notice a listed property that looks like it might fit your requirements, do *not* call the agent. Do *not* call or stop by to talk to the owners. Instead write the owners a letter stating the price and terms that you would consider paying. Then ask the owners to contact you *after* their listing has expired. (If a seller goes behind his agent's back and arranges a sale while the property is listed, the owner is legally obligated to pay the sales commission.)

> **Ask sellers to contact you after their listing has expired.**

An example: Sellers have listed their property at its market value of $200,000. The listing contract sets a 6 percent sales commission. The sellers have told themselves that they will accept nothing less than $192,500, which means that after selling expenses they would receive around $180,000. You offer $175,000. Would the sellers accept your offer? Or would they relist, postpone their move, and hold out for $5,000 to $10,000 more?

It would depend on the sellers' finances, their reason for moving, and any other pressures they may face. But you can see that even though your offer is low relative to the market value of the property, your price gives the sellers almost as much as they could expect if their agent found them a buyer. (Naturally, your letter would not formally commit you to the purchase. It would merely state the price or terms that you have in mind.)

Real Estate Agents

Do not conclude from the above technique that you should never use a real estate agent to help you find bargain-priced investment properties. A top agent can assist you in many ways. However, agents do deserve to

> **Real estate agents can provide you many valuable services.**

be paid for their services. So if you're planning to buy at a bargain price or buy on bargain terms (especially with low- or no-down-payment financing), where's the agent's fee going to come from? To pursue the best deal possible, at times you may have to forgo an agent's services and do your own legwork.

Cruise the Information Highway

Today's investors not only cruise neighborhoods, they also cruise the Internet to look for properties. Thousands of websites now list properties for sale. Property buyers (or browsers) can access the Realtor's Multiple Listing Service (MLS) through Realtor.com.

There is also a budding entrepreneurial industry that is accumulating specialized listings of everything from foreclosures to distressed properties to FSBOs. Going online you can locate investors looking for money—or money looking for properties.

> **Shop and compare properties on the Internet.**

Virtually all real estate information that in the past has been available from Realtors, public records, newspaper ads, newsletters, and other sources is now accessible on the Internet. Nobody today knows exactly where technology will lead us tomorrow. But electronic shopping for real estate (and mortgages) has made the MLS book as obsolete as a slide rule. (For a listing of websites useful to real estate investors, see the Internet Appendix. For a quick check of techniques you can use to find owners who will sell at a bargain price, see Box 9.1.)

---

1. Advertise "I buy properties" in the real estate classifieds.
2. Advertise on your car or truck with a magnetic "I buy properties" sign.
3. Make your car or truck a mobile billboard. Paint it with an "I buy houses" advertising message.
4. Mail out "I buy houses" postcards to owners in your farm area.
5. Mail out "I buy houses" postcards or letters to owners who are being foreclosed.

(continued)

Box 9.1   Quick Check List to Find Bargains

(Continued)

6. Advertise your property needs to real estate agents.
7. Contact attorneys (real estate, divorce, bankruptcy, estate, tax settlement specialists).
8. Contact yard care companies that maintain properties for lenders after the owners have abandoned them.
9. Network with friends, family, acquaintances.
10. Agree to pay bird-dog fees to anyone who refers you to a great buy.
11. Approach other investors who have just bought a property at a foreclosure sale. They may be willing to quick-flip for a small profit.
12. Contact the mortgage loss mitigation (REO) departments of mortgage lenders.
13. Follow closely the foreclosure postings.
14. Keep your eye out for properties in disrepair, especially those that are vacant or occupied by renters.
15. Contact out-of-town owners of properties in disrepair.
16. Get to know real estate agents who specialize in distress sales, foreclosures, and REOs. These types of agents frequently run ads publicizing their specialty—or you can just notice which agents tend to run ads for distressed properties such as HUD homes.

For a more extensive discussion of these and other similar techniques, see Peter Conti and David Finkel, *Making Big Money Investing in Foreclosures* (Chicago: Dearborn, 2003), pp. 91–132.

Box 9.1 Quick Check List to Find Bargains *(Continued)*

CHAPTER 10

Make Money with Foreclosures and REOs

If you've watched some of the real estate infomercials, you might believe that it's easy to buy a property at a foreclosure auction for just pennies on the dollar—then quickly resell that property for a large and easy windfall gain. Not true.

The Stages of Foreclosure

In fact, buying foreclosures "on the courthouse steps" represents just one type of foreclosure possibility. And that widely promoted approach entails big risks and uncertain profits. Consequently, experienced and successful investors usually buy *before* or *after* a foreclosure auction—not during. As a beginner, that, too, is where you should place your efforts.

Owner's Default (the First Stage)

When property owners fail to pay their mortgage payments, at first their lender will encourage, coerce, or threaten them through "reminder" letters, telephone calls, or credit counseling. If those efforts don't produce results, the lender's lawyers take over. Talking tough, the lawyers usually threaten foreclosure and warn the property owners to either pay up or face serious trouble.

Lenders favor loan workouts over foreclosure.

Typically, lenders may continue their loan workout efforts for anywhere from one to six months, or maybe longer. In contrast to the late 1980s and early 1990s, most lenders today do tend to give borrowers generous opportunity to reinstate or even refinance their delinquent mortgages.

As a result, fewer properties now end up at foreclosure sales—especially compared with the tidal wave of foreclosures that flooded the market 10 to 15 years ago. Even so, lenders will get the keys to more than 100,000 properties this year. And the number of borrowers who fall behind in their payments (and are in need of a loan workout) exceeds 2 million people a year. So, even though pickings aren't as good as they once were, beginning investors can still locate great foreclosure buys.

Near-record numbers of property owners need loan workouts.

Filing Legal Notice

When a lender does finally give up on a workout, its lawyers either file a legal "notice of default" or a "lawsuit to foreclose" (depending on the state). The lender then posts notice of this suit on the Internet and in newspapers. These postings tell the property owners, any other parties who may have legal claims against the owners or their property, and the public in general that legal action is moving forward to force a sale of the property.

The Foreclosure Sale (the Second Stage)

Eventually, when the defaulting borrowers run out of time, legal defenses, or delaying maneuvers, the foreclosure sale date arrives. At this point, the court trustee auctions the property to the highest cash bidder.

Lenders often win the bid at the foreclosure sale.

On occasion, a real estate investor (a foreclosure speculator) submits the winning bid. More likely, though, the lender who has forced the foreclosure sale bids, say, one dollar more than the amount of its unpaid claims (mortgage balance, late fees, accrued interest, attorney fees, foreclosure costs) and walks away with a "sheriff's" deed to the property. From then on until the lender sells the property, that property remains on the lender's books as *real estate owned*—an REO.

Lender's Don't Want REOs (the Third Stage)

The most important thing to know concerning foreclosure should be written in capital letters: LENDERS DO NOT WANT TO OWN FORE-CLOSED REAL ESTATE. For lenders—including such institutions as the Federal Housing Administration (FHA), the Department of Veterans Affairs (VA), Fannie Mae, and Freddie Mac—holding onto an REO that they have acquired through foreclosure rarely seems like a good idea. No matter how much potential the property offers, lenders who own REOs want to sell quickly. For you, their desire to sell quickly may mean their loss and your gain.

In sum, the three stages of the foreclosure process offers you these possibilities to gain a bargain price or bargain terms:

1. You can negotiate with the distressed property owners and, if necessary, the foreclosing lender.
2. You can bid at the foreclosure auction.
3. You can negotiate and buy directly from the lender or its insuring agency (FHA, VA, Fannie Mae, Freddie Mac) that owns the property as an REO.

Approach Owners with Empathy: Step One

There's no magic system that you can use to buy a property from owners facing foreclosure. These owners are plagued with financial troubles, personal anguish, and indecisiveness. In addition, they probably have been attacked by innumerable foreclosure sharks, speculators, bank lawyers, and recent attendees of "get-rich-quick" foreclosure seminars. These owners are living with public shame. For all of these reasons and more, they are not easy people to deal with.

Yet when you develop a sensitive, empathetic, problem-solving approach with people suffering foreclosure, you may be able to come up with a win-win agreement. Just keep in mind that more than likely you won't be the only investor who pays them a visit. A "Here's my offer—take it or leave it" approach will undoubtedly antagonize owners. This approach will not favorably distinguish you from a dozen other potential foreclosure buyers (sharks). So develop your offer and negotiations to preserve what little may be left of the owner's dignity and self-esteem.

> **"Take it or leave it" rarely works in negotiations with distressed owners.**

Perhaps you can share personal information about setbacks you have lived through. Above all, emphasize win-win outcomes. Dire straits or not, no one wants their property stolen from them.

Meet the Property Owners

When you visit with the property owners, you will try to make a good buy. But also, approach the troubled owners with aid that will end their distress. When everything goes right, the owners will receive cash for some of their equity, their credit will be salvaged, and you will acquire title to the property.

Here are several approaches you can use to open negotiations with an owner in foreclosure:

> "If you'll allow me to make a complete financial analysis of the property, I can be back within 24 hours with a firm offer that might solve your current dilemma.
>
> "I would like to figure a way to give you some cash for your equity, which you will otherwise lose in a foreclosure sale. By working with me you can save your credit, leave this property financially better off, and start your life over.
>
> "May I review the loan documents on your home? Do you have a copy of the mortgage and the loan payment record?"

With an empathetic, win-win manner, you will more often succeed where the foreclosure sharks fail.

Don't Fear Run-Down Properties

Do not be put off by cosmetic damage to the house as long as the house is structurally sound. A run-down house usually gives you more chance to profit. In fact, the more cosmetically run-down, the better. Every easily curable defect offers profitable opportunity to the shrewd distressed-property investor and renovator.

> **Cosmetic fixers offer big potential for profit.**

Thoroughly check out the entire property. Carefully analyze it. Then accurately evaluate the selling price that you could get after you've completed your fix-up work. If you've worked the numbers and the total costs of purchase and fix-up *exceed* your probable resale value, don't necessarily abandon the project. Go back to the troubled owner (or mortgage lender) and reopen negotiations. Point out that you must make a reasonable profit. If still you're unable to arrive at a good deal, then look elsewhere.

Vacant Houses

To discover a vacant house in foreclosure means to discover both a problem and an opportunity. It's a problem because you may have to do some detective work to locate the owners. Unless the owners have purposely tried to disappear, though, you can probably locate them in one of the following five ways:

1. Contact nearby neighbors to learn the owners' whereabouts, or the names of friends or family who would know.
2. Call the owners' telephone number and see if you get a "number changed" message.
3. Ask the post office to provide the owners' forwarding address.
4. Find out where the owners were employed and ask co-workers.
5. Contact the school that the owners' children attended and ask where their school records were sent. (However, with today's concerns about privacy, I've found that many school personnel will no longer give out school transfer information.)

> **Owners of abandoned properties seldom hold out for top dollar.**

After you locate the owners comes opportunity. Because they have abandoned the property, they probably aren't entertaining any pie-in-the-sky hopes for a sale at an inflated price. At this point, they may view any offer you make them as "found money."

In some cases, you will learn that the owners have split up and gone their separate ways. This situation raises another problem: Especially in hostile separations, working out an agreement with one owner in the belief that you can convince the other to go along often proves futile. To avoid this difficulty, *negotiate with all owners simultaneously*—or don't negotiate at all, unless you're just trying to sharpen your skills and you won't mind failing to close the deal.

Sometimes Losing Less Is Winning

If the property goes to the foreclosure sale, more often than not, the lender and the property owners will lose money. But think what happens when all parties agree to work with each other, rather than against each other. You can create an outcome where everyone walks away better off. Maybe they receive less than they hoped for, certainly less than they were theoretically entitled to, but far more than they could expect from a bidder at a foreclosure auction.

Some Investors Do Profit from the Foreclosure Auction: Step Two

Although foreclosure sales typically lose money for lenders, lienholders, and property owners, savvy bidders can turn these sales into big profits. But it's not easy. Bidding blind doesn't work. You have to do your homework.

Why Foreclosures Sell for Less than Market Value

A typical foreclosed property does sell at a price less than its market value. Why? Because foreclosure auctions don't come close to meeting the criteria of a market value transaction (see Box 10.1).

Market Value Sale	Foreclosure Auction
No seller or buyer duress	Forced sale
Buyer and seller well informed	Scarce information
60 to 120 day marketing period	Five minutes or less selling time
Financing on typical terms	Spot cash (or within 24 hours)
Owners agree to move	Owners or tenants may have to be evicted
Marketable title	No title guarantees
Warranty deed	Sheriff's (or trustee) deed
Seller disclosures	No seller disclosures
Close inspection of physical condition	No physical inspection
Yard sign	Rarely a yard sign
"Homes for sale" ads	Legal notice listing

Box 10.1   Characteristics of a Foreclosure Sale

As you can see, foreclosure auctions seem purposely designed to yield the *lowest possible sales price.* They take place under conditions that violate all principles of effective marketing.

Make the Puny Sales Efforts Work for You

For most would-be buyers, the potential risk, expense, and aggravation of foreclosure sales deter them from even showing up to bid. When you consider the lame marketing efforts, the adverse conditions of sale, and the potential owner (tenant) eviction problem, is it any wonder that foreclosed properties deserve to sell at a "fraction of their market value"?

Indeed, you might look at the foreclosure sales process and say, "Too many potential problems. No way do I want to take those kinds of risks. Besides, how could I ever come up with so much cash on short notice?" Clearly, that's the attitude of the great majority of real estate investors. It explains why at most sales the foreclosing lender "wins" the bid at a price equal to (or slightly above) the accumulated balance on the borrower's outstanding debt.

> **Great uncertainty produces low sales prices.**

Overcome the Risks of Bidding

RISK looms large to block your path to foreclosure sale profits. So the key to savvy bidding lies in knowing as much about the property as due diligence demands.

How can you get this information? First, meet with the property owners to talk over possibilities for working out a deal before foreclosure. Even when those discussions end without agreement, you've still been able to learn about the property (market value, fix-up needs, improvement opportunities), the neighborhood, and the owner's intentions. This step alone puts you way ahead of the game.

Second, quickly research liens against the title to the property at the courthouse—or online. You want to list every claim or judgment that you will have to satisfy to clear title. If you decide to pursue the property, you will need to verify the quality of the title with a lawyer or title insurer. I have usually found the clerical workers at the courthouse helpful when I'm unfamiliar with the record-filing procedures in an area.

How to Arrange Financing

After you gather information to manage the risks of buying at foreclosure, you still face the problem of financing. How are you going to get the cash to close the sale? If you lack wealth or credit, you're probably out of luck. Unless you bring in a money partner you really can't play the foreclosure game.

However, if you can even temporarily raise cash—such as a home equity loan, credit card cash advances, selling (or borrowing against) stocks, or maybe a signature loan—you can bid at a foreclosure auction. Then, after the foreclosure paperwork clears, you can place an interim or longer-term mortgage loan against the property and pay off your short-term creditors.

> **Raise the cash to bid via partners or short-term credit.**

Established investors who routinely buy foreclosed properties generally establish a line of personal credit at a bank. Then they can draw on the money whenever they need it. Or they maintain cash balances (money market funds) in amounts sufficient to cover their usual buying patterns.

The Foreclosure Sale: Summing Up

If you are willing to learn the foreclosure game (as it's played in your local area), do your homework on properties, and manage your risks, you can build profits quickly. You can buy properties at foreclosure auctions "for a fraction of their market value." Your challenge is to learn which of these properties meet the test of a true bargain—and which ones to avoid because they carry severe risks or expensive problems.

The Benefits of Buying REOs: Step Three

You can say one thing for certain about an REO: That lender wants to sell the property as quickly as possible. Mortgage lenders like to make loans and collect monthly payments. They do not like to own and manage properties. As a result, they often grant buyers of their REOs a bargain price, favorable terms such as low or no closing costs, below-market interest rates, and low down payments, or even some combination of all of these benefits.

If the property needs fix-up work that the lenders would prefer not to remedy, they may accept offers at deep discounts from market value. Just as important, prior to closing the sale of their REOs, lenders normally clean up title problems, evict unauthorized occupants, and bring all past-due property tax payments and assessments up to date. Some lenders, too, permit buyers to write offers subject to an appraisal or professional inspection (contingency clauses).

Safer than Buying at the Foreclosure Sale

Buying an REO directly from a lender typically presents no more risk than buying directly from any other property owner.[1] Normally, you can

---

1. Several exceptions might include: (1) states where the foreclosed owners may have a right of redemption; (2) if the foreclosed owners still retain some legal right to challenge the validity of the foreclosure sale; or (3) if a bankruptcy trustee or the Internal Revenue Service (tax lien) is entitled to bring the property within their powers. Rarely would any of these potential claims be worth losing sleep over. But prior to closing an REO purchase, you might want to run these issues by legal counsel.

buy an REO much more safely than you could have bought the same property at its foreclosure sale. Depending on the lender's motivation, its internal policies and procedures, and the property loan-to-value ratio (LTV) at the time of the foreclosure sale, you might even be able to buy at a price lower than market value.

Why a Lower Price?

Let's say the market value of a property at the time of its foreclosure sale was $165,000. The lender's claims against the property totaled $160,000. To win the property away from the lender, you would have had to bid more than $160,000—a price that's too high to yield a profit.

> **It costs lenders big money to hold on to their REOs.**

However, once the lender owns the property and tallies its expected holding costs, Realtor's commission, and the risks of seeing the (probably) vacant property vandalized, it may decide to cut its losses. It may accept an offer from you within the range of $140,000 to $150,000 (especially if you offer cash, which you may borrow from some other mortgage lender).

In desperate times REO lenders may turn to mass marketing and highly advertised public auctions to unload their REOs. In stable to strong markets, they generally (but not always) play it low key. If it can be avoided, no lender wants to publicize the fact that it's "throwing down-on-their-luck families out of their homes." So, absent tough times and mass advertising, you can find REOs in three different ways:

- ◆ Follow up after a foreclosure sale.
- ◆ Cold-call lender REO personnel.
- ◆ Locate Realtors who typically get REO listings.

Follow Up After Foreclosure

You can easily learn of lender REOs by attending foreclosure auctions. When a lender casts a top bid for a property in which you're interested, buttonhole the bidder and start talking business. Or try to schedule an appointment to see the officer who takes charge of the management and

> **Open discussions with a lender immediately after the foreclosure sale.**

disposition of REOs. When you show the lender how your bargain offer will actually save, perhaps even make the bank money, you'll be on your way to closing a deal.

Beware of the stall. Nearly every financial institution is run by standard operating procedures, management committees, and other precautionary rules that frequently work against sensible decisions. If you run into a bureaucratic stonewall, you must persevere. The reward of following through doesn't just lie in getting a good deal on a property now. More important, you will build personal relationships that will open the bank's doors for you in future transactions.

Cold-Call REO (Loss Mitigation) Personnel

All mortgage lenders experience at least a few borrower defaults. No one has yet designed a foolproof system for predicting which loan applicants will fail to pay. It follows, then, that at one time or another all mortgage lenders must end up with REOs—even if eventually they pass them along to HUD, VA, Fannie Mae, or Freddie Mac.

Sometimes, too, lenders pick up REOs without going through foreclosure. During the last real estate downturn, many lenders would open their morning mail to find the keys to a house, a deed, and a note from the distressed owners saying, "We're out of here. It's your problem now."

To find REOs that lenders have acquired through foreclosure or "deed-in-lieu" transfers, you can cold-call mortgage lenders. You might ask for a list of their REOs. This technique, though, seldom turns up much. For various reasons, lenders may keep a tight hold on this information. Nevertheless, it doesn't cost to ask.

> **Cold-calling lenders for REOs requires persistence.**

Until you establish relationships with REO personnel, you may find the following approach works better: Rather than ask for a complete list of REOs, narrow your focus. Tell lenders what you're specifically looking for in terms of location, size, price range, floor plan, condition, or other features. In that way, a lender can answer your request without disclosing the full number of REOs within its inventory.

Locate Specialty Realtors

Many mortgage lenders *avoid* selling directly to REO investors (though they do make exceptions) for two reasons: (1) as mentioned, they don't like the unfavorable publicity, and (2) they want to promote good relations with Realtors.[2] Because most mortgage lenders expect Realtors to bring them new loan business, these same lenders can't then turn around and become FSBO (for sale by owner) dealers. "You scratch my back and I'll scratch yours" sets the rules in business.

As one part of your efforts to find REOs, cultivate relationships with Realtors who specialize in this market. (In fact, HUD, VA, Fannie Mae, and Freddie Mac almost always sell their REOs through Realtors.) In most cities, you can easily find REO specialists by looking through newspaper classified real estate ads.

Hire a Real Pro   Once you have identified several foreclosure specialists, give each one a call. Learn their backgrounds. Do they only dabble in the field of REOs and foreclosures? Or do they make this field their full-time business? When I recently telephoned REO specialist John Huguenard, for example, he talked with me for an hour and a half about property availability, detailed financing and purchase procedures, hot areas of town, rehab potential, estimating repair costs, portfolio lenders, strategies for buying and managing properties as well as selecting tenants, and a dozen other related topics.

> When searching for REOs, talk with an REO specialist.

At one point during our conversation, he asked, "I'll bet you haven't talked to any other agents who know as much as I do about REOs and foreclosures, have you? I've been doing this 23 years. Last year, I sold 90 houses and rehabbed 16 others for my own account." John was right. I hadn't.

Beware of False Experts   John's the kind of real estate professional you want to find. Although many realty agents claim expertise in REOs and foreclosures—"Sure, I can do that for you"—only a few make it their prime activity, day in and day out, year after year. When you work with an

---

2. Also, most lenders don't want to waste time with all of those investor "wannabes" who have just read a "nothing down" book or "graduated" from a foreclosure guru's seminar.

agent who's really in the know, you won't have to do your own legwork and door knocking. Your agent will screen properties as soon as—if not before—they come onto the market. You will then be notified immediately.

Plus, specialty agents with in-depth knowledge also will stay on top of the finance plans that portfolio, government, and conventional lenders are offering to home buyers and investors. (Again, for example, John Huguenard knew of portfolio lenders doing 100 percent LTV investor loans for investor acquisition and rehab.)

Avoid the foreclosure dabblers. Work with a real pro, someone who knows all of the current rules, regulations, and operating procedures.

HUD, VA, Fannie, and Freddie Won't Sell Direct to Buyers   No matter what approach to acquiring REOs and foreclosures you choose to follow, you will benefit by talking with realty pros who make the business a career. As noted earlier, though, if you buy an REO from HUD, VA, Fannie Mae, or Freddie Mac, you *must* process your offer through a lender-authorized real estate agent. Only in certain exceptional circumstances would any of these organizations negotiate with you directly. Your REO specialist will know all of the ins and outs necessary to deal with these agencies and firms.

More Sources of Bargains

You may think that we've exhausted the possibilities for finding bargain deals. But no. You've got at least 11 more sources of bargains.

Federal Government Auctions

Each year agencies of the federal government (in addition to HUD and the VA) sell all types of seized and surplus real estate including homes, apartment complexes, office buildings, ranches, and vacant and developed land. Among the most active sellers are the Internal Revenue Service (IRS), General Services Administration (GSA), and the Federal Deposit Insurance Corporation (FDIC). On occasion, you can also find properties offered by the Small Business Administration (SBA). Although space here doesn't permit full discussion of each of these agencies, you can locate their properties and sales procedures at the following websites:

> Internal Revenue Service at www.treas.gov/auctions/irs
> General Services Administration at http://propertydisposal.gsa.gov/propforsale
> Federal Deposit Insurance Corporation at www.fdic.gov/buying/owned/real/index
> Small Business Administration at http://app1.sba.gov/pfsales/dsp

Sheriff Sales

In addition to foreclosures, you might want to follow sheriff sales or other legally mandated involuntary property sales. These sales may result from property tax liens, civil lawsuit judgments, and bankruptcy creditors.

Because of the local nature of these types of forced sales, I can't go into the details that relate to specific sales procedures or the relative possibilities for finding bargain prices. I can only say, "It all depends." Yet if your goal is to leave no stone unturned in your attempt to locate good deals, talk with real estate lawyers, courthouse officials, foreclosure speculators, and others who are in the know about these types of sales. Because these sales take place under less than ideal marketing methods, it's only natural to expect selling prices that fall substantially below a property's market value.

Buy from Foreclosure Speculators

Another way to profit from foreclosure and forced sale auctions without actually bidding is to buy from a winning bidder shortly after the foreclosure sale.

Say a foreclosure speculator puts in a winning bid of $145,000 on a property that seems to have a market value of $195,000 if it were fixed up and marketed effectively. After the auction, you offer the speculator $170,000 (or whatever). To minimize risk, you attach several contingencies to your offer that permit you to get the property thoroughly inspected, evict any holdover owners or tenants, clear up title problems, seek title insurance, and arrange financing. If the property checks out, the sale closes and the speculator makes a quick $25,000 (more or less). You get the property at a discount without the costly surprises that can turn a superficially promising foreclosure buy into a big loss.

> **Ask a speculator to flip you a property at a wholesale price.**

Probate and Estate Sales

Probate and estate sales present another potential source of bargain properties. When owners of properties die, their property may be sold to satisfy the deceased's mortgagee and other creditors. Even when the deceased leaves sufficient wealth in cash to satisfy all claims against the estate, heirs still normally prefer to sell the property rather than retain ownership.

Probate

To buy a property through probate, generally you submit a bid through the estate's administrator (usually a lawyer) or executor. Then all bids are reviewed by the probate judge assigned to the case. Depending on local and state laws, the judge may then select a bid for approval or reopen the bidding. Because of legal procedures and delays, bidding on probate properties can require perseverance. Judges wield substantial discretion in deciding when and whether to accept a probate bid. You can never tell for sure where you stand.

An acquaintance of mine tells of a probate property that came up for sale in an area of $150,000 homes. The probate administrator listed the house for sale at $115,000. A flurry of bids came in that ranged from a low of $105,000 up to a high of $118,000. Several months later the judge looked at the bids, rejected the high bid of $118,000, and solicited additional offers. Eventually, the judge approved the sale at a price of $129,850 to someone who had not even been involved in the first round of bidding.

> **Probate judges may exercise arbitrary power.**

After all was said and done, the successful buyer did achieve a bargain price. (Unlike forced sales "on the courthouse steps," in a probate sale, you generally can enter and inspect the properties prior to submitting a bid.) To learn about probate in your area, talk with a probate lawyer or the clerk of the county court. Also look at local newspapers that announce upcoming probate sales.

Estate Sales

In some situations, an estate's assets need not be dragged through the probate process. You may be able to buy directly from the heirs or the executor of the estate. In fact, some buyers of estate properties follow the obituary notices, contact heirs, and try to buy before the property is

> **When you contact heirs, you often find eager sellers.**

listed with a real estate agent. To succeed in this approach, you would, naturally, need to develop an empathetic demeanor.

Estate sales frequently produce bargains because heirs eagerly want cash. They also may need the money to pay off a mortgage, other creditors, or estate taxes. Out-of-town heirs (especially) may not want to hold a vacant property for an extended period until a top-dollar buyer is found. Once again, pressures of time or money can lead to sales prices that fall below a property's market value.

Private Auctions

Increasingly, many sellers who want to liquidate their properties turn to private auctions. During the last economic downturn in California, banks and thrifts were pooling their REOs and jointly auctioning off dozens (sometimes hundreds) of properties at a time. New homebuilders, too, have increased their use of auctions. Sometimes homebuilder auctions involve closeout sales where a builder wants to get out of a current project to devote time and energy to a new development. On other occasions, a homebuilder's auction may represent a last desperate attempt to raise cash to head off project foreclosure or company bankruptcy.

> **Homebuilders (or their lenders) may auction off excess inventory.**

In Dallas, a wealthy homeowner tired of trying to sell his $1.6 million (listed price) home through a brokerage firm and was eager to move into his newly built $4.4 million home. So he hired an auctioneer. On a pleasant Saturday morning, hundreds of people showed up and within minutes of the opening bid, the home had a new owner. The winning price: $890,000.

Prepare for an Auction

Attend a major real estate auction. You'll have fun. Often a band is playing, food and drinks are served, and a festive mood prevails. The auction company wants to make potential bidders feel good. But beyond this dis-

Private auctions make for festive events.

play of cheer, the auction company is promoting one goal: Get every property sold at the highest possible price. Auctioneers get paid a percentage of the day's take, plus perhaps a bonus for exceeding a certain level of sales.

To find a bargain, don't get caught up in the festive frenzy and abandon good sense (as the auction company wants you to). Instead, attend the auction armed with information. Prepare to walk out a winner—not simply a buyer. Here's how you can make that happen:

- ◆ *Always thoroughly inspect a property.* During the weeks before most private auctions, the auction company will schedule open houses at the properties to be sold. If you can't visit an open house, contact a real estate agent and ask for a personal showing. (Most auction companies cooperate with Realtors. If an agent brings a winning bidder to the auction, that agent is paid a 1 percent or 2 percent sales commission.) Sometimes auction properties sell cheap because they are nothing more than teardowns waiting for a bulldozer. Or they may suffer any of a number of other problems. Even new properties aren't necessarily defect free. Check them out before you bid.
- ◆ *Appraise the property carefully.* Even if free of defects, you can't assume value. You must figure it out by studying recent selling prices of comparable properties. Don't count on list price to guide you. Just because you buy a property 25 percent below its previous listing price doesn't mean you have bought at 25 percent below the property's market value.
- ◆ *Set a maximum bid price.* Remember, you're looking for a bargain. Market value tells you what a property might sell for if fixed up and marketed by a competent and aggressive real estate agent. Market value *does not* tell you the price you should bid. Before the auction, set your maximum bid price. Don't let the auctioneer's "boosters" cajole, excite, romance, bamboozle, or intimidate you into going higher.
- ◆ *Be aware of the buyer's premium.* At many auctions, you will be required to pay a 5 or 10 percent "buyer's premium" fee in addition to your bid price.
- ◆ *Review the paperwork that will accompany a successful bid.* Before the auction begins, review the property tax statements, environmental reports, lot survey, legal description, and the sales contract you'll be asked to sign.

◆ *Learn what type of deed the seller will use to convey the property.* With a general warranty deed, the seller guarantees clear title subject only to certain named exceptions. Other types of deeds convey fewer title warranties. Don't accept a deed without an understanding of its limitations (liens, easements, encroachments, exceptions, missing heirs, etc.). All in all, title insurance is your best guarantee. If a property's title is uninsurable, consult a real estate attorney to obtain an opinion of title.

◆ *Be prepared to pay the deposit.* To become eligible to bid, register with the auction company before the auction begins and show proof of deposit funds or cashier's checks (amount varies by auction). You then will be issued a bid card that will tell the auctioneer you are an approved bidder. Without a bid card, the auctioneer won't recognize your bid.

◆ *Find out if financing is available.* Often auction companies prearrange financing on some or all of their properties. If so, find out the terms and qualifying standards. If not, determine how much time the auction company gives you to arrange your own financing. Unlike most government agency property auctions, private auction companies typically do not expect their successful bidders to pay cash for their properties.

◆ *Learn whether the sale is absolute or subject to a reserve price.* Usually auction properties are either offered absolute or with reserve. If absolute, a property is sold no matter how low the top bidder's price. With a reserve price, the top bid must exceed a prearranged minimum amount or the property is pulled out of the auction. On occasion, though, the owner of a property may "nod" to the auctioneer and approve a bid that does not meet the reserve price.

How to Find Auctions

Most auction companies advertise their upcoming auctions in local and sometimes national newspapers (such as the *Wall Street Journal*). Auction companies not only want to attract as many bidders as possible, they want to draw large crowds so they can create a sense of anticipation and excitement. In addition to advertising, most auction companies will place your name on their mailing lists.

Local auction companies are listed in the phone book. Large-scale auctions, though, are frequently handled by auction companies that operate nationwide. These include Fisher Auction Company, Hudson & Marshall, JP King, Kennedy-Wilson, Larry Latham, NRC Auctions, Ross Dove & Company, and Sheldon Good & Company. Even if you decide not to bid, large auctions are fun to attend. Try one. Plus, you'll learn the tricks of the trade as you watch the professional auctioneers and investors vie with one another.

Short Sale Bargains

Up to this point, you've discovered multiple ways to find properties that you can buy at a bargain price. You've learned about motivated sellers, foreclosures, REOs, auctions, probate, and estate sales. Now, you're going to see how to *create* a bargain price by negotiating with a lienholder. Investors call this technique a short sale.

What Is a Short Sale?

> **Upside-down property owners create the need and opportunity.**

> **Upside-down owners owe more than their property is worth.**

In the late 1980s and early 1990s, the "short sale" technique gained momentum in the serious real estate recession that plagued California, Texas, and several other parts of the country. Investors and lenders used the short sale to help rescue *upside-down* property owners who had fallen behind on their mortgage payments (or in some cases, where they were about to fall behind).

Let's say that during a speculative real estate boom you buy a home for $300,000. You put 5 percent down and borrow $285,000 from a lender. After three years of owning the property, you get laid off. Even worse, the market value of your property falls to $265,000. You would like to sell the house, but now you owe more than it's worth. You're upside down.

Even if you found a buyer to give you a full price offer, you wouldn't net enough to pay your lender, closing expenses, a real estate commission, and accumulated deferred maintenance (repair) costs. What can you do?

Unfortunately, without a job, you can no longer make your mortgage payments. Nor is it likely that you can refinance. Your lender threatens to foreclose. Your situation looks bleak.

Lender, Too, Faces Bleak (Money-Losing) Outcome   The lender is threatening to foreclose, but it doesn't really want to. If the lender forecloses, it will surely lose money.

In your present difficult situation, you owe the lender a total of $280,000 (mortgage balance, missed payments). If the lender goes through foreclosure, it will want to collect not only this $280,000, but also numerous other costs such as . . .

- ◆ Attorney fees
- ◆ Court costs
- ◆ Lost interest
- ◆ Property insurance premiums
- ◆ Property tax payments
- ◆ Miscellaneous costs (staff time, property upkeep, paperwork, bad publicity)

If these other costs total $20,000 through the date of the foreclosure sale, the lender would have $300,000 sunk into this property.

How much would a foreclosure speculator bid for the property at auction? Maybe $200,000. If the lender lets this speculator take the property, the lender loses around $100,000.

Total sums owed	$300,000
Speculator bid	200,000
Lender loss	100,000

Alternatively, the lender may choose not to let the property go to a foreclosure speculator. It could shut out the speculators with a bid of $300,001. If the lender wins its bid, it then owns the property as an REO.

Does acquiring the REO solve the lender's problem? No. The lender will continue to lose interest earnings on the money it has put out

REOs don't end the lender's misery.

thus far on the property. Plus, it must still pay property taxes, premiums for property insurance, property upkeep, and repairs. To actually get the property sold, the lender will probably pay fix-up costs and a real estate commission.

Lenders Lose with REOs   After all of these efforts and costs, will the lender eventually come out ahead with its REO? Still, the answer is no. Remember, at most, the property will bring a price of $265,000. Here's how the numbers might look.

Balance owed at foreclosure	$300,000
REO costs	15,000
Real estate commission @ 6%	15,900
Total	$330,900
REO sales price	265,000
Lender loss with REO	(65,900)

Even with the REO alternative, the lender loses $65,900 (and that assumes an REO sale at full market value—which is not likely). So, ask yourself if, as an investor, you could work out a way for lenders with bad loans to lose less money. Would the lender accept your solution? In many instances, the answer to that question is yes.

The Pre-Foreclosure Workout   What if, before the lender filed foreclosure on a bad loan, you could get the lender to accept a short payoff—some amount less than the total balance the borrower owes? Quite likely you could save the lender from losing as much money as it otherwise would by going through with its foreclosure. You would help the borrowers salvage what's left of their credit record. (Late payments don't bring down a credit score nearly as much as would a foreclosure.)

What's in it for you? You acquire a property for less than its market value. Let's go back to the earlier example at the point in time when the borrowers owed $280,000—only now we'll assume that you're the investor.

How the Numbers Look   You talk with the borrowers. You learn their bleak upside-down situation. You offer them $1 for their property with the proviso that you can work out a short payoff on their loan with their lender. You succeed. Their lender agrees to accept $230,000. In exchange, the lender grants a full release of the mortgage lien it held against the property.

In a short sale, the lender accepts less to lose less.

The sellers/borrowers get to begin a new financial life free of mortgage debt, free of mortgage payments they cannot make, and free of waking up in the middle of the night and flipping on the TV to find nothing but Carleton Sheets and Ron Popiel infomercials. The lender loses only $50,000, instead of the $65,900 (or more) that it would have lost by foreclosing the borrowers and eventually ending up with another REO that it does not want.

As for you, the investor, you've just become the owner of a $265,000 property for an outlay of $230,001. Everybody comes out ahead.

How to Actually Complete a Short Sale

To complete a short sale, you will typically need to negotiate well and diligently persevere. To earn your gain of $25,000 to $100,000 from this technique may require anywhere from several weeks to several months of back-and-forth talks and proposals. And even after this effort, you may still fail to put all of the pieces together.

> **Short sales yield big profits for investors—but require effort.**

But when you do succeed, all of those efforts do pay off handsomely. So let's look at the steps you can take to beat the odds.

Find Sellers in Financial Distress (or Otherwise Motivated to Deal) To complete a short sale, you first need to find sellers who are financially distressed or otherwise eager to cut a deal that frees them from their property and their mortgage obligations. How can you find these motivated sellers?

You've got dozens of possibilities. Just revisit all of the techniques we've discussed so far, and especially those shown in Box 9.1. Remember, every day some people's lives change to make property ownership a burden. When you figure out a way to relieve that burden, you help the sellers and you help yourself.

Review the Sellers' Mortgage Payment Records After you've established rapport with the sellers and set the tone for productive discussions, you need to review their mortgage payment records and all collection letters thus far sent by their lender. Specifically, you want to learn:

- ◆ The current payoff amount on the loan including all back payments, late fees, and legal fees assessed by the lender (if any).

◆ Where the lender is in its collection efforts. In my experience, I've found lenders are more inclined to complete a short sale when the borrowers have missed multiple monthly payments. The borrowers are so seriously delinquent that the lender believes the property will almost certainly end up in foreclosure.

◆ How the full amount the borrowers owe compares with the likely selling price of their mortgaged property.

◆ Whether it appears that a foreclosure will lose the lender a lot of money, after adding in continued lost interest and other expenses. If so, you've located a hot prospect for a short payoff.

Review the Sellers' Total Financial Picture   Before a lender will accept a short payoff, the borrowers must prove destitution. By destitution, I don't mean that the borrowers will soon be living on food stamps in the back of their car. But the lender will probe to determine whether the borrowers own any valuable assets that they could sell to raise money.

> **Lenders won't let borrowers just walk away from their mortgage.**

The lender also will look at the borrowers' earnings history and career prospects. If the borrowers look like they're merely trying to shirk their mortgage obligations, the lender won't likely negotiate (unless you persuade the collections staff to rethink their position).

Place the Property Under Contract   When your preliminary talks and investigation show that the borrowers really can't pay and that the lender is heading toward big losses, get the property under contract.

Offer the sellers some token amount ($1) in exchange for a deed to their property. In addition, you agree to permanently get the lender off their backs. By doing so, you save the sellers' credit and restore their peace of mind (at least as it relates to this imminent foreclosure).

However, because at this point you don't know whether the lender will accept a short payoff, you must also include a contingency in your offer to the sellers that reads something like this:

> This agreement between ___you___ and ___sellers___ is subject to ___you___ obtaining full satisfaction of all claims levied by ___lender___ for an amount not to exceed $_____.

The maximum amount you actually commit to pay the lender will depend on the amount of profit you plan to earn and the riskiness of the property (current condition, certainty with which you can achieve your desired selling price). Do not agree to pay the sellers any real money, because the lender won't approve it. Only rarely will a lender permit borrowers to put cash in their own pocket from a sale when at the same time the lender agrees to take a loss.

Obtain Permission to Negotiate with the Lender   At the time the sellers accept your offer, you also will get them to sign a form that authorizes the lender to release the sellers' loan information to you. This form allows you to verify all of the mortgage payment data that the sellers have provided you. Plus, it gives the lender authority to negotiate a payoff with you.

> **Lenders require you to provide them a seller release form.**

Without this form, the lender will not share otherwise confidential loan data about its borrowers with you. Make sure the sellers understand the need for this release. Without it, you're just shooting blanks.

Approach the Lender   When you first approach the lender, do not—I repeat, do not—even suggest the mortgage payoff price that you have in mind. During this preliminary meeting (most probably with a staff officer in the lender's loss mitigation department), learn the lender's views about short payoffs. Learn the criteria the lender applies. Learn the lender's standard policies and operating procedures.

Different lenders try to settle their bad loans in different ways. Some hardballers won't budge. Others are glad to see you. Some (perhaps the majority) will act standoffish but can be persuaded to negotiate when you show them why your solution will work to their advantage. (Never assume that all of the bank personnel who staff loss mitigation departments understand why short payoffs can benefit the lender.)

> **Bank staff may not immediately open up to you.**

Prepare and Submit Your Offer   You've opened discussions with the lender and gathered information about its payoff policies. Ideally, during these talks, the lender will have given you clues as to how much discount it's willing to accept. (Regardless, though, always offer far less than you're willing to pay.) You're now ready to prepare and submit an offer.

But wait. You don't want to just give the lender a number. In most instances, you will need to first build your case. You will need to submit a full package of persuasive evidence. This package should include:

- ◆ *Cover letter.* Here's where you lay out in summary form all of the evidence that you've submitted to prove why a short payoff now will benefit the lender. However, do not put precise figures in this letter. Build up the merits of the idea before you start talking numbers. Talk benefits before price.
- ◆ *Condition of the property.* Take as many *unflattering* photos of the property as you can. Submit those that look the worst. Also, submit repair cost estimates (as high as you can reasonably justify).
- ◆ *Comparable sales.* Choose the lowest-priced, best-looking comparable sale properties that you can find. Use these comp sales to support the lowest possible estimate of market value for the mortgaged property. The less the lender thinks the property will bring at foreclosure (or as an REO), the more willing it will be to accept your short-sale offer.
- ◆ *Owner distress pleas.* In this part of the offering package, you will include a hardship letter from the borrowers. This letter will explain all of the tough times these folks are experiencing. For support, include those threatening letters the borrowers have received from the IRS, those large unpaid medical bills, the electricity cutoff notice from the utility company, and the newspaper article that explains why 400 laid-off workers at the local textile plant (where both of the borrowers worked) will never be called back.
- ◆ *Credibility.* As in all negotiations, provide evidence to the lender that as soon as the lender accepts your offer, you are ready, willing, and able to close. Prove to the lender that you will perform as promised.
- ◆ *Your offer.* On this final page of your package, calculate the amount of losses the lender will suffer if it continues the foreclosure process. Then, show your bid payoff amount. The figures should show that the lender will net more if it acts now to accept your offer.

◆ *Persistently follow up.* Do not get discouraged if the lender doesn't immediately respond to your offer. Follow up, follow up, follow up. If the lender won't accept, then weasel, cajole, or persuade the loss mitigation officer to suggest a number that might look good. Do whatever you can to keep the dialogue alive.

Coming Up with the Money   To maximize the attractiveness of your offer to the lender, talk cash. Lenders typically prefer to cash out their bad loans. Rarely would a lender agree to a discounted payoff *and* carryback financing. (Yet, if necessary, you can still ask.)

How can you raise this money if you don't already have it? Return to Chapters 3–8. Given the bargain deal that you've just negotiated, you should be able to easily flip the property to another buyer (who has the cash to close), secure low- (or no-) down-payment financing from another lender, or bring in a money partner.

With a near-sure profit from the transaction, you will find the money. Nevertheless, don't wait to the last minute. Not only do you need to prove your credibility in your bid package, but after a lender accepts your offer you can't delay. Line up a *sure* source of cash *before* you submit your bid.

CHAPTER 12

Run Numbers Like a Pro

In this chapter, you're going to see some easy ways to figure out whether a property you're looking at will really give you a great buy. If your property looks good on all (or even most) of these benchmarks, you're almost certain to make a lot of money.

- The construction cycle
- Per-unit measures
- Gross rent multipliers
- Capitalized value
- Cash flow returns
- Potential for creating value

After you learn these value benchmarks, you'll see that contrary to popular belief, at times you can achieve a great return plus a margin of safety—even if you pay above market value.

The trick, of course, is to know what you're doing and why you're doing it. Too many beginning investors merely chase after "below-market" buys, and reject in knee-jerk fashion all properties priced at or above market. Instead, as a savvy, entrepreneurial investor, you'll want to run your potential buys through a variety of financial tests. High passing grades will tell you when you've really found a property that will prove to be a star performer.

Certainly, buying below market can give you a great bargain. But that's not the only way to score a good deal.

170

Follow the Construction Cycle

When you invest, you expect to profit as the property appreciates in value. Over the long run, as construction costs go up and population increases, property values nearly always increase. In the short run, though, current market values sometimes jump too far above construction costs. Eyeing large profits, builders rush to construct new houses, condominiums, and apartments. They glut the market with too many new houses and rental properties. Journalists proclaim, "Real estate's no longer a good investment." The foreclosure rate begins to climb.

> **Over time, higher building costs pull up property values.**

The market heads toward the ebb of the construction cycle. Guess what? You're now facing the perfect time to buy.

How to Profit from the Construction Cycle

Here's how the construction cycle works: Typically, a city, town, or vacation area begins to boom. Jobs and wages go up. More people move in. Interest rates decline. Apartment rents and home prices climb higher. Apartment vacancies disappear. The number of homes up for sale begins to decline. Pretty soon, *existing* houses or apartments that could be constructed *new* for say, $100,000 per unit begin to command prices of, say, $120,000, $130,000 or more.

Builders Spy Opportunity

With prices of existing properties well above their construction costs, builders can quickly make a lot of money. Build at $100,000; sell at $130,000. Great! $30,000 profit. Naturally, too many builders rush in to grab a pile of profits. Because of these optimistic builder expectations, the supply of new homes shoots up. What was recently a shortage becomes a surplus.

> **High builder profit margins may lead to overbuilding.**

Buyers who bought near the top of the cycle face disappointment (or worse) as rent levels and property prices temporarily stagnate or slide back to lower levels.

Recovery   Over time, banks pull back their mortgage lending. Builders sharply cut their new developments. Rental vacancies begin to tighten; the number of unsold homes begins to fall. Potential renters and home-buyers again outnumber the supply of available properties. Property prices and rents stabilize and then edge up. Eventually, as shortages again loom on the horizon, vacancies fall further. Prices take off on another rapid run-up. The construction cycle turns another revolution. Prices set new record highs.

Implications for Investors

The classic major boom-bust construction cycle occurred in Texas in the mid to late 1980s. Properties that could be built new for $75,000 to $100,000 sold for as much as $125,000 to $150,000. Condominium and apartment projects multiplied like dandelions after an April rain. Back then, large real estate tax shelter benefits added fuel to the fire. In a situation similar to the dot-coms and tech stocks in the late 1990s, rapid price increases fed on themselves—until the real estate bubble burst.

Pitfalls   Could Texas *investors* have avoided getting caught in this downdraft? Absolutely. Had they kept an eye on construction costs, they could have anticipated problems. For whenever the market prices of properties push more than 10 to 15 percent ahead of their new replacement costs, the market is flashing yellow. Yet, rather than cautiously slow down, most would-be investors (and builders) speed up.

> **Large profits for builders can bring too much new supply to market.**

Savvy *investors,* though, pay attention to this warning sign. They back off from new acquisitions or buy only when they can get their price—not the inflated (and soon-to-be-deflated) market price.

The moral: Stay in touch with local builders or others who are in the know about contractor costs (building suppliers, lumber yards, real estate appraisers, building contractors, construction lenders). Also, you might consult one or more construction cost services. You can easily follow your local building costs through cost manuals (at your library) or websites. When builder profit margins grow ever fatter, oversupply becomes a real threat.

Profit When Values Drop Below the Costs to Build New   Rents low? Vacancies climbing? Unsold houses and condos piling up in the Realtors' Multiple Listing Service? Builders going bankrupt? Lenders foreclosing? Great! That's the perfect time for investors to buy—especially when market prices end up below replacement costs. Because that means few builders will build. Builders will not knowingly pay more to build a house than they can get from its selling price.

As long as longer-term trends in an area point to a larger population, more jobs, and a desirable quality of life, prices (rents) are guaranteed to rise. More people, growing incomes, higher construction costs. You can profit from the construction cycle because decade-by-decade property prices will continue to set new peaks.

> **Depressed markets**
> *reduce* **risk.**

Have Money, Will Travel   Will local or regional shakeouts occur in the future? Probably. Although builders and construction lenders have supposedly entered a new era of disciplined building and lending, that story's been told before. It seems that each generation forgets the mistakes of the past. They must relearn the lessons taught in earlier years.

Stay informed. Keep tabs on various cities and real estate markets around the country. Should property prices again plunge below their cost of replacement, don't miss that opportunity. Adopt the motto, "Have Money (Credit), Will Travel." If the bargains don't come to you, then, as a entrepreneurial investor, prepare to go to the bargains.

> **Stay informed**
> **about out-of-town**
> **markets.**

Local (Regional) Recessions

Even without serious overbuilding, property prices can sometimes fall below replacement costs due to job declines and recession. During the early 1990s, large layoffs in the defense and aerospace industry created the housing troubles experienced in Southern California. But as with Texas and New York City, the Southern California economy had to bounce back. And when it did, we witnessed a great boom in property prices. Follow the real estate cycle and you, too, can earn those big bucks that recovery brings about.

Construction Costs > Market Price = Bargain Hunter's Delight

Per-Unit Measures

In addition to tuning in to the construction cycle, savvy real estate investors rely on various per-unit measures to help them decide whether a property looks like a good buy. Like all rough measures or rules of thumb, per-unit figures signal whether a property *tends* to be priced over or under some benchmark norm. Though never compelling on their own, these measures will give you another important test to apply to your potential investments.

> **To compare properties, use per-unit prices.**

Per Apartment Unit

When you look at multiunit apartment buildings, divide the asking price by the number of apartment units in the property. For example, for an eight-unit property priced at $450,000, you would calculate:

$$\text{price per unit} = \frac{\$450,000}{8}$$
$$\text{price per unit} = \$56,250$$

If you know that other similar apartment buildings have typically *sold* for $60,000 to $70,000 per unit, you may have found a bargain. This and other per-unit measures also give you a quick way to compare prices when rental properties differ in the number of their units. Say you're comparing a 6-unit, a 9-unit, and an 11-unit property at the respective prices of $275,000, $435,000, and $487,500. By figuring per-unit prices, you can easily rank the properties from the lowest priced to the highest.

No. Units	Price	Price per Unit
11	$487,500	$44,318
6	$275,000	$45,833
9	$435,000	$48,333

Size, Quality, and Location   Ideally, the units you compare should closely match each other. However, if that's not possible, adjust your valuations to reflect size, quality, and location differences among properties. Especially consider important location, site, and building features. Although I'm not trying to push you into the "analysis paralysis" so common in MBA programs, do try to spot those "differences that make a difference." When you use a checklist to compare building features, you can better rank properties according to their profit potential. (See the checklist at my website, stoprentingnow.com.)

> Arbitrage your
> investments. Buy
> in one market, sell
> in another.

Opportunity Knocks (Arbitrage) Primarily, price-per-unit measures can help you find "bargain" buildings. But this measure can also help you spot opportunities in two other ways:

- ◆ *Size.* Change the size of the units from larger to smaller, or vice versa. Imagine that smaller 700- to 800-square-foot units sell and rent at substantial premiums over larger units of 1,200 to 1,400 square feet. So, if you buy a building of predominantly larger units, you could earn a big payoff when you redesign the building's space into smaller units.
- ◆ *Conversion.* You might also profit by noticing that buildings with two-bedroom rentals typically sell in the $40,000 to $50,000 per-unit range. Yet, in similar condo buildings, two-bedroom units sell in the $70,000 to $80,000 range. Or this price difference might appear in the opposite direction. Either way, you may be able to buy at the lower-priced use, convert, then sell (or rent) at the high-priced use.

Although arbitrage opportunities don't occur everyday, they do come up every now and then. So, pay attention to relative prices. Prepare to jump when you can buy a building at a low price and then convert it to a use that sells at a higher price.

Per-Square-Foot (p.s.f.) Measures

You've probably heard property buyers and sellers remark that a property sold for say, $135 per square foot. Price per square foot (p.s.f.) represents one of the most widely used methods of benchmark pricing. Investors and homebuyers alike rely on it to ballpark values. When you calculate a per-square-foot figure, you simply divide the total square footage of the unit (house, apartment, or total building) into its price:

$$p.s.f. = \frac{\text{asking price}}{\text{square footage}}$$

$$p.s.f. = \frac{\$285,000}{1,900}$$

$$p.s.f. = \$150$$

If comparable sale properties typically have sold at $170 to $180 p.s.f., a price of $150 p.s.f. may represent a great bargain.

Unfortunately, naive investors can go wrong using per-square-foot figures because no uniform standards apply. All square feet are not created equal in terms of quality, design, and usability. So calculate p.s.f. figures with caution. For example, unless designed with market appeal, converted garages, basements, and attics are worth far less per square foot than a property's original living areas.

Not all square footage counts equally.

Also, look out for mismatches of size. Some buildings are constructed with room counts or room sizes far out of proportion to each other, or to competing properties.

Gross Rent Multipliers (GRMs)

To value rental houses and small apartment buildings, you can also divide the property's price by its total (gross) rent collections. As shown below, this calculation gives you a gross rent multiplier. Consider these market data:

	Sales Price		Annual Rent Collections		GRM
College Terrace	$434,500	÷	$55,000	=	7.9
Bivens Lake Apts.	$526,680	÷	$62,700	=	8.4
Four Palms	$323,610	÷	$48,300	=	6.7

If you find an income property with a relatively high GRM, it could signal either a price too high, or rents too low. Further checking would reveal the answer. Throughout the United States and Canada,

> **GRMs vary by neighborhood. Check sales of comparable properties.**

I've seen annual gross rent multipliers as low as 4.0 (such as rundown properties or unpopular neighborhoods), and as high as 13 (coastal California cities). In my present university town, annual gross rent multipliers typically range from a low of 6.0 (unexceptional student housing) to 8.2 (newer units in professional, but not premier, neighborhoods).

As a rule, when annual gross rent multipliers go much above 8.0, you're often looking at negative cash flows—unless you increase your down payment to 30 percent or more.[1] Because big cities and vacation towns with high housing prices often produce GRMs of 10 or higher, cash-flow investors who live in those areas should buy their rental houses and apartments elsewhere. Or, in high-priced areas, you can look for neighborhoods or market niches (condominiums, lower-middle income segment, outlying suburbs) that offer a more profitable balance of property prices and the level of the rents.

> **High GRMs signal negative cash flow.**

Capitalized Value

As you've already seen, you can also appraise an income property by figuring its capitalized value:

$$V = \frac{NOI}{R}$$

Where V represents the estimated market value of the property, NOI (net operating income) represents the property's rents less expenses, and R equals the market capitalization rate. To illustrate, here's how this technique would look for a six-unit apartment building:

---

1. Based on current mortgage rates for creditworthy investors of around 6.0 to 7.0 percent on small rental properties.

Six-unit Income Statement (Annual)

1. Gross annual potential rents ($725/mo. × 12 × 6)	$52,200
2. Income from parking and storage areas	5,062
3. Vacancy and collection losses @ 7%	(4,009)
4. Effective gross income	**$53,254**
Less operating and fixed expenses	
5. Trash pick-up	$1,080
6. Utilities	450
7. Licenses and permit fees	206
8. Advertising and promotion	900
9. Management fees @ 6%	3,195
10. Maintenance and repairs	3,000
11. Yard care	488
12. Miscellaneous	2,250
13. Property taxes	3,202
14. Property and liability insurance	1,267
15. Reserves for replacement	1,875
16. Total operating and fixed expenses	$17,914
Net operating income (NOI)	**$35,340**

You can easily *compute* NOI. But, if you're not careful, you can still err. To alert you to these possible traps, think about the following warnings (which match up numerically with the entries shown on the income statement):

1. ***Gross potential rents.*** For this figure, use the property's existing rent levels. If its current rents sit above market, use *market* rent levels. Verify all leases for rental amounts and lease terms. Do not use a rent figure based on your anticipated rent increases (if any).
2. ***Extra income.*** With many properties, you can charge for rental application fees, parking, storage, laundry, party room, garages, and so on. Verify all of this income. Don't count extra income that's not been proven by past operating experience or reasonable market data.
3. ***Vacancy and collection losses.*** Use market vacancy rates, or the current owner's vacancies for the past year—whichever is *higher.* Also, when judging market vacancy rates, take your figures from the market niche in which this prop-

erty currently operates. Vacancy rates may vary significantly by neighborhood, apartment size, quality, and rent level. As you compare vacancy rates by market niche, try to spot those segments that are experiencing the greatest shortages.

4. ***Effective gross income.*** It is from this cash that you will pay property expenses and mortgage payments. If you overestimate rent levels or underestimate vacancies, you may end up cash-short.

5. ***Trash pick-up.*** Verify rates and permissible quantities. Look for lower-cost alternatives.

6. ***Utilities.*** In addition to common area lighting, some buildings include centralized heat and air systems. Verify the amounts of these expenses with utility companies.

7. ***License and permit fees.*** On occasion, owners of rental properties are required to pay municipal fees of one sort or another.

8. ***Lease-up expenses.*** Ideally, you will generate a good supply of rental applicants from free postings, referrals, and inquiries; otherwise, you may need to advertise. Also, you'll probably need to pay for credit checks on potential tenants.

9. ***Management fees.*** Even if you self-manage your units, allocate some expense here for your time and effort. Don't confuse return on labor for return on investment.

10. ***Maintenance and repairs.*** Enter an expense to pay yourself or others. "I'll take care of that myself" shouldn't mean, "I'll work for free."

11. ***Grounds maintenance.*** Yard care entails mowing the lawn, trimming hedges, removing snow, cleaning up leaves, tending to the flower beds, and so on.

12. ***Miscellaneous.*** You will incur such odds-and-ends expenses as lease preparation, auto mileage, and long-distance telephone charges.

13. ***Property taxes.*** Verify amount, tax rate, and assessed value. Check accuracy. Note whether the property is subject to any special assessments (sewer, sidewalks, water reclamation).

14. ***Property and liability insurance.*** Verify exact coverage for property and types of losses. Increase deductibles and limits on liability.

15. ***Reserves for replacement.*** Eventually, you'll need to replace the roof, HVAC, appliances, carpeting, and other limited-life items. Allocate a pro rata annual amount here.

16. ***Net operating income (NOI).*** Subtract all expenses from effective gross income. You now have the numerator for V = NOI/R.

As a rule, figure a building's NOI conservatively. Don't make grand assumptions about potential rent increases. Don't understate or omit necessary expenses. Verify, verify, verify. Allocate reasonable amounts for replacement reserves. Ask to see the sellers' Schedule E where they have reported property revenues and expenses to the IRS. (You may get resistance on this request. But listen carefully to the sellers' excuses. Are they plausible?)

> **Ask for the sellers' Schedule E.**

Estimate Market Value

After figuring NOI, you next need to come up with an accurate capitalization rate (R). To figure this cap rate, compare the NOIs (net operating incomes) of similar properties to their selling prices. You can get this information when you talk with realty agents who regularly sell (and preferably own) small rental properties, or from other investors (a local realty investment club, for example). Competent property management firms also stay informed about local cap rates. After learning the market in your area, list your cap rate data as follows:

> **Cap rates are set by local markets.**

Property	Recent Sales Price	NOI	R
Hampton Apts. (8 units)	$452,900	$43,211	.0954
Woodruff Apts. (6 units)	360,000	35,900	.0997
Adams Manor (6 units)	295,000	28,440	.0964
Newport Apts. (9 units)	549,000	53,700	.0978
Ridge Terrace (8 units)	471,210	42,409	.09

From this comparable sale data, you might think that Ridge Terrace and Hampton Apartments seem most like the property that you're valuing. So, you select cap rates of .09 and .095. Then, you calculate a value range for the property you're looking at:

$$1. \quad V = \frac{\$35,340 \text{ (NOI)}}{.09 \text{ (R)}}$$

$$V = \$392,666$$

$$2. \quad V = \frac{\$35,340 \text{ (NOI)}}{.098 \text{ (R)}}$$

$$V = \$360,612$$

You now know the market value range for your property falls between $360,000 and $390,000.

Throughout the country, cap rates for small rental properties may run from as low as .06 or .07 up to .12, .14, or higher. Generally, a *low* cap rate occurs when you're valuing highly desirable properties in good to top neighborhoods. Apartment buildings with condo conversion potential also tend to sell with low cap rates. Remember, a low cap rate will create a relatively high property value and a high cap rate yields a relatively low property value. Relatively high cap rates apply to less desirable properties in so-so neighborhoods.

> **The lower the cap rate, the higher the value of a property.**

Anticipate the Future; Pay for the Present

In the previous NOI example, you relied on verified income and expense figures drawn from the property's current operating history and your knowledge of competitive properties. Yet, as an entrepreneurial investor, you will improve your properties through fix-up work and renovations, better property management, and perhaps even neighborhood revitalization. Your improvements can dramatically boost your property's net income and at the same time lower the property's cap rate. Your property's value can quickly jump by 20 percent, 30 percent, or more.

> **Sellers will ask you to pay for potential. Savvy investors pay only for "as is."**

Here's how you need to exercise caution. When you negotiate to buy, focus on the present, not your (or the seller's) vision of the future. Investors who anticipate great profits often pay too much. They let the sellers capture the value potential that they plan to create.

Mum's the Word: Don't Tell Sellers Your Plans

Beginning investors, especially, tend to reveal too much of their plans for a property. To gain a bargain price, don't turn your cards so that the sellers (or their sales agent) can see them. If you explicitly question the sellers in ways that reveal your value-creating ideas, the sellers will likely use that potential to strengthen their own negotiating position.

> **Avoid signaling your plans to a seller.**

In most cases, sellers already hold inflated ideas about all the great things you can do to enhance their property—which regrettably, they say, they never had the time (or money) to accomplish. With such ploys common, you need not load the sellers with even more ammunition to fire back at you. As much as possible, negotiate for the property as it currently is operated. Reap any future upside as your bonus for entrepreneurial insights.

Cash Flow Returns

In addition to market value, you should also judge your properties by the cash flow returns they will yield. To illustrate, let's bring forward that six-unit apartment building from several pages back. Assume you can buy that property for $350,000 (around $60,000 per unit). You talk to a lender and tentatively arrange a mortgage for $280,000 (an 80 percent loan-to-value ratio). The lender wants an 8.0 percent interest rate with a 25-year term. You would need to put $70,000 down. Here are the relevant figures:

Loan amount	$350,000
Annualized mortgage payments @ 8.0%; 25 years	25,932
Net operating income (NOI)	35,340
Less mortgage payments	25,932
BTCF (before tax cash flow)	9,408

$$\text{Cash flow return} = \frac{\text{BTCF}}{\text{Down payment}}$$

$$= \frac{\$9,408}{\$70,000}$$

$$= 13.44\%$$

Not bad. But say your minimum required return (hurdle rate) equals 15 percent. What might you do to boost your cash flow returns? For starters, you could try to get the lender to extend the loan term to 30 years. If successful, your payments (assuming no change in interest rate) would drop to $24,652 a year; your annual pretax cash flow would increase to $10,688 (35,340 minus 24,652):

$$\text{Cash flow return} = \frac{\$10,688}{\$70,000}$$

$$= 15.3\%$$

If you don't like extending the loan term to 30 years, you could try to push the lender down to a 7.625 percent interest rate. In that case, your mortgage payments (25 years) would total $25,102 per year. Your cash flow would equal $10,237 (35,340 – 25,102):

$$\text{Cash flow return} = \frac{\$10,237}{\$70,000}$$

$$= 14.28\%$$

Oops, that lower interest rate won't quite do it. But as an enterprising investor, you've got a number of other options:

◆ Try for an even lower interest rate (7.5 percent would work).
◆ Ask the seller to take back an interest-only balloon note for five years at 7.0 percent in the amount of, say, $20,000.
◆ Negotiate a lower price for the property.

◆ Switch from a 25-year, fixed-rate mortgage to a 7.0 percent 5/20 adjustable-rate mortgage. This tactic would work especially well if you planned to sell (or exchange) the property within five years.

◆ Look for reasonable and certain ways to boost the property's net income. Increase rent collections, raise occupancy. Cut expenses.

◆ Agree to pay the seller a higher price in exchange for owner financing on terms more favorable (lower interest rate, lower down payment) than a bank would offer.

> **You find a property. You negotiate and structure a good deal.**

Any or all of these techniques *could* work. Experiment with the numbers and negotiate some mutually agreeable solution. As an investor in real estate, the "market" will never provide you a return. You earn your return based upon the price, terms of financing, property improvements, and market strategy that you put together.

Don't Settle for Market Rates of Appreciation: Create Value

But here's even better news. You never need to passively accept market rent increases or property appreciation rates of just 3 percent, 5 percent, or even 7 percent a year. You can use your entrepreneurial skills to study the market, improve the property, develop a competitive edge for your target market, and locate communities and neighborhoods that are poised to "beat the market." Any or all of these efforts will quickly shoot up your net worth.

> **Create your own appreciation.**

Yes, I love to buy properties that score high on all of the value benchmarks that you've just learned. But just as much—and sometimes more—I love to buy properties that include large doses of hidden value, value that I can bring to life through market-researched, profit-yielding improvements. In fact, in sellers' markets (when too many buyers are chasing too few properties), it's often easier to discover hidden value begging to be realized than it is to find properties that can be bought at below-market prices.

CHAPTER 13

How You Can Greatly Increase the Value of Your Investment Property

Want to immediately jump your net worth by $25,000, $100,000, $250,000, or more? Then put to work this simple method for figuring out the value of a property:

$$\text{Value} = \frac{\text{Net Operating Income (NOI)}}{\text{Capitalization Rate (R)}}$$

To refresh your memory, let's go through another example. Assume that you find a six-unit apartment building. This rental property currently brings in a net income (NOI) of $48,000 a year. Based on talks with real estate agents, appraisers, and other investors, you figure this property "as is" should sell with a cap rate of 9 percent (.09). With these two numbers you can calculate the "as is" value of these six units at $533,333.

$$\frac{48,000 \text{ (NOI)}}{.09 \text{ (R)}} = \$533,333 \text{ (V)}$$

If you could somehow boost that property's NOI to say, $60,000 a year, you would jump its value by 25 percent. You would quickly gain another $133,000 in equity.

$$\frac{60,000 \text{ (new NOI)}}{.09 \text{ (R)}} = \$666,666 \text{ (V)}$$

Even better, if you can reduce the riskiness of the property, you might be able to justify a lower cap rate than .09, say, 8 percent (.08). With a higher NOI and a lower cap rate, the value of that property skyrockets from the original $533,333 up to $750,000—an immediate gain in value of $212,000.

Are such large increases in value possible within a period of 6 to 18 months? Absolutely! Why? Because many owners of small investment properties still think of themselves as "landlords" (with the accent on "lord") and their residents merely as "renters" who don't deserve "customer care." But just the opposite is true. Today (and in the future) market conditions require savvy investors to treat their tenants as valued customers—not serfs.

Search for Competitive Advantage

> **Boost your property values by outperforming your competition.**

Most small investors mismanage their properties because they do not intelligently survey and inspect competing properties. Without this market knowledge, they can't strategically customize their properties to make them stand out from other rentals. In other words, these owner-investors fail to monitor their competitors and they fail to carefully adapt their market and management strategies to wow their customers (tenants, buyers).

Your Properties Should Stand Above the Competition

> **Never think of yourself as a landlord.**

As a mental starting point for creating value, remember, never think of yourself as a landlord. Never define what you do as "owning rental properties." Instead, think of yourself as providing your customers with a product (housing) that stands out and stands above your competitors. If you adopt this modern attitude, your profits (and the value of your properties) will shoot far above average for two reasons:

1. ***Better resident relations.*** The residents of your properties will reward you with lower turnover, fewer problems, and higher rents.
2. ***Alert to opportunities.*** With a customer-oriented, constant-improvement attitude, you will consistently look for and come up with ideas that will add value to your property operations.

A Strategy of Your Own

Good management and marketing depend on good knowledge of competing properties and resident (tenant) preferences. You want to create a *specific* strategy that will yield *you* the highest profits. Certainly, you can read a dozen books on "landlording" and most of them will give you a precise list of do's and don'ts that may cover every topic from applications to waterbeds. While ideas from these books often prove suggestive, never accept them as the final word.

What works today may not work tomorrow. What works in Peoria may not go over in Paducah. What works in a tight rental market may prove less effective in a high-vacancy market. What works best with HUD Section 8 tenants may actually turn away those upscale young professionals who live in your more expensive buildings. Should you accept pets, smokers, or college students? It all depends.

> **Adapt your property to your local market.**

Offer your selected target market of renters (or buyers) the value proposition that they will prefer—yet, at the same time, a value proposition that fattens your bottom line (NOI). In practice, you can find that profit-maximizing value proposition by knowing the competition. Then create your own competitive advantage.

Here's the $100,000 question: What can you actually do to boost your property's investment value? Here are some ideas.

First, Verify Actual Rent Collections, Not Merely Rental Rates

Before you buy, verify. Too many new investors merely accept an owner's rent figures and then subtract a so-called standard 5 percent vacancy factor. In truth, many property owners do not *collect* 95 percent of their scheduled rents—even if they achieve 95 percent occupancy. To verify rents, first verify the lease rates the tenants have agreed to pay. Second, realistically estimate vacancy and collection losses. Your profits, and the building's value, rest upon bankable funds, not leaky leases. If you over-pay for a property because you overestimate the property's current rent collections, you are trying to increase value in a headwind.

Talk with Tenants

Prior to buying any investment property, I always talk with a sampling of the renters who live in the building. This practice serves four purposes.

- Identify problems in the building.
- Identify problems with tenants.
- Verify lease application data.
- Generate ideas for improvement.

Problems in the Building

"Not enough parking." "Too much noise." "The bills for heat and air are outrageous—$277 last month." "These walls are paper thin." "This place lacks security. We've had three break-ins during the past six months." "The closets in this apartment are too small, and there's no place for long-term storage." "No place to park or store my boat—or even my bicycle." "Cockroaches, ugh. This place is crawling with cockroaches."

To really learn about a building, talk with the tenants. You can gain valuable insights by asking tenants, "Tell me, what don't you like around here?" On occasion, the tenants will speak well of the building (or its owner). But more often they like to complain. Will you hear glowing praise? Not likely. Tenants know that too many good comments might bring on a rent increase.

> **Ask tenants, "What don't you like?"**

Problems with Tenants

Bad tenants can ruin a potentially good building. If some tenants create hassles for others, you want to know about it before you offer to buy the property. Problems within a building *and* problems with disruptive tenants can stir up vacancies, turnover, and rent collections. Solve these problems and you create value.

Verify Lease and Application Data

Leases and tenant application data do not always portray the true facts about a property's tenants. Do you realize that some sellers actually show beginning investors phantom leases with false data? Aside from outright fraud, your talks with tenants might reveal rent concessions that aren't recorded in the written file that the sellers gave you to review. You might also find that some tenants are subletting their units. Or maybe they've let additional friends and family move in with them.

> **Closely review the rent roll.**

Before you buy, put together a rent roll that's as accurate as possible. Otherwise, both your NOI and cap rate (risk rate) figures may err.

Generate Ideas for Improvement

Whenever you value a building, divide the "problems" you find into two piles: (1) economically unsolvable and (2) opportunity-laden. As your talks with tenants reveal the strengths and weaknesses of the "as is" property, you're valuing the property as it stands today. But at the same time, you're constantly rolling ideas through your mind. How might you profitably improve the property tomorrow? Through the eyes of a critical buyer, you find faults and profit-draining negatives. Through the alert eyes of an entrepreneurial investor, you visualize ways to turn a lump of coal into a diamond.

> **Critique the property, but also look for opportunities to create value.**

Set Your Rents with Market Savvy

Many owners of rental properties devote far too little effort to figuring out the rental rates that they should charge for their units. They underprice.

They overprice. They don't make rent-enhancing improvements. They fail to adequately segment their tenants. They spend too much money on ineffective advertising. They devote too little time and money to target marketing. If they experience high vacancies, they blame a soft market. If they experience low vacancies, they pride themselves on their skill as a landlord.

All in all, these mistakes (and many others) flow from the same source. Property owners just don't realize the great profits they're missing when they set their rents to reflect their own personal whim or arbitrary judgment rather than market reality.

> **Mispricing your rents will cost you dearly.**

Think of missed opportunities like this. You own a 12-unit building. You underprice each unit by $25 a month. The cap rate is .09 (9 percent). How much does this underpricing error cost you?

$$\text{Lost income} = \$25 \times 12 \text{ units} \times 12 \text{ months}$$
$$= \$3,600 \text{ per year}$$
$$\text{Lost building value} = \frac{\$3,600}{.09}$$
$$= \$40,000$$

You've lost $40,000 of value just by underpricing $25 per month! Move that rent shortfall up to $50 or $100 a month, and you lose $100,000 to $200,000. Make no mistake: Underpricing rents can cost you a bundle of money. Overpricing, too, can also cost you plenty. By trying to charge too much, your vacancies, turnovers, advertising costs, conversion rates (meaning that you must show the property 15 to 20 times before you find a willing tenant), malicious tenant damage, and bad debts will probably shoot up. Before you set your rent rates, inspect competing properties. Acquire personal knowledge of competing properties and competitor pricing. Then you will be able to adopt a pricing strategy that maximizes your net income (NOI) and property value.

Your Apartment Checklist

If rental houses and apartments were like cans of Campbell's tomato soup or bottles of Coca-Cola, you could expect every unit to rent for the same price. You could discover an actual "market" rent level. But, in fact, houses and apartment buildings differ in dozens of ways that their potential tenants find appealing or unappealing. Mentally tour properties. What do you see? How do the properties differ with respect to these features?

❑ Views
❑ Energy usage/efficiency
❑ Square footage
❑ Natural light
❑ Ceiling height
❑ Quiet/noisiness
❑ Parking
❑ Room count
❑ Appliances (quality, quantity)
❑ Landscaping
❑ Quality of finishes
❑ Heat/air conditioning
❑ Decks/patios/balconies
❑ Cleanliness
❑ Carpeting/floor coverings
❑ Electrical outlets
❑ Emotional appeal
❑ Color schemes/aesthetics

❑ Living area floor plan
❑ Closet space
❑ Storage space
❑ Kitchen functionality
❑ Kitchen pizzazz
❑ Entryway convenience
❑ Tenant demographics
❑ Tenant lifestyles, attitudes
❑ Lighting
❑ Security
❑ Laundry facilities
❑ Fireplace
❑ Physical condition
❑ Window coverings
❑ Types/style of windows
❑ Image/reputation
❑ Furniture

And this checklist doesn't even mention other important tenant concerns such as the amount of the security deposit (total move-in cash), the terms of the lease, the quality of the management, and last but far from least, location. Before you think through all of these possible differences, you can't intelligently say that your two-bedroom, two-bath units should rent for $675 a month. First, you want to compare and contrast your units feature by feature to a broad sample of competing properties.

> **Profit-maximizing investors pay attention to every detail of their properties.**

With good competitive information about property features and rent levels, you not only improve your ability to evaluate your property. Just as important, you prime your mind to spot opportunities to increase its value.

Give the Interior a Martha Stewart Makeover

As you walk into the unit, are you met with a bland neutrality? Do you see faded paint, scuff marks, outdated color schemes, cheap hollow-core doors, nail holes in the walls, worn carpeting, torn linoleum, old-fashioned light fixtures, cracked wall switch plates, or stained toilets, bathtubs, and sinks? If you answer yes to any or all of these questions, great! You've found the easiest path to creating value.

Pay Special Attention to Kitchens and Baths

To really wow your potential tenants, bring in Martha Stewart to redo the kitchens and bathrooms. Flip through the pages of kitchen and bath magazines. Look for that right combination of materials and colors that will create a light, bright, cheerful, and inviting look. Eliminate those harvest-gold appliances, the chipped and stained sinks, and that cracked glass in the shower door.

As you inspect these key rooms, focus on each of the following features for at least 30 seconds:

❑ Floors
❑ Ceilings
❑ Sinks
❑ Toilet bowl
❑ Windows and window sills
❑ Electrical outlet plates
❑ Lighting
❑ Faucets
❑ Walls
❑ Cabinets
❑ Cabinet and drawer handles
❑ Appliances
❑ Counter tops

By focusing for 30 seconds on each feature of these rooms, you will notice everything that blends together to give these rooms their overall feel. Throughout the entire apartment or house, details count. But they especially count in the kitchens and bathrooms. The right pizzazz in the kitchens and bathrooms can transform a ho-hum unit into a showplace.

> **Focus gives you the ability to see what others miss.**

How much will this transformation cost? If you've recently spent $25,000 to remodel your own kitchen, you may think pizzazz in a rental unit would run you into the poorhouse. Not true. You can accomplish wonders with an outlay of between

$2,000 and $5,000. Replacing sinks, hardware, toilet bowls, and toilet seats requires relatively little money. As to the cabinetry itself, often a lower-cost refinish (not a full replacement) can work wonders.

Cleanliness Generates Profits

Do you want to attract tenants who will care for your properties? Then thoroughly clean the units as if a drill sergeant were about to perform a white-glove inspection. Do not think "rental property." Think "home."

> **Clean units attract clean tenants.**

Clean everywhere. Remove the dirt, dust, cobwebs, and dead bugs from all corners, baseboards, light fixtures, and shelving. Pull out all kitchen drawers. Dump the bread crumbs and other accumulated debris. Make sure all windows and mirrors sparkle and shine. Look closely for grime in the shower and shower door tracks. Scrape the rust out of the medicine cabinets and repaint where necessary. Eliminate all odors. Each unit should not only look fresh and clean, it should smell fresh and clean.

Natural Light and Views

If your units seem dark, brighten them up. In addition to color schemes, add windows or skylights. If you're lucky, you might find one of those older buildings with 10-foot ceilings—now reduced to 8 feet via suspended acoustical tile. For a reason unknown to me (energy conservation?), dropped ceilings became popular in the 1960s and 1970s. Today, they're considered ugly and outdated. Rip out those dropped ceilings. Your rooms will seem larger and brighter. Also, in rooms with high ceilings, you can install clerestory windows to bring in more light.

> **Create a view with landscaping.**

For first-floor rooms, see if you can enhance the view with landscaping or fencing. To create views for upper-story units, think long term. Plant trees. When financially feasible, you might create a view by moving a window. Ugly views turn off most tenants. Pleasant views provide good selling points. Do as much as you can to give your tenants better views than dumpsters, parking lots, high-traffic streets, and the rooftops of other buildings.

Special Touches

For those special aesthetic touches, try chair railings, wallpaper borders, upgraded door handles, paneled doors, and wood stains (instead of paint). Upgrades in light fixtures, too, can help you add pizzazz. The newer forms of track lighting seem to be gaining popularity for both form and function.

You can get ideas for special touches from home decorating and re-modeling magazines. Also visit new model homes and newer upscale apartment, townhouse, and condominium developments. Don't go too far with special touches or you will cut into your profitability. Still, a few "gee whiz" features will help rental prospects differentiate and remember your units.

> **Create a few "gee whiz" features.**

Safety, Security, and Convenience

Often safety and convenience go together as with the number and capacity of electrical outlets. Older buildings, especially, lack enough outlets and amperage to safely handle all of the modern household's plug-in appliances, computers, printers, fax machines, and audio/video home entertainment centers. Many renters don't notice this type of functional obsolescence until after they move into a unit. Then they "solve" the problem with adapter plugs and roaming extension cords. If the unit lacks electrical capacity, plan an upgrade.

Other Issues of Safety and Security

> **Get an expert to assess the risks of an environmentally suspect property.**

Other safety issues include smoke alarms, carbon monoxide detectors, fire escape routes, door locks, first-floor windows, and first-floor sliding glass doors. Environmental health hazards may exist because of lead paint, asbestos, or formaldehyde—any of which may be found in building materials used in construction (or remodeling) prior to 1978. When buying, insist on seller disclosures about the presence of any of these hazards. If the building is suspect, don't buy it without advice of an environmental expert.

Costly remedial improvements in these areas will seldom pay off with much higher rents. You can, though, profitably deal with environmental issues by negotiating a large discount in your purchase price. As to security against break-ins, make sure all windows and doors lock securely and cannot be jimmied with a credit card (as in the TV shows), or even a screwdriver. Deadbolt locks are best. Entry-door peepholes also give tenants a sense of security.

In our criminal-infested world, tenants want to feel safe in their homes. If doors, door locks, and windows seem flimsy, many tenants won't rent the unit—regardless of its other oohs and aahs.

Stairs, Carpets, and Bathrooms

Pay particular attention to any steps or stair railings that may be loose or dangerous. Frayed carpets and bathtubs that lack no-slip bottoms and handrails can provoke falls. Remedy every safety or security hazard within the property. Even when a repair doesn't add to your rent collections, it will protect your tenants. It will reduce the chance that you could end up on the wrong end of a tenant's lawsuit for damages.

> **Unsafe properties invite lawsuits.**

Rightsize the Rooms

Have you ever walked into a house and found some rooms too large and others too small? It seems today that in many houses builders construct a huge great room along with a huge master bedroom and bath, and then finish off the house with three or four dinky bedrooms. The house lacks a sense of proportion (which evidently is what some homebuyers like).

Create a Sense of Proportion

What sense of proportion should a house or an apartment unit display? The answer varies by tenant segment, price range, and timing (because tastes today differ from those of 10, 20, or 30 years ago). As people and property change, opportunities arise for you to notice possibilities for improvement. Buy an out-of-style building, then rearrange the internal floor plan to better appeal to the intended market segment of renters or buyers.

Postwar Units Are Modernized

I once bought an older eight-unit apartment building. It had been built in 1949 to house the veterans of World War II and their fast-growing families. The units were arranged in a "3BR/1BTH" style (common to that period) with one moderate-sized bedroom for the parents and two small bedrooms for those recently born baby boomers. In the early 1990s (when I bought the property), most tenants looked at the units and said, "Ugh, no way could we live here."

Because the owner had trouble keeping the units rented, I got a bargain price. To create value, I split up one of the small bedrooms. I used half of that space to enlarge the other small bedroom, and half to add a second bathroom. I then rented the building to tenants looking to share their rentals with a roommate. Rent collections jumped by $175 per unit per month—a very profitable return on my investment and renovations.

Create More Storage

Self-storage (mini-warehouses) now represent one of the fastest growing types of properties in the United States. We've all become pack rats. "Throw it away? Why I might need that sometime."

Talk with tenants. Talk with homeowners. Many will tell you the same thing. "I like my home, but we lack space for storage." If you want to add appeal to your rental houses and apartment units, add storage space. To do so, think about storage in three ways:

- ◆ Bring dead space to life.
- ◆ Increase the capacity of existing space.
- ◆ Create new storage space in basements or attics. Install storage sheds.

Bring Dead Space to Life

Let me first illustrate with an example that may seem trivial, but it never fails to mildly impress prospective tenants. Look in the cabinet under your kitchen sink. You will see a small gap between the front panel of the cabinet above the door and the sink. In other words, dead space. How might you use that space? Install a small pull-down compartment to stow away soap, sponge, and scrubbing pads. No more sink clutter. Whenever I show this little innovation to other people, I always get an approving response.

Okay, I admit, it's trivial. But it illustrates the point. All houses and apartments include generous amounts of dead spaces (large and small) that you can bring to life.

- Under stairs and stairwells
- Bay windows with storage built under the window seat and under the outside of the window
- Garden windows
- On the tops of kitchen cabinets
- Dead-end cabinets
- Walls suitable for shelving
- Recessed storage between studs (as with an in-wall medicine chest)
- Kitchen hanging bars for pots and pans

These ideas merely sample the possibilities. If you go through any house or apartment and ask, "Where are the dead spaces that I can bring to life for purposes of storage?" you will find them.

Increase the Capacity of Existing Storage Space

My favorite examples to illustrate how to achieve "more with less" come from the California Closet Company (CCC). As ideas from this innovative firm have proven, you can double (or triple) your storage capacity without adding even one square inch of new space. Simply reorganize and redesign the raw space that already exists. Although founded as a closet company, CCC now redesigns garages, offices, workshops, and kitchens. Put these same reorganizing principles to work and you'll really wow your prospective tenants. You will give your rentals a sought-after benefit.

> **Let the California Closet Company guide your ideas to add space for storage.**

You could also make some space serve multiple purposes. The most common way to multipurpose is through use of a Murphy bed that folds up against a wall. A Murphy bed not only adds usable floor space, it also opens up the possibility of shelving alongside the bed. You can either use the wall cavity or create a new, larger cavity by bringing a new wall out even with the Murphy bed.

Check Noise Levels

No one likes noise. Before you invest, test the units for soundproofing. Will noise from a television or stereo carry throughout the house or apartment? When you inspect properties, bring along a portable radio. Test various rooms. Turn up the volume. Do the walls provide enough soundproofing? Families and roommate tenants want privacy and quiet. If your rental property fails to offer quiet, your units will lose appeal.

Check for Neighborhood Noise

Just as important, will your tenants hear neighbors or neighborhood noise from inside their units? Again, people pay for quiet. They discount heavily for noise.

> **Check noise levels at various times.**

No doubt, you'll typically hear more noise in neighborhoods filled with apartment buildings. But single-family neighborhoods can also suffer from loud stereos, barking dogs, and unmuffled car engines. Does the drum corps of the nearby high school practice outside three hours a day? When possible, visit the property during periods of high traffic or peak noise. Don't assume that a neighborhood offers peace and quiet. Verify.

Ask for Written Disclosures

Seek written disclosures from the seller of the property. Talk with tenants and neighbors. Find out whether anyone has tried to enforce quiet by complaining to city government, a homeowners association, or by filing a nuisance suit. If you invest in the property, could you effectively invoke noise ordinances against these noisy tenants (or homeowners)

> **Seek disclosures about noise.**

who live nearby? Can you add features to the property (soundproof windows, heavy doors, more wall insulation, or tall, thick hedges) to reduce the noise that arises from either outside or inside of the building? When you suppress noise, you create value.

Overall Livability

Never think "rental property." Always remember, you are providing people a home. As you design the overall appeal of a property, imagine how the units will be for your intended target market of residents.

- Do the units offer enough square footage?
- Are the units spotlessly clean, fresh, and bright? Do they smell clean and fresh?
- Do the room counts and room sizes represent the most profitable use of space?
- Do the aesthetics of the units excite with emotional appeal?
- Does the unit bring in enough natural light?
- What views will the tenants see from inside the units looking out?
- Do the units offer generous amounts of closets and storage space?
- Are the units quiet?
- Will tenants feel safe and secure within the units?
- Do the kitchens and baths offer eye-pleasing pizzazz?

Experience proves that *homes* rent faster and enjoy lower vacancies than mere rental houses and apartments. Give your tenants something special. You'll earn higher profits. You'll boost the value of your properties.

CHAPTER 14

Twenty-One More Ways to Boost the Value of Your Properties

You're now well on your way to create instant wealth. Your great livable units sparkle with pizzazz and emotional appeal. These units will keep your building full of tenants who will gladly pay premium prices.

Yet, before sharp interiors can woo your prospective tenants, you must get them to keep their appointments to inspect the homes that you are offering. Nothing will accomplish this goal better than curb appeal.

Create Strikingly Attractive Curb Appeal

> **Position your property with a well-kept outstanding exterior.**

You can write an award-winning newspaper ad that will make your phone ring. But your Madison Avenue talents will fall flat when great tenants pull up in front of the building and immediately begin to ask themselves, "What are we doing here? This place is nothing like I imagined. Do you think we should go in?"

"Nah, why waste our time? This place is a dump. We shouldn't even think about living here."

Your Building Is Your Best Advertisement

More than likely, hundreds (maybe thousands) of people will pass by your property each week. What will they notice about the property? Will it appear as that run-down rental of the neighborhood, a nondescript plain Jane? Or will it cause passersby to remark, "Isn't that building kept up well? Those flower gardens and brick walkways seem to reach out and invite us to come inside."

If you want your building to generate more income, create an inviting exterior. Create award-winning publicity with knockout curb appeal. Not only will an attractive, well-kept exterior appeal to a better class of tenants, it will also increase tenant satisfaction and reduce turnover. To create strikingly attractive curb appeal, make these improvements:

1. *Clean up the grounds.* When you first take over a property, get busy with a meticulous cleanup of the grounds, parking area, and walkways. Pick up trash, accumulated leaves, and fallen tree branches. Build a fence to block that view of the dumpsters. Tell tenants to remove their inoperable cars from the parking lots, parking spaces, or driveways. If abandoned cars are parked on the street, ask the city government to post them and tow them.

2. *Yard care and landscaping.* Tenants and homebuyers alike love a manicured lawn, flower-lined walkways, mulched shrubs, and flower gardens. With landscaping, you can turn an ordinary building into a showcase property. With landscaping you can create privacy, manufacture a gorgeous view looking out from the inside of the units, or eliminate an ugly view. Especially if you're looking at a holding period of three to five years (or longer), put in those small plants, shrubs, flower gardens, and hedges now. When you sell, those mature plantings will easily earn you a return of at least $10 for each $1 the landscaping cost you.

3. *Sidewalks, walkways, and parking areas.* Replace or repair major cracks and buckling that may appear in your sidewalks and parking areas. Remove all grass or weeds growing through the cracks. Edge all of the areas where the yard abuts concrete or asphalt. Neatness pays. Overgrown grass and weeds really stain the curb appeal of a rental property—

precisely because these types of blemishes signal that the property is a rental.

4. ***Fences, lampposts, and mailboxes.*** For purposes of good looks, privacy, and security, quality fencing can enhance the value of a property. Just as certainly, a rusted, rotted, or tumbledown fence blemishes the property; likewise rusty lampposts with broken glass light fixtures. For a nice decorative touch, add a white picket fence or a low stone fence in the front of the building. If the building houses a cluster of mailboxes, make sure the mail area is kept neat and the mailbox lobby or porch area present a good first impression.

5. ***The exterior of the building.*** Now, turn your attention to the exterior of the building itself. The building must signal to prospective tenants that you take good care of your property. Paint where necessary or desirable. Repair wood rot. Clean roof and gutters. Next, imagine ways to enhance the building's appearance with shutters, flower boxes, a dramatic front door and entryway, and new (or

> **Clean up the mailbox area and keep it clean.**

additional) windows. Can you add contrasting color for trim or accent the building design with architectural details? How well does (or could) the property's exterior distinguish it from other comparably priced rental properties?

Here's How You Can Achieve That Dazzling Curb Appeal

Unless you're creatively gifted, you may not be able to spontaneously generate *great* ideas for improving a property. Creative design certainly doesn't come easily to me. I rank high among the artistically challenged. So here's how I compensate for my dull artistic vision.

> **To generate ideas, snap photos of role-model properties.**

I carry a camera in the glovebox of my car. Often when I see a building or yard that displays eye-catching features, I snap a picture. Over time, I've put together a large collection of photos. When I'm trying to figure out how to give a property strikingly attractive curb appeal, I pull out some of these photos and select model properties to compare feature to feature with my investment property. Comparing better to worse always brings forth a rush of value-creating ideas.

You don't even have to rely on your own snapshots. Dozens of "house and home" types of books and magazines fill the shelves of grocers and bookstores. I regularly buy these publications. Their articles and photos will definitely enlighten your creative thinking and aesthetic sensibilities.

> **Look closely for ways to generate extra income.**

Collect More than Rent

When you review the income statements of apartment buildings, you will sometimes come across a line-item entry called "other income." These amounts may include money earned from laundry machines, parking, storage lockers, or various services and amenities.

1. *Laundry.* Ideally, your rental units will each include space for washer and dryer hookups. But if they don't, look for space somewhere else on the property where you can install coin-operated (actually electronic card-operated) washers and dryers. Without on-premises laundry facilities, your building will suffer a serious competitive disadvantage. Today, most tenants have been raised in homes with washers and dryers. These tenants do not want to cart their washing to a laundromat.

2. *Parking.* If parking spots are scarce in the neighborhood where you own properties, consider an extra charge for parking (or perhaps an extra charge for a second car). Do not arbitrarily give one parking space per unit. Some tenants may not have cars. Others may be willing to park on the street. By pricing your scarce parking separately from the units, those tenants who want it most will pay more.

3. *Build storage lockers.* Back to the idea of adding storage space. You create value any time you can squeeze some profitable use out of every nook and cranny within the building, and within every square foot of the site. One such profitable use is storage lockers. Does the property include an attic, basement, or crawl space where you could carve out room for more storage? You can easily rent such lockers for $10 to $20

per month. Generally, you can achieve payback in less than four years. If no existing space within the building can serve this purpose, install several of those prefabricated storage sheds.

4. ***Add other amenities or services.*** Whenever you take over a property, think through a list of services or amenities that you could provide (preferably at a price) that would increase your revenue *and* strengthen your competitive edge. Consider services such as cleaning, day care, or transportation. In terms of amenities, would your tenants appreciate (and pay for) a swimming pool, tennis courts, racquetball (or squash) courts, a fitness center, or a study room? As the widely known investor, Craig Hall, advises, "Keep an open and searching mind. Seek out things you can do to attract and satisfy the best tenants for each specific investment." Amen!

Convert a Garage, Attic, or Basement

> **Add quality space, not space that looks weird.**

As you shop for properties, look for those with an attic, garage, or basement that you can convert to *quality* living space. I emphasize the word *quality* because beginning investors often convert as cheaply as possible. As a result, their finished spaces not only look cheap, they may lack natural light, the ceilings may hang too low, or the newly created floor plans and traffic patterns may seem weird, convoluted, or garbled.

In contrast, savvy improvers who design and finish their conversions to wow potential tenants or buyers can and do make serious money for their efforts. To earn good profits, your space conversion should achieve the following objectives:

- Fit the needs of the target market
- Please the senses
- Integrate the new with the overall plan and design of the existing property

Target Market Needs

> **Ask yourself, "What would tenants pay most for?"**

When you remodel only for personal use, it's OK to convert your basement into a recreation room that mimics the look of your favorite tavern. For profitable remodeling, though, aim to please your target market. What type of highly valued space can you offer that competing properties lack? A dynamite home office, a study, a playroom for the kids, a workout area, a library, an entertainment center, a seductive master bedroom and bath? Think visually. What can you imagine?

Aesthetics: Pleasing to the Senses

> **Can you make a basement seem homey?**

Basement conversions often fail because they lack windows and give off that damp, musty odor so common to below-ground living areas. To overcome these problems, use window wells and carve-outs to bring in natural light. To eliminate the musty smell and dampness, use high-quality sealants and fresh air ventilation. Follow the same general ideas for attic and garage conversions. You want these finished areas to look, live, feel, and smell as good as the rest of the house. You want light, height, warmth, and color. You do not want to merely tack up cheap paneling, hang acoustical tile ceilings, or lay down a roll of indoor-outdoor carpeting. Romance the space. Think pizzazz!

Integrate the Conversion into the House

> **Well-designed conversions do not announce themselves as conversions.**

When you evaluate houses for their conversion potential, don't just think of added living space as an independent area. Work to expand the total integrated living area of the house. The best conversions flow smoothly to and from the original living areas. Think access and flow. How well can you blend the conversion into a natural traffic pattern?

As much as possible, avoid signaling to your prospects, "Now entering a converted garage (basement or attic)." Or "Watch your head. The ceiling's a little low in here." Look for properties that are currently designed with potential for an integrated addition. A well-planned conversion can easily pay back two dollars (or more) for every dollar invested.

Create an Accessory Apartment

Accessory apartments pay back large returns.

Variously called in-law suites, basement suites, garage apartments, mortgage helpers, or accessory apartments, these separate living units can easily pay back their cost many times over. Depending on the city and neighborhood, an accessory apartment can bring in rents that range anywhere from $250 to $750 per month. And unless you build from scratch, you can typically create desirable space for as little as $5,000 and certainly no more than $15,000.

In other words, viewed in terms of return on investment, $10,000 in renovation costs can often generate a rental income of $4,000 to $6,000 per year. You can search the world over and never find as much return for so little risk.

Create a Special Purpose Use

Tailor unique features of a property to niche segment of buyers (tenants).

You may find that renovating toward some special purpose use can generate a premium resale price or rental rate. Most fixer-upper investors go generic. In return, they receive a generic profit. But when you renovate toward the specific needs of a bullseye segment of seniors, the disabled, children, home businesses, college students, or any other specialized target of tenants (buyers), you favorably differentiate your product.

To discover a profitable niche, talk with people at social service agencies, hospitals, and local colleges. Imagine the special needs of single parents, multigenerational households, hobbyists, roommates, group homes, and shelters. Always stay alert to markets where demand runs strong and supply falls short. Whereas most run-of-the-mill investors know how to fix up a property, entrepreneurs search for a special niche of customers. Then they tailor the features of the property to perfectly fit that target market.

Change the Use of a Property

> **To maximize value, convert to a more profitable use.**

Apartments with new life as condominiums . . . gas stations now operating as retail outlets . . . old homes converted to office space . . . what was once farm acreage is now a sprawling urban shopping center. These properties are examples of adaptive use of both land and buildings brought about by a city's growth and change.

Conversions provide boundless opportunities for the creative investor. Converting an old house located in the downtown area can earn good profits. Office space sometimes rents at twice the rental rate of housing. The opposite also can occur. Recently, in London, housing prices have climbed so high that all types of retail, warehouse, and offices are being converted to apartments.

Condominium Conversion

To plan for a condo conversion, study the local area to learn the sales prices of comparable condo units. If you can purchase a similar apartment building at a low enough price, renovate and sell the converted units as condos to earn a profit.

Here's how you might calculate the potential profits of converting rental units into individually owned condominiums for a 16-unit apartment building:

Acquisition price	$480,000
Rehab at $7,500 per unit	120,000
Attorney fees (condo document preparation, government permitting process, sales contract preparation, closing document review)	40,000
Marketing costs (advertising, sales commissions)	45,000

Mortgage interest (12-month renovation and sellout)   50,000
Incidentals (architect, interior design, landscaping,
    government permits)   35,000

Total costs $770,000
Cost per unit $48,125

> **Condo conversions can offer a risky opportunity for quick profits.**

In this example, you paid $480,000 ($30,000 per unit) to acquire this 16-unit rental property. After all costs of conversion, your total investment increased to $770,000 ($48,125 per unit). But these figures haven't yet considered profits. If you want to net $10,000 per unit, you will need to sell the units at a price approaching $60,000 each (twice your purchase price).

To decide whether such a project is feasible in your area, research rental properties, condo prices, and conversion laws. Do some scratch-pad feasibility calculations. If preliminary estimates look promising, talk with an investor, contractor, attorney, or real estate consultant experienced in the conversion process. With the knowledge gained from these talks (and perhaps some follow-up research), you can decide whether this investment approach offers you enough profit potential to offset risks such as cost overruns, slow sales, and bureaucratic delays.

Convert Apartments or Houses to Office Space

Sometimes it's profitable to convert apartments or houses to office space. To mull over this possibility, answer these questions:

1. Is the property in a commercial zone? If not, can you get the property rezoned?
2. What is the current vacancy rate for office space in the area of the subject property? If too much space is already available, can you identify an underserved niche?
3. Do you have adequate parking for office space? The city may require one parking space for every 250–500 square feet of rentable office space.
4. How much will it cost to convert? Could you borrow the money to finance such a conversion? And, finally, will the cost,

legal procedures, and time and effort be worth the eventual profit you will realize?

Study the property and the market carefully. Thoroughly figure the finances of the projected conversion. Keep in tune with the requirements. If you can convert at a reasonable cost and earn a good profit, take a chance. You'll also gain valuable experience.

(Don't forget, for more complex investments, partner with someone who is more experienced. Place the promising property under option or purchase contract with contingencies. Then line up your partner and proceed.)

Cut Operating Expenses

As a rule of thumb, every dollar you slice from your property's operating expenses can add $10 or more to your building's value. With gains like that, you should meticulously keep track of all expenses. Then make continuous efforts to reduce or eliminate them. Here are some ideas.

Energy Audits

Nearly all utility companies will help you discover ways to reduce your gas or electric bills. Some will even audit and inspect your property. Others will provide booklets or brochures and, perhaps, a customer service department to answer specialized questions. You can also find dozens of articles and books at your local library that discuss energy conservation.

Energy-audit a building before you buy it. Then you can judge beforehand the extent to which you can feasibly reduce these costs.

Maintenance and Repair Costs

Savvy investors also need to reduce or eliminate money-wasting property maintenance and repair expenses. From my experience, I would encourage you to focus on five things:

1. ***Low-maintenance houses and apartment buildings.***
   When shopping to buy, favor those properties that are con-

structed with materials, HVAC, and fixtures that require less maintenance. Nothing beats a property that's built to last with minimal care. Ditto for yards, shrubs, and landscaping.

2. ***Tenant selection.*** Just as there are both low- and high-maintenance houses and apartment buildings, so too are there low-maintenance and high-maintenance tenants. Avoid the latter and select the former. Personally, I watch out for chronic complainers and people who show no "house sense."

3. ***Repair clauses.*** To further promote tenant responsibility, a growing number of property owners shift the first $50 or $100 of every repair cost onto their tenants' shoulders. Also, I favor high security deposits.

4. ***Handyman on call.*** Nothing eases the drain on your time and pocketbook as much as having a trustworthy and competent all-around handyman (or persons) to take care of your property maintenance and repairs.

5. ***Preventive maintenance.*** You inspect and maintain your car. Do likewise with your investment properties. Anticipate and alleviate when the cost is relatively small. Always ask your maintenance experts how you might replace high-maintenance items with low-maintenance items.

Property Taxes

"If you think that your property taxes are too high," writes tax consultant Harry Koenig, "you're probably right! Research shows that nearly half of all properties may be assessed illegally or excessively." While Koenig probably overstates the situation somewhat, millions of property owners do pay more in property taxes than they need to. With just a little attention and planning, you can avoid this trap by taking several precautions:

1. ***Check the accuracy of your assessed valuation.*** Usually tax assessors base their tax calculations on a property's market value. Look closely at the assessor's value estimate on your tax bill. Can you find comparable sales of similar properties that would support a *lower* value for your property? If so, you may have grounds to request a tax reduction.

2. ***Compare your purchase price to the assessor's estimate of market value.*** Apart from providing comp sales, if

you can show the assessor that you recently paid $190,000 for a property that the assessor appraised at $240,000, you can make a good case for lower taxes.

3. ***Look for unequal treatment.*** Under the law, assessors must tax properties in a neighborhood in a fair and uniform manner. You can argue for lower taxes by showing that the assessor has assigned lower values to similar nearby properties.

4. ***Learn tax assessment laws before you improve or rehabilitate a property.*** The property tax laws of every state list the types of property improvements that are taxed and the applicable millage rates. Once you discover the detailed nature of these laws, develop your property improvement strategy to add value without adding taxes.

Gentrification and Other Value Plays

In large and midsized cities across the United States and Canada, gentrification has pushed property prices through the roof in neighborhoods like Kerrisdale (Vancouver), Buckhead (Atlanta), South of Market (San Francisco), Chicago North Side, Chicago West Side, College Park (Orlando), "M Street" (Dallas), and Coconut Grove (Miami). Most of these neighborhoods have become name brands.

In earlier years, though, most of these neighborhoods were modest, even lower-priced neighborhoods. Several areas such as Chicago Near North and San Francisco South of Market included industrial and commercial properties.

> **You can find the next Buckhead or College Park.**

In each instance, however, the in-close accessibility of these neighborhoods overwhelmed their negatives. Prior to gaining cachet, these neighborhoods still gave residents an easy walk, drive, or commute to major job districts. And their prices looked dirt cheap when compared with conveniently situated premier neighborhoods.

Unfortunately for you, many gentrified name brand neighborhoods no longer represent good value. That's not to say that these areas won't show strong future appreciation. But that, as a rule, their high prices mean that your rent collections probably won't cover your mortgage payments plus property expenses.

The Good News

But here's the good news. All across the country, other emerging neighborhoods are poised for turnaround, revitalization, and rapid appreciation of property values. By becoming a neighborhood entrepreneur, you can score the same large gains that those early investors have earned in College Park, Near North, and Thorton Park.

Revitalize the Neighborhood

I know that you've probably heard it said 100 times: "Buy in the best neighborhood you can afford. You can change anything about a property except its location." At first glance, this advice seems plausible. But rethink what the term "neighborhood" actually refers to:

- Convenience
- Aesthetics
- People: attitudes, lifestyles
- Legal restrictions
- Schools
- Taxes/services
- Microclimate (weather)
- Safety and security
- Image/reputation
- Affordability

> The "best" neighborhoods don't always appreciate the fastest.

Even *Money* magazine agrees. In an article on home buying, *Money* advised its readers, "With interest rates sinking, it's a great time to shop for your dream house. . . . You'll need to seek out the neighborhoods where property values are rising faster than your community average." Surprising to many investors, though, is the fact that the neighborhoods where prices are positioned to rise fastest may not be the most prestigious or well-established neighborhoods. Often, the largest price increases can be expected in areas that are poised for turnaround or renewed popularity.

Entrepreneurs Improve Thorton Park (and Make a Killing)

"Florida's new urban entrepreneurs have the vision to see a bustling district of sushi bars, loft apartments and boutiques on a glass-strewn lot or rat-infested warehouse," writes Cynthia Barnett in the August 2001 issue of *Florida Trend*.

Phil Rampy is proud to have been one of those early entrepreneurs. Twelve years ago, Rampy bought a property in the then-shunned Thorton Park neighborhood near trash-strewn Lake Eola (or as they used to call it, Lake Erie-ola). Today, Thorton Park has climbed up the status ladder to rank among "the trendiest addresses" in Orlando. That $60,000 bungalow that Rampy renovated is now valued at more than $200,000. Although Thorton Park still sits on this Earth in the same place it did 10 years ago, nearly everything else about this neighborhood has changed.

> **Which neighborhoods do you believe will gentrify within the next decade?**

Many Neighborhoods Show Potential

When you compare neighborhoods, don't just look at the present. Imagine potential. List all of a neighborhood's good points. How could you and other property owners join together to highlight and improve these features? List the neighborhood's weak points. How can you and others eliminate negative influences? Who can you enlist to promote your cause? Can you mobilize mortgage lenders, other investors, homeowners, Realtors, not-for-profit housing groups, church leaders, builders, contractors, preservationists, police, local employers, retail businesses, school teachers, principals, community redevelopment agencies, elected officials, civic groups, and perhaps students, professors, and administrators of a nearby college or university? People can make a difference.

> **Learn what people are saying about different neighborhoods.**

How You Can Become a Neighborhood Entrepreneur

You don't have to live in a big-trouble, inner-city location to become an urban entrepreneur. You can do it anywhere. No neighborhood is perfect. I suspect that even Beverly Hills and Scarsdale could stand improvement in at least a few ways.

Because neighborhood quality drives up property values and rent levels, keep yourself alert for ideas to initiate (or join in) to make the neighborhood a better place to live. When you simultaneously improve your property *and* its neighborhood, you more than double your profit potential. Would any of the following suggestions work for the areas that you're considering?

> **Values jump with neighborhood improvements.**

Add to Neighborhood Convenience   Would a stoplight, wider road, or new highway interchange improve accessibility to the neighborhood? Where are the to and fro traffic logjams? How can they be alleviated? Is the neighborhood served as well as it could be by buses and commuter trains? How about social service transportation? Could you get the vans that pick up seniors or the disabled to place this neighborhood on their route? What about the traveling bus for the library? Does it stop in the neighborhood?

> **Try to attract new retailers, coffee houses, and restaurants.**

Improve Appearances   Put together a civic pride organization. Organize a cleanup and fix-up campaign. Plant trees, shrubs, and flowers in yards and in public areas. Lobby the city to tear down or eliminate eyesore buildings, graffiti, or trashy areas. Try to reduce on-street parking. Get abandoned vehicles towed. Enforce environmental regulations against property owners and businesses that pollute (noise, smoke, odors).

> **Fix-up becomes contagious.**

Zoning and Building Regulations   Are too many property owners in the neighborhood splitting up single-family houses and converting them into apartments? Do too many residents run businesses out of their homes and garages? Are high-rise or midrise buildings planned that will diminish livability? Are too many commercial properties encroaching on the area? Then lobby for tighter zoning and building reg-

> **Enlist the help of the code enforcers. Change the zoning.**

ulations. On the other hand, do areas within the neighborhood and those nearby make more intense use of properties desirable? Then lobby the city to rezone the area to apartments or commercial.

Eliminate Neighborhood Nuisances   Do one or more households in the neighborhood make a nuisance of themselves? Junk cars in the driveway, barking dogs, loud stereos, constant yelling and shouting, out-of-control yards littered with debris—you and other property owners can force them to clean up their act or suffer severe and continuing legal penalties.

> **Rules seldom permit nuisances to continue if neighbors register complaints.**

Pore over your local ordinances and any pertinent private rules and restrictions. Sift through the regulations for zoning, aesthetics, occupancy, use, parking, noise, disturbing the peace, health, safety, loitering, drug dealing or possession, extortion, and assault. You can nearly always find some regulatory violations under which you can file a complaint.

If after receiving a citation the nuisance neighbors continue to offend common decency, a judge can issue an order to cease and desist (or something similar). Further violations would then bring the scalawags a citation for contempt of court. They've now angered the judge. Each day the breach persists could rack up multiple fines, and possibly jail time. In some cases the government will even remedy the problem—cut the weeds, haul off a junk car—and then bill the offenders.

> **Improve school performance and watch property values set new highs.**

Upgrade the Schools   The *Wall Street Journal* (August 23, 2001, p. A-1) reports that all across the country "parents and property owners have become increasingly aggressive about trying to improve their public schools." When you think that in many areas parents spend $3,000 to $10,000 a year to send their kids to private schools, why not rechannel those monies and support into the neighborhood schools?

Safety and Security   In addition to reducing crime, you can bolster the safety within the neighborhood (especially for children and seniors) by slowing down or rerouting traffic. In fact, if you can get the city to lay down speed bumps, you achieve both objectives at the same time. Speed bumps not only force motorists to let up on the gas pedal, they tell drivers who want to speed that they'd better travel a different street.

You might also try lower posted speed limits and more intense enforcement. In Berkeley, California, neighborhoods lobbied the city to erect traffic barriers at residential intersections. This effort converted many formerly through streets into cul-de-sacs.

> **Insist on the government services for which you and other property owners pay taxes.**

Lobby the Politicians   Property owners pay taxes. Now insist that you get what you pay for. As the Berkeley experience proves, when property owners and neighborhood residents join together to form a political force, they can push the city politicos to alleviate traffic problems, clean the streets, enforce ordinances, upgrade the schools, beef up police patrols, create parks, and provide other services that neighborhoods should expect.

Add Luster to Your Image   Some good friends of mine used to live in Miami, Florida, but now they live in the upscale Village of Pinecrest, Florida. Did they move? No. They and their neighbors persuaded the post office to give them a new address so they could distinguish themselves from that diverse agglomeration known as Miami. As part of their efforts to create an improved neighborhood, some residents of Sepulveda, California, have formed a new community and renamed it North

> **Give your neighborhood or community a new name.**

Hill. In Maryland, Gaithersburg has changed its name to North Potomac, attempting to capitalize on the prestige of its nearby neighbor. Some residents of North Hollywood got the official name of part of their community changed to Valley Village. "With the name change," says Realtor Jerry Burns, "residents take more pride in their neighborhood."

Talk Up the Neighborhood   Most people learn about various neighborhoods through word of mouth and articles they read in their local newspapers. As all good publicists know, you can influence these methods of "getting the word out." Talk up the neighborhood to opinion leaders. Comment to friends, coworkers, relatives, and acquaintances about the great improvements of the community.

Convince a reporter to play up the neighborhood's potential for turnaround, quality of life, convenience, or affordability. Let everyone know that the area deserves a better reputation. When you revitalize a neighborhood, your properties can double or triple in value within just 8 to 10 years.

PART FOUR

Onward and Upward to Building Wealth

15

Win What You Want through Negotiation

Sometimes you can *find* great deals in real estate. But more often, you must help *create* your great deals through negotiation.

> **You create great deals through negotiation.**

Think about it. Whenever you buy or sell, arrange financing, obtain bids from contractors, or write out a lease, your skills as a negotiator will influence what you get and what you give up. As Herb Cohen, the widely respected negotiating trainer, says, "You can get anything you want in life, but you must do more than ask. You must negotiate."

So, in this chapter, you're going to see how you can win what you want through negotiation.

How to Define Win-Win

You've probably heard of the negotiating style called win-win. But do you really know what that negotiating style implies? Most people don't—even though they think they do.

Myth Versus Reality

In the fairy-tale world of win-win, you and the other party to the negotiation sit down together, openly share information about each other, explore options and possibilities, express concerns, focus on goals, and then come up with a solution that truly satisfies both of you. Maybe in the land of Oz negotiations proceed this smoothly, but not in the real world.

"Why not?" you ask.

Because in the real world, we all want the best deal we can cut. You want to pay less. I want you to pay more. I want possession within 30 days; you do not want to give up the property for 90 days. I want you to finance the deal with 10 percent down. You're insisting on 30 percent. I want to pay you 6 percent interest. You think I should pay 8 percent. The list of potential deal points for controversy goes on and on.

> **Real-world negotiators go for *almost* as much as they can get.**

Forget "What's Fair"

At least 9 out of every 10 times, the people with whom you negotiate will try to pull more chips into their own pile and leave you with less. Likewise (unless you're sporting a halo), you'll also want the larger pile. Maybe this sounds crass, but that's the way most investors play the negotiating game. Forget "what's fair" as the deciding arbiter.

To succeed as a wealth-building real estate investor, cast aside your illusions. To get what you want, you must go well beyond the idealized view of win-win.

The Real Meaning of Win-Win

Yes, win-win does foster cooperation. It does foster mutual problem solving. And it does require you to think up more deal points to (as they say) make the pie bigger.

But let's face facts. No matter what negotiating style you choose to get what you want, you will run bluffs, drag red herrings across the other party's path, create subtle ways to extract information, and protest that you cannot pay more even though you know full well that you are willing and able to do so.

You Win; the Other Party *Feels* Like a Winner   In the real world version of win-win, you avoid the hostile, "rip your face off" negotiating style so common to New York lawyers. You do not try to disrespect, belittle, denigrate, or put down the other party. You do not press the other party against a wall, pick his pockets of everything you can find, and then let him loose just to watch him fall to the floor.

You choose to avoid this win-lose style of negotiating not because you're a nice guy or gal (although you may be) but because you can get more of what you want by adopting a softer, more conciliating manner.

> **People want to *feel* like they've won the negotiation.**

As Zig Zigler is noted for saying, "You can get anything you want in life, *as long as* you help the other fellow get what he wants."

What is it that people want most from a negotiation? They want to *feel* like a winner. They want to *feel* like they cut the best deal they could.

Who Feels Most Like a Winner?   Imagine that you're negotiating with a seller. You're going back and forth on price. Finally, the seller gives in to give you almost everything you're asking for. You're pleased as punch.

Then, after closing, you learn that the seller was really pressed for cash. Had he not bluffed you into believing that he would go no lower, he would have sold for $50,000 less than you agreed to pay.

Now, how do you feel? How would most people feel? Right. Their sense of victory just melted away.

I have negotiated hundreds of agreements, and I can assure you that most people value their feelings more than the objective deal points. Naturally, exceptions occur. But more often than not, you win the most deal points when you encourage the other party to *feel* like he or she is winning the negotiations.

Experience Rules   I know of no serious real estate investor who enters a negotiation to strike a "fair" agreement in any objective sense. Rather, they enter negotiations to extract (almost) as much from the other party as possible. These investors differ primarily in the way they try to win these deal points.

- ◆ *Win-lose style.* The egocentric dealmaker wants to win while forcing the other party to admit defeat. These investors want the other party to know that they've been outmaneuvered, outsmarted, and overpowered.
- ◆ *Win-win style.* The investor who puts this style to work remains content to know that he persuaded (not forced) the other party

to push the chips in his direction. But this negotiator never lets on that he got the best of the deal. He allows the other side to win that prize. That ploy stands as the real-world meaning of win-win.

> **Win-win does not imply an objectively fair agreement.**

Which negotiating style works best? Each method has its advocates and practitioners. Personally, I favor win-win. Not because it's the nice-guy, "how to win friends and influence people" approach. Rather, my experience tells me it's the best approach to win what I want. Try it, and I'm sure you will agree.

Now let's see what methods, tactics, and gambits you can draw on to win more deal points.

Know Thyself

To get what you want from negotiations, you must first know what you want. As you envision it, does this potential deal fit into your wealth-building goals? Does it fit within your frame of time, money, and talents? If completed, will this deal move you closer to where you want to go?

Many beginning investors jump to buy a property because in some way it seems like a good deal. But before you rush into something because it seems to look good, figure out whether the deal will be good for you. Evaluate the deal in terms of your longer-term personal and financial goals.

Know the Property and Neighborhood

Prior to talking with the sellers, learn as much about the property as you can. Here's a sampling of the information you should try to discover.

- ◆ How is the property zoned? Are more profitable uses possible?
- ◆ How large is the lot? What are its dimensions and boundaries?
- ◆ When did the property last sell? At what price?
- ◆ Is there a mortgage on the property? What's the amount of the outstanding balance? What interest rate?

- ◆ What school districts apply to the property?
- ◆ What employers are located nearby?
- ◆ What are the neighborhood demographics? Who's moving in? Who's moving out?
- ◆ What percent of neighborhood residents rent versus own?
- ◆ What range of rents and property prices apply to the neighborhood?

> **Every time you ask the sellers a question, you may tip off your intentions.**

You might wonder why you should go to all of this trouble. Why work to discover this property and neighborhood information on your own when you could easily ask the sellers (or their real estate agent)? But here's the downside to that approach. You might alert the sellers to some piece of information that they could use to strengthen their own negotiating position. You might tip your hand about some hidden value potential you see in the area or the property.

Know the Sellers

Have the sellers accepted or declined any offers on the property? If so, what were the terms and price? (Sometimes agents will disclose this information. Sometimes you can learn it from a lender, an appraiser, the sellers' neighbors, or even the sellers themselves.) If a previous deal fell through, find out why. Will this past experience influence the sellers' negotiating positions with you?

Do the Sellers Face Pressure?

Nearly all real estate books advise you to find "motivated" sellers. Who are these wonderful folks who will gladly give you a good deal? Generally, they're sellers who face severe pressures of time, money, or family situation (divorce, death, job move, retirement).

Know the sellers' personal or financial circumstances and you'll learn the deal points that they might value most. You'll also discover those issues the sellers might be willing to resolve in your favor (bargain price, owner financing, lease option, "subject to" purchase).

Get the Sellers to Like You

People give better deals to people they like. So try to build rapport with the sellers. Read a copy of Dale Carnegie's *How to Win Friends and Influence People* (New York: Pocket Books, 1936, 1990). Don't insult, argue, contradict, or directly challenge anything the sellers say. Always hedge your differing views with statements such as "Have you considered," "It seems to me," "In my experience," "Oh, it was my understanding that," and "What if I were to . . ."

> **Sellers give better deals to buyers they like.**

When sellers like you, they will help you get what you want. If they dislike you, they will favor other buyers—even though the other buyers are proposing what objectively appears to be a less attractive offer. Never come at sellers from sharp angles.

Tact, Not Ultimatums

When you're negotiating with sellers in distress, never use the cliché, "Take it or leave it." Apart from proving you to be a tactless amateur, such a ploy seldom works. In most cases, even property owners under duress would sooner lose their money than part with their ego and self-esteem. The same negativity attaches to out-of-the-blue, lowball offers that shoot out untethered by reason, empathy, and understanding. To work best with a troubled owner, work with, not against. With these types of sellers (as well as nearly all others, too), mutual problem-solving outperforms one-upmanship. Don't conquer, conciliate.

> **Don't conquer, conciliate.**

Negotiate an Agreement, Not Just Price

In contrast to buying stocks where transactions take place according to a set price and essentially fixed terms, in real estate almost anything's negotiable. If the sellers seem inflexible on price, look for other value-added concessions. Or if it is they who require a quick close or sure sale, oblige their demands in return for requests of your own.

For purposes of bragging rights, some sellers insist on a "high" price. Okay, give them what they want. Then take back more in favorable financing, closing costs, possession date, warranties, inspections, repairs,

> **Willingly trade
> your white chips
> for the seller's
> blue chips.**

personal property, title insurance, or other terms and conditions of value. Remember, in real estate you can negotiate a winning agreement without directly negotiating a bargain price. As a win-win negotiator, remain alert to white-chip issues and concerns that you can trade off to win the blue chip issues that you prize most.

Establish Favorable Benchmarks

Sellers often entertain some strange ideas about why their property warrants a particular price. If you encounter such a situation, don't argue. Seek information. Ask the sellers (or their agent) how they arrived at such a value. Frequently, you will find their benchmark either inaccurate or irrelevant. For example:

1. *Add-in costs.* "We paid $25,000 for that kitchen remodel," the sellers might say.
2. *The Joneses' house.* "The Joneses down the street just got $245,000 for their house, and it's 400 square feet smaller than ours," is a frequently heard rationale.
3. *The appraisal.* "$185,000 is a great price for this property. Look, here's an appraisal. The appraiser says it's worth $205,000."
4. *Their past purchase price.* "We paid $425,000 a year and a half ago. At $445,000 you're getting a steal. Properties in this neighborhood are going up 10 to 15 percent a year."

To negotiate successfully with owners who use these and other familiar types of benchmarks, subtly undermine their accuracy or relevance, but not with direct "put-you-on-the-spot" challenges. Rather, tactfully phrase your investigative questioning. Lead the sellers to doubt the applicability of their benchmark "facts." Then supply your own more appropriate (and more favorable) benchmarks.

> **Avoid direct
> argument, try to
> change the
> benchmarks to
> those that favor
> your interests.**

When you can get the sellers to recognize and accept your benchmarks, you go a long way toward getting them to accept your price (or other terms and conditions). When you merely try to pull down the seller's price while leaving them to hold tightly to their benchmarks, you'll usually find it tough to break their grip. (For various legitimate benchmarks of value, see Chapter 12.

Tit for Tat

Never concede without asking for a return concession. "If I can meet your need on point X, would you be willing to accept Y?" To concede without a return request invites continued "nibbling." In addition, agreement without request gives the seller second thoughts. "Why is Mr. Buyer jumping at this? Am I selling too low?" Do the sellers a favor. For each concession you give up, ask the sellers for something in return.

Get Seller Concessions Early

In their eagerness to entice your interest, many sellers will begin to concede deal points well before you formally open negotiations. During your initial casual discussions, test the waters. "Have you thought about carrying back financing? I know you're asking $415,000, but what kind of price would you be happy with? Which of the appliances are you willing to leave? How much of the closing costs had you planned to pay?"

> **Guide the sellers into making early concessions.**

By *casually* asking these types of questions, you lower the floor on which later negotiations will stand. Once negotiations begin, sellers tend to play their cards closer to the table.

Come Ready to Buy

Know the sellers. Know the property. Know the neighborhood. Know the market. Know values. Know your finances. Know what you're looking for. Then, when you see it, move, move, move. The "well-let-me-think-it-over" investor won't score nearly as many great buys as that investor who comes into the game ready to play. You can't expect good buys to remain unrecognized for long. During the past year, I've looked at around a dozen properties that I considered good-to-great buys. Nearly all of them sold within four weeks (or less) of hitting the market. Several sold the first day their "For Sale" signs went up.

Ask for More than You Expect

Ideally, you want the sellers to begin sweetening the deal before you write up your first offer. But at some point, you will need to submit a written purchase contract. When you do, ask for much more than you could possibly expect to eventually settle for.

Your Goal Is to Make Money

Remember, as an investor, you are doing deals primarily to make money. Don't become emotionally attached to an investment property as you might a house that you intend to occupy as your long-term home. With an investment, the numbers either work to give you a great buy, or they don't. When they don't, keep on negotiating—or look elsewhere.

> **Go for more than you expect to get.**

If you're negotiating to buy a *home* that truly suits your personal needs like no other, I would caution you to avoid a lowball offer because—unless presented tactfully—that offer could backfire. It could offend the sellers. In response, the sellers might either reject you as a buyer or accept another offer. You could end up severely disappointed. You missed the home of your dreams.

Not so with an investment property. With an investment property, alternatives always exist. With investment properties, you're negotiating for financial reward, not any one property per se.

The Benefits of Asking for More than You Want or Expect

How would you feel if you offered $200,000 and the sellers quickly said, "We'll take it. When do you want to close?" Undoubtedly, you would soon regret your offer. You tell yourself, "That was a dumb move. I bet the sellers would have accepted a lot less."

Likewise, the sellers will begin to question the wisdom of their decision. They begin to think, "If this buyer was willing to open with an offer of $200,000, he surely would have been willing to go up to $210,000, maybe even $225,000. We acted too hastily. We should have countered."

When you ask for a better deal than you could possibly expect to get, you actually promote your goals in several ways.

◆ It gives you room to negotiate.
◆ It reduces the sellers' expectations.
◆ It permits you to make concessions and helps the sellers feel like they have won.

And last, but far from least,

◆ The sellers may surprise you. They might fulfill your wish list with only minor changes.

In that pleasant situation, you would still want to assure the sellers that they got nearly all that you were willing to give. Had they not accepted, you would have bought that other fourplex you were looking at. "In fact," you tell the sellers, "I now wish I had tried to make that other deal. I think those sellers were willing to carry back financing at 6 percent interest with just 10 percent down."

Establish Credibility

No one wants to negotiate with a flake. To entice the sellers, let them know that they can count on you to do what you say. Remember, emphasize your strong points:

◆ Character
◆ Credit
◆ Capacity
◆ Consistency

If your record is weak in any particular area, emphasize whatever compensating factors you can think of.

What evidence might you keep on hand to bolster your ability to close a deal and perform as promised? To the extent these documents would help your case, you might set up a file for seller review (when necessary) any or all of the following items:

- ◆ FICO score and credit reports
- ◆ Past payment records on other real estate (rent or mortgage)
- ◆ Experience with contractors, rehabs, renovations
- ◆ Bank statements to prove you have more than enough cash to close plus substantial reserves
- ◆ A letter of intent from your partners or a copy of your partnership agreement
- ◆ Testimonials and references from others who have worked with you
- ◆ Prior real estate ownership or management experience

Before you try to sell your offer to the property owners, sell yourself as a credible, trustworthy investor.

Never Offer to Split the Difference

To bring a perceived deadlock to an end, you may be tempted to blurt out, "Okay, let's just split the difference." Resist this impulse.

You want the *sellers* to propose this solution. Because once they've put this offer out, they've essentially announced that they will accept this new lower price.

Now you can counter the sellers' "split the difference" offer. "I don't know," you say. "I really can't go any higher than the $290,000 figure that my calculations require. Your new price of $310,000 won't give me the return I must have. But here's what might work. If you can carry back $50,000 at 7.0 percent instead of 7.75, I think I can barely squeeze out my minimum return at a price of $300,000."

> **Get the sellers to first offer to "split the difference."**

The Mental Commitment

Now, you're within $10,000 and 0.75 percent of agreement. The sellers have mentally moved their position from $330,000 to $310,000. It's almost certain that your deal will end up closing at a price less than $310,000 and at an interest rate of less than 7.75 percent.

You win the deal points. The sellers—provided you have protested long and loud enough—feel they won the negotiation. They managed to extract from you your absolute best offer—or so they believe. Then when you congratulate and compliment them on their tough bargaining skills, you put the icing on their cake.

The Price Dilemma

Avoid suggesting a split-the-difference solution for one more reason. It tends to focus the negotiations on price. When possible, rather than let price alone create a deadlock or impasse, keep searching through your total bundle of possible deal points. Keep looking for those high-value, low-value tradeoffs. What might you or the sellers need or want besides money?

List Your BATNAs

> **With other options in view, you strengthen your walk-away willpower.**

In negotiating lingo, BATNA stands for your best alternative to a negotiated agreement. To negotiate a winning agreement, you must maintain your walk-away willpower. When you negotiate to buy an investment property, always explicitly list your other potential choices. Always say to yourself, "If I can't get the deal I'm looking for here, what other opportunities can I pursue?"

Remember, you're not negotiating to buy a property. You're negotiating to earn a good profit.

Negotiate for Yourself

Writing in *Real Estate Today,* a national trade magazine for Realtors, sales agent Sal Greer tells of an offer he received on one of his listings. Sal says that after receiving the purchase offer from a *buyer's agent,* this agent told Sal, "This is their [first] offer, but I know my buyers will go up to $150,000."

"Of course," Sal adds, "I told my sellers that information, and we were pleased with the outcome of the transaction."

The lesson for you is very plain. Never let your agent do your negotiating for you. Don't give your agent information you do not want the other side to learn. Do not let on to your agent that you're willing to pay a higher price than your first offer. Use your agent as a fact finder and intermediary. But guard your emotions, confidences, and intentions.

Many first-time investors mistakenly rely too heavily on their agents to actually come up with the terms of their offer and carry out their negotiations. These investors will ask their agents, "What price do you think I should offer? What's the most you think I should pay? Will the sellers pay closing costs or carry-back financing?" The buyers then follow whatever the agent recommends.

> **Never abandon control of negotiations to your agent (or your attorney).**

Such buyers abdicate their negotiating responsibilities. If you follow their example and shift decision making to your agent, you run the following risks.

You May Be Working with a Subagent

Remember, you may be working with the sellers' listing agent or a subagent. Often "your" agent's legal duty is to the seller. In favoring the sellers' interests, the agent may persuade you to boost the price or terms of your offer. Or the agent my disclose your confidences to the sellers.

> **Agents may violate the confidences of you or the sellers.**

As a practical matter, many sellers' agents don't strictly follow the letter of the law. Even though technically they're representing the sellers, in their heart and efforts they may feel more loyalty to you. I know many subagents who work hard for their investors—even to the detriment of their sellers.

Nevertheless, because you don't know for sure how an agent will use the information you share, carefully limit your disclosures. Likewise, when it comes to offering price and terms, rely on an agent for facts about the sellers, selling prices of comparable properties, neighborhood statistics, and general market conditions. Listen to the agent's price recommendations and accept the benefits of his or her knowledge and experience. But don't delegate your decision making. You may be led into giving up more than you need to.

Be Cautious of Buyers' Agents

Increasingly, brokerage firms and sales agents have been promoting buyers' agency. Because sellers are represented by their listing agents, buyers presumably need someone to look out for their interests. Marilyn Wilson, a Bellingham, Washington, real estate broker, says, "Buyers should think of their agents as attorneys. Would you want to have one attorney representing both parties in a divorce settlement?"

> **Buyer's agents, too, face conflicts of interest.**

Superficially, the idea sounds reasonable. But even if you choose to employ a buyers' agent, you still need to guard your disclosures and negotiating strategy. First of all, like the buyers' agent Sal Greer referred to earlier, even *your* agent may disclose confidences—either intentionally or unintentionally.

Second, we're all subject to subtle influences. A buyers' agent may talk you into offering a higher price or better terms because it will make his or her job easier. Under which scenario do you think your agent will work the hardest for you: When the agent knows you offered $385,000 but you've said you're willing to go up to $410,000, or when you offer $385,000 and say, "If they don't accept this offer, there's four or five other properties I'd like to look at"?

Watch What You Say

Regardless of whether you're working with a sellers' agent, a buyers' agent, a dual agent, or a facilitator, watch what you say. Don't tell an agent everything and then turn the negotiations over to her with the simple instructions, "Do the best job you can," or "Why don't you try $235,000 and if that doesn't fly, we can go up to $245,000."

In fact, it doesn't matter whether we're talking about lawyers, insurance agents, mortgage brokers, financial planners, real estate agents, or any other type of professional relationship, conflict of interest always lurks in the background. You must walk a fine line. Release enough information to achieve the results you want, but not so much that you invite an agent to sacrifice your interests to the interests of someone else (including herself).

> **All types of agents compromise their principals (and principles).**

Leave Something on the Table

Negotiating expert Bob Woolf says, "There isn't any contract I have negotiated where I didn't feel I could have gone for more money or an additional benefit." Why leave money on the table? Because skilled negotiators know, "The deal's not over til it's over." If you push too hard, you create resentment and hostility in the other party. Even if they've signed a contract, they'll start thinking of all the ways they can get out of it. Even worse, if you stumble on the way to closing, they won't help you up. They'll just kick dirt in your face.

> **Push the sellers' limits and later they may shove you back.**

Especially in the purchase of real estate—where emotions run strong—you're better off leaving something on the table. The purchase agreement only forms stage one of your negotiations. Later, you might encounter problems with respect to property inspections, appraisal, financing, possession date, closing date, surveys, zoning, building permits, or any number of other things. Without goodwill, trust, and cooperation, unpleasant setbacks on the way to closing can throw your agreement into contentious dispute.

As a win-win negotiator, make the other parties feel they've won. Even though you're persistently pulling more chips into your own pile, assure the sellers that they've never given up more than they had to. When you leave something on the table, the sellers will feel more committed to the agreement.

CHAPTER 16

How to Write Your Purchase Offer

Quite likely, when you get ready to make your offer to buy a property, you'll be handed a so-called standard purchase agreement to fill out and sign. But wait. Before you blindly accept that form, read it closely.

No Single Contract Form

No all-purpose form contract has ever been written. Just as important, the form used in your area may not fully serve you or the sellers' interests. Although space here doesn't permit a detailed discussion of every contract term that you might see, I'll go over many of those terms that you should pay special attention to.

Indeed, before you even think about putting in an offer on a property, ask a real estate agent to provide you with a blank copy of the form contract(s) that the agent typically relies on to complete a purchase agreement. Then read each clause. Compare it to the discussions in this chapter. Ask the agent (or legal counsel) to clarify any terms or clauses that you don't fully understand.

> **Review a blank contract form long before you need it.**

Make Sure You Draft These Clauses with Care and Understanding

Although there's no such thing as a "standard" purchase offer, the discussion here does explain those clauses that you should make sure you (your agent, your lawyer) draft with care and understanding.

Names of the Parties

Your agreement should include the names of all parties to the transaction. It is especially important that your agreement name all owners (sellers) and make sure all are available to sign your offer as soon as you reach agreement. Be wary of negotiating with a seller whose spouse or partners do not actively join in the negotiations. If they don't later agree to sign, you have no deal.

Some sellers will claim that their co-owners will go along with whatever they say. Yet, after you commit, the seller will come back and say, "Gee, I'm terribly sorry. My partner refuses to sign. He thinks I'm giving the property away. He wants another $25,000, but I've told him I can't renege and change the terms. But he insists. So I'll tell you what, if you can agree to another $10,000, I'll go back to my partner and do my best to convince him to go along. I'm really sorry, but sometimes my partner gets obstinate and there's little I can do to reason with him."

> **Don't fall for the "good guy–bad guy" gambit.**

This ploy is one of the oldest tricks in the book. But it often works. So sellers (and buyers) continue to use it. Just don't be surprised when you have it pulled on you—if you've proceeded to negotiate with someone who lacks the legal authority to carry out the agreement. (Or some sellers might say, "Gee, I'm sorry. I know I agreed to these terms, but my lawyer says 'no way.'")

Site Description

Identify the property that you're buying by street address and legal description. As a safeguard, walk the boundaries of the property as you follow the lines on a survey or a plot plan. When you walk the boundaries, note any encroachments. Does the neighbors' garage overlap the

> **Walk and confirm the boundaries of the site.**

property line? Is there a crooked driveway, a misplaced fence, or overhanging tree limbs that could create a problem?

Make sure the lot size you think you're buying actually measures up to the size you're getting. Especially where a property site borders a vacant lot, field, or creek, don't merely assume the lot lines run where they seem to run. Sometimes, too, what appears to be the subject property's yard actually belongs to the neighboring property. Visually verify where the surveyed boundaries really lie.

Building Description

Often, your real estate agreement needs to identify only the lot, not the building. That's because the legal definition of real estate (the surface of the Earth) automatically includes all structures permanently attached to the land.

If the seller, though, has represented to you that the buildings are of a specific size or are built of certain materials, or of a certain historic date or design, then write those features (whatever they are) into the property description. In Berkeley, California, buyers sued the sellers of a gracious old home because the sellers had (mistakenly) told the buyers that the home had been designed by Julia Morgan, a famous San Francisco Bay Area architect of the early 1900s.

> **If you think you're buying a Julia Morgan design, write it into your purchase offer.**

The buyers claimed that they had not just agreed to buy a house on a specific site. Rather, they had offered to buy a Julia Morgan house. Lacking the Julia Morgan prestige, the buyers believed they were entitled to damages. (The court agreed and awarded damages to the buyers.)

If you think you're buying a prewar brownstone, or maybe the house where Elvis Presley was raised, write it into your agreement. Let the sellers know exactly what you expect to receive in all its critical details. Verify that the building you think you're buying actually fits the description of the property that you're relying on. Should your expectations (the seller's representations) prove incorrect, you may be able to rescind the agreement, sue for damages, or both.

Personal Property

Although the legal definition of real estate applies to land and buildings, it does not necessarily include the personal property that the sellers have promised to leave for you. (Generally, the term personal property refers to items that are not "permanently" attached to a building or the land.) Say the sellers of a fourplex provide their tenants window air conditioners, miniblinds, gas ranges, refrigerators, and ceiling fans. In your written offer to buy that property, expressly list these additional items.

Courts Have Extended the Definition of Real Property   While it's true that some courts have extended the concept of real estate to include personal property that is "adapted for use" with a specific building, don't depend on litigation to force the sellers to convey the personal property that you believed to be included in the sale. Leave no doubt—write it out. Go through every room of the property. List every item that the sellers might plausibly maintain was not a part of your agreement because it was their "personal property" and therefore not included with the sale of the real estate.

Who Owns What? Sellers or Tenants?   Listing personal property serves another purpose as well. It requires the sellers to clearly point out what personal property belongs to them and what belongs to their tenants. Property investors who do not obtain an accurate list of the seller's personal property may later find themselves in dispute with tenants when the tenants claim, "That refrigerator is ours. That junk icebox the landlord provided was carted off to the dump two years ago. We bought this refrigerator from Betty's parents."

> **Ask the tenants to verify the list of owners' items.**

To be safe, ask the sellers' tenants to okay any list of personal property that you and the sellers prepare. After you have closed on the deal is not the time to learn that the furniture and appliances that you thought you bought actually belong to the tenants.

Price and Financing

When you prepare your offer, spell out the precise purchase price and the terms of the financing. List the amounts payable, how payable, when payable, and the interest rate(s). Make interpretation easy for a disinterested third party. Leave nothing to decide at some later date. "Seller agrees to carry back $20,000 on mutually agreeable terms" leaves too much ambiguity.

When planning to borrow new financing, or even if you're assuming the seller's mortgage, this same advice holds: Don't leave the amount and terms of financing open to question. If you need a 5 percent down loan at 6.0 percent interest, write those terms into your financing contingency.

Earnest Money Deposit

Contrary to popular belief, the validity of your purchase offer does not depend on the amount of your earnest money deposit, or for that matter, whether you've even paid a deposit. Earnest money is nothing more than a good-faith showing that you intend to complete your purchase. More than anything else, choose your deposit amount as part of your negotiation strategy.

> **Earnest money signals your intent and credibility.**

Size of the Deposit   Large deposits signal to the sellers that you are a serious buyer. Some investors use large deposits to offset their lowball offers. A large earnest money deposit tells the sellers, "You can count on me to buy your property. This large deposit proves that I mean what I say. Wouldn't you rather go for a sure thing now rather than wait for a better offer that may never come along?"

On the other hand, a small deposit may signal that you're financially weak, or that you're trying to tie up the property cheaply while you mull over other options. But here's the rub: Smart sellers won't accept purchase offers that don't truly commit you to buying their property.

Learn Local Custom   To some degree, whether the sellers think your deposit large or small, serious or trifling, depends on local custom. So gauge the impression you will make with your deposit by the amounts local sellers and realty agents think reasonable for the type of property that you're buying.

Just keep in mind that a deposit that seems low tarnishes your credibility. A high deposit brightens your credibility. You could employ a low deposit strategy and rely on other factors to support your credibility as a buyer (current ownership of multiple properties, strong FICO score, high net worth, person of integrity). But this trick is difficult to pull off. As a rule, few things speak louder than ready cash.

Quality of Title

> **Always rely on legal counsel or title insurance for opinions of title quality.**

Many arcane legalities surround the issue of title quality. To get good title, you need a real estate attorney or, better, a title insurer. However, your purchase agreement will state the title guarantees and exceptions that govern your transaction. Make sure you know what these are before you sign. Especially exercise caution when you buy a property through foreclosure, tax sale, sheriff's auction, probate, or some other type of sale where the previous owner of the property does not sign the deed.

Property Condition

Your purchase offer should address the issue of property condition in two ways. First, ask the sellers to complete a property disclosure statement that lists every conceivable problem or defect that now or ever has affected the property and the neighborhood.

Second, while you can learn a great deal from seller disclosure, you can't learn everything. Generally, sellers must disclose only what they know. As added protection, include a property inspection contingency in your offer. Then, check out the property with one or more pros who can verify the condition of the plumbing, heating and air conditioning, electrical system, roofing, and foundation.

You can write your inspection contingency to set a cost limit on needed repairs (e.g., $1,000). Ideally, the sellers should pay these costs. But if you've negotiated a bargain price, you might accept responsibility. If repair costs go over your stated amount, your contingency clause should give you the right to withdraw your offer and get back your earnest money deposit.

Preclosing Property Damage (Casualty Clause)

Your purchase offer should require the sellers to deliver their property to you on the date of closing (or the date of possession) in the same condition as it stood on the date the sellers accepted your offer. If the property suffers damage (fire, earthquake, vandalism, hurricane, flood) after the purchase contract has been signed, but prior to closing, the sellers must repair the property at their expense. Alternatively, in the event of damage, you or the sellers may be allowed to pull out of the agreement, and you will get back your deposit.

Closing (Settlement) Costs

Many real estate transactions involve thousands of dollars in closing costs. You or the sellers might pay for title insurance, an appraisal, mortgage points, buy-down fees, application fees, lender-mandated repairs, lawyers' fees, mortgage assumption fees, recording fees, transfer taxes, document stamps, survey, property inspections, escrow fees, real estate brokerage fees, and other expenses. These costs can quickly add up to a fair-sized chunk of money. Who pays each of these costs—you or the sellers? Local custom frequently dictates, but negotiation can override custom. If the sellers won't drop their price as low as you'd like, ask them to pay more of the settlement costs.

> **Some cash-short investors trade off a higher price for seller-paid closing costs.**

Closing and Possession Dates

Your offer to buy a property should set dates for settlement and possession. When you or the sellers place great importance on either a quick (or delayed) closing date, that date can play a valuable role in your negotiations. Because of a need for ready cash, the sellers might trade a lower price for an early closing date. Or for tax reasons, the sellers may prefer to delay settlement until after they've begun a new tax year.

Likewise for the date of possession. The sellers might want a fast closing, but they also may want to keep possession of the property (especially if it's their home) for some period that extends beyond the settlement date. Maybe their new home isn't yet completed. Maybe they would like to postpone moving until after their children finish the school term. Their reasons vary, but as a smart negotiator, feel out the sellers on their preferred closing and possession dates. Then use this information to shape your offer. If you're willing to meet the sellers' needs on this issue, they may meet your requests on price or terms.

Leases

When you buy a rental property, you must abide by the valid leases and promises that the sellers have entered into with the tenants. Especially investigate these issues:

- ◆ *Rent levels.* How much do the tenants pay in rents? Are any tenants in arrears? Have any tenants prepaid? How long have the current rent levels been in effect?
- ◆ *Concessions.* Did the tenants receive any concession for signing their leases such as one month's free rent, a new 18-speed bicycle, or any other incentives that lower the effective amount of rents the tenants are paying?
- ◆ *Utilities.* Do the leases require the tenants to pay all of their own utilities? If not, for what utilities do the owners pay?
- ◆ *Yard care, snow removal, other services.* Who provides yard care, snow removal, or other necessary services such as small repairs within the rental units? Who pays for garbage and trash pickup? Do the leases obligate the sellers to provide laundry facilities, off-street parking, a club house, exercise room, child-care center, or commuter transportation?
- ◆ *Furniture and appliances.* Check the leases to determine whether the owners are required to provide tenants with furniture or appliances. If so, which ones, what quality, and who is responsible for maintenance, repairs, and replacement?
- ◆ *Duration.* What term is remaining on each of the leases? Do the tenants enjoy the option to renew? If renewed, does the lease (or rent control laws) limit the amount of rent increase that you can impose?
- ◆ *Security deposits.* How much money has the owner collected from the tenants in security deposits? Have any tenants prepaid their last month's rent? Does the seller have an inspection sheet

that shows the condition of each of the units at the time the tenants moved in? Have the tenants signed those inspection sheets?

♦ *Tenant confirmation.* Whenever feasible, ask the tenants to confirm the terms of the lease as the sellers have represented them. Make sure the sellers (or their property manager) have not entered into any side agreements with tenants that would modify or override the terms of the lease. Learn whether the sellers have orally promised any of the tenants special services, rent relief, or other dispensations.

Never forget: Even though you will own the property, the tenants were there first. For the remaining term of their leases, their leasehold rights may trump your rights of ownership.

Contingency Clauses

Typically, you will hedge your purchase offers with a financing contingency and a property inspection contingency. If you can't get financing on the terms you want, or if the condition of the property doesn't meet your standards (as written into your purchase offer), you can call the deal off. The sellers must return your earnest money to you.

> "No strings attached" offers can persuade sellers to accept a lower price.

Nevertheless, even though you *can* condition your offer on anything you want, that doesn't mean the sellers will accept it. They may tell you, "No way are we going to take our property off the market for several months while you try to put together a syndication deal. Come back and talk to us after you've raised the money." The more you hedge your offer with deal-threatening contingencies, the less likely the sellers will sign it.

On the other hand, a clean "no strings attached" offer may gain the sellers' approval even when your price or terms don't meet their hopes and expectations. Sellers prefer firm offers.

Assignment and Inspection

In many states, buyers may freely assign their real estate purchase contracts. However, assume nothing. Talk this issue over with a lawyer. As a buyer who (at least on some occasions) may want to "flip" a contract, make sure that the sellers cannot legally object. As a safeguard, you can insert an assignment clause into your offer similar to the following:

> Buyers may assign this Contract and all rights and obligations hereunder to any other person, corporation, or trustee.

The sellers may oppose such broad language and try to negotiate language such as:

> Buyer may assign this Contract only with the written approval of the sellers. Consent by the sellers shall not be arbitrarily withheld.

The sellers may want the right to approve your assignees just to satisfy themselves that the assignees possess the money and credit to complete the purchase. The sellers also may want you to remain liable for damages (or specific performance) should your assignees default. Obviously, you would like to avoid (or limit) this liability. If you assign the purchase agreement, you want out of the deal permanently.

When you do obtain the right of assignment, insert a clause that gives you access. Your potential assignees must be able to inspect and evaluate the property. Otherwise, only speculators would show any interest in buying the contract from you.

Recording in the Public Records

If you are writing up a lease option, lease purchase, contract-for-deed, or some other type of purchase offer that delays closing of title for, say, more than six months, make sure you can record the signed contract in the public records. This recording serves notice to the world that you hold rights in that property.

Without this notice, the sellers may place mortgages or other liens against the property that could jeopardize your legal interests. Also, without a public record, the sellers' judgment creditors, or perhaps the Internal Revenue Service, might stake a priority claim to the property.

You need to discuss these issues with competent legal counsel. You do not want to make payments to the sellers only to find years later that the sellers cannot deliver good title to you.

Systems and Appliances

Regardless of whether your closing will take place within 30 days or 3 years, your purchase offer should clearly spell out who is responsible in the interim for maintenance, repair, and replacement of any malfunctioning systems (heating, air conditioning, electrical, waste disposal, well water) or appliances. To the extent possible, spell out how to resolve the "repair or replace" dilemma.

> **Sellers should guarantee the condition of all appliances and HVAC systems.**

For example, if the air conditioning goes out, the sellers may want to repair it at a cost of $450 in lieu of a total system replacement that would cost $3,200. Yet, if the repairs will only keep it clanking and clunking for, at best, 6 to 12 months, you would want to insist on replacement.

Environmental Hazards

Today, with both heightened costs for environmental cleanups and extensive regulatory controls, your contract needs to address any environmental hazards that may affect the property. Lead paint, asbestos, mold, urethane formaldehyde, underground heating oil tanks, radon, and who knows what other dangers the Environmental Protection Agency may discover, can cost property owners thousands in remedial or replacement expenses.

> **When possible, make the seller responsible for environmental risks.**

Ideally, you might like your purchase offer to read as follows:

> Sellers warrant that the property complies with all current federal, state, or local environmental laws, rules, or regulations. Sellers agree to indemnify buyers for all required cleanup costs that shall be necessary to remedy environmental hazards (known or unknown) that existed during the sellers' period of ownership.

This language only suggests, but it covers two main points: (1) Is the property free of hazards? and (2) If hazards are discovered, who is going to pay for the cleanup? Under federal (and many state) laws, as owner of a property, you may have to pay for its environmental cleanup—even when you are innocent of creating the hazard.

Summing Up

Your offer will include many important terms that control the relationship between you and the sellers. Read these terms and conditions before you sign your offer. Then with counsel, add, rewrite, amend, or strike out terms and conditions as you see fit.

Once you and the sellers sign, you're both bound to the extent of the law. To protect yourself, draft your offer so that you understand your agreement—including what recourses, legal remedies, and costs apply if you or the other party pulls out of the deal without a legitimate reason.

CHAPTER 17

Craft Your Lease to Increase Profits

Most small property owners try to use their leases to strictly control tenant behavior. Although imperfect, a written lease does legally protect your interests—more so than an oral agreement. But your lease can serve another important purpose: It can help you achieve a competitive advantage over other property owners.

Achieve Competitive Advantage

Before you decide on the specific clauses within your lease, closely review the leases of other property owners. Look for ways to differentiate your rental agreement that would encourage tenants (your target market) to choose your property over competing properties. For example, to gain competitive advantage, you might

- Lower your upfront cash requirements.
- Offer a repair guarantee.
- Shorten your lease term.
- Guarantee a lease renewal without an increase in rent.
- Place tenant security and rent deposits in an investment of the tenant's choice. Accumulate interest for the tenant's benefit.

Or you might develop a "tight" lease and position your property as rentals that cater to more discriminating and responsible tenants. You could include severe lease restrictions on noise and other nuisances common to other rentals. Then, promote your property as "the quiet place to live." When you adapt leases to fit your target market, you can increase your rental revenues, achieve a higher rate of occupancy, and lower your operating expenses.

Craft Your Rental Agreement

As you think about your lease, look for ways to creatively adapt (or omit) specific clauses to better appeal to your tenants. Properly crafted, your lease will not only protect you legally, but also help you attract topflight tenants.

Names and Signatures

Most property owners require a lease to name all residents who are permitted to live in the unit—including children, if any. All adult residents should sign the lease. As a general rule, investors do not permit tenants to freely bring in additional tenants or to substitute new co-tenants for those moving out. Normally, all new tenants are required to fully satisfy the application and qualification process.

Joint and Several Liability

When you rent to co-tenants (even if husband and wife—divorces do happen), include a "joint and several liability" clause. This clause makes all tenants individually and collectively responsible for all owed rents and tenant damages.

> **Make each tenant responsible for all rents and damages.**

Without this clause, individual co-tenants often claim that they're liable only for "their part of the rent." Or, maybe you'll hear, "I didn't burn that hole in the carpet. Jones did. Collect from him." Most of the time, Jones has already moved out and disappeared. Joint and several liability gives you the legal right to collect payment from the other co-tenants who have the money.

Guests

To get around signing up their roommates, some tenants won't officially bring in new or additional *co-tenants*. When you show up and wonder who these new people are, you'll be told, "They're *guests*.""Joe's just staying here for a couple of weeks until he's called back to work at Ford." Two months later, Joe's still there and now his girlfriend, Jill, has also taken up "guest" status.

> **Be wary of "guests" who become undocumented tenants.**

Whether you might get these kinds of tenants depends on the type of people your property attracts as well as your tenant-screening standards. As a precaution, place a "guest clause" in your lease that limits the number and length of time guests can stay.

Term of Lease

Many landlords reflexively set the term of their leases at one year. In some markets, though, this tendency creates too few properties available for shorter (or longer) terms. Because short-term (especially seasonal) tenancies bring in higher rents, you might boost your income by appealing to this potentially underserved market. Another possibility: To reduce turnover and vacancy, give tenants a slight discount if they sign up for a lease term of, say, two or three years.

Property Description

Precisely describe the property rights you're giving your tenants. For example, do they receive the right to use the garage, parking spaces, attic, basement, or outdoor storage shed? Or should you rent those areas at an additional price? Can you convert any of these spaces to a higher, better, and more profitable use?

Inventory and Describe Personal Property

If you provide personal property for your tenants (washer, dryer, refrigerator, stove, microwave, blinds, drapes, curtains, furniture), inventory and describe (with photographs or serial numbers where possible) each separate item and include the list as a lease addendum. Unbelievable as it may sound, I know of vacating tenants who have taken their landlord's almost-new appliances and left in their place appliances that ranked just above junk.

Rental Amounts

Some owners set their rent levels low to reduce turnover, vacancy losses, and tenant complaints. (Complaints fall because tenants don't want to give you reason to raise their bargain rent.) Also, slightly below-market rents will give you a large pool of applicants from which you can select topflight tenants. Nevertheless, lower rents may not be necessary. With scarce and desirable features, your units will attract quality tenants even with rents that sit at the top of the market.

Late Fees and Discounts

To encourage tenants to pay their rent early, some owners offer an "early payment discount." Others levy late fees if the tenant's check comes in, say, three to five days past its due date. In recent years, more owners have adopted the "carrot" approach over the "stick" approach. These owners claim that discounts create better tenant relations, work more effectively, and are easier to enforce.

> **Rent only to people who pay on time, every time.**

Regardless of which method you choose, never, never, *never* allow tenants to get behind in their rent. Begin an eviction as soon as your lease and local ordinances permit. Tenants who can't pay today will rarely pay tomorrow.

Multiple Late Payments

What about the tenant who regularly pays on the eighth or ninth every month—even though the rent falls due on the first? As long as the late fee is included, some owners tolerate this behavior. I would not. I want my rents paid on time, every time.

To enforce the "on time, every time" requirement, I either work out a new payment date with the tenants that better matches their cash flows or I enforce the "multiple late payment" clause. This clause sets forth a "three strikes and you're out rule." When tenants won't pay on time, kick them out and keep their security deposit (if local law permits). Ditto for repeated bad checks.

Tenant "Improvements"

"If we buy the paint, is it OK for us to paint the living room?" As an owner of rental properties, you will receive requests like this from tenants. Or you may end up with tenants who don't ask. They redecorate first and wait for you to ask questions later—like, "How could you paint the living room deep purple?" or "What happened to the oak tree that was in the back yard?" To stop tenants from diminishing the value of your property with their weird "improvements," require them to obtain your written permission before they paint, wallpaper, redecorate, renovate, repanel, remove, or in any other way modify your property.

> **No tenant improvements without permission.**

Owner Access

Under the laws of most states, you may not enter your tenants' home (except for emergencies) without their permission. If you do want access to make inspections and repairs, take care of damages (like an overflowing toilet), show the unit to prospective tenants (or buyers), or for any other reason, include a reasonable and nonintrusive "owner access" clause in your leases.

Quiet Enjoyment

Do you want to guarantee your tenants that they will not suffer from noise and disturbances created by other tenants? Then tightly restrict their neighbor-disturbing partying, fighting, arguing, and loud lovemaking. Allow them to play their television, radio, and stereo only at low volumes. You could place a general clause in your lease such as:

> Residents agree not to create, generate, broadcast, or otherwise cause sounds or disturbances to emanate from them-

selves, their guests, or their residences into the residences of others. All residents agree to supremely respect and promote the quiet enjoyment of the building by all other residents.

Beware of buying buildings with those notorious "paper-thin" walls. Unless you can solve this problem (without spending much money) your tenants will constantly complain to you.

Noxious Odors

As with noise and disturbances, noxious odors wafting throughout a building can stir up tenant dissatisfaction and complaints. Leading sources of noxious odors include smoking, cooking (especially some types of ethnic foods), and heavy users of perfumes. If any of these (or other types of noxious odors) seem like they could present a problem, then your lease should include a clause that limits or excludes the causes of these odors.

> **Noise and noxious odors drive away good tenants.**

Tenant Insurance

Your property owners' insurance policy will not cover the personal property of your tenants, so you may want to require them to buy a tenants' insurance policy. Many investors have learned through experience that when uninsured tenants suffer damage to their property (through fire or other peril), they sue the owner for negligence. Even if the building burns after being hit by lightning, the tenants (or their lawyers) will claim that you should have installed a better lightning rod.

> **Ask your tenants to buy insurance to cover their own possessions.**

Sublet and Assignment

When tenants plan to be away from their home for an extended period (summer in Europe), they may want to *sublet* their unit. When tenants plan to relocate permanently (job change, bought a house), they may want to *assign* their lease to someone else. To address this issue, you can adopt one of these positions:

1. No right to sublet or assign.
2. Right to sublet or assign with owner's written permission. Original tenants and new tenants both assume liability for rent payments and damages.
3. Right to sublet or assign with owner's written permission. Original tenants released from any liability for future rent payments or damages. Owner must look exclusively to new tenants for financial performance.
4. Unlimited right to sublet or assign. Original tenants remain liable.

Without a lease restriction, some courts rule that tenants may freely assign or sublet their units. You don't want that outcome. So to protect yourself, include a sublet and assignment clause in your lease.

Pets

Too many property owners prohibit pets. In my experience, responsible tenants care for their pets in a responsible manner. Irresponsible people treat their pets irresponsibly. If you select responsible people, you usually can eliminate your "pet problems" without excluding all pets. By accepting responsible people with well-behaved pets, you can boost profits. Often, you can charge a "pet premium" that requires higher rents and a higher security deposit.

If you do accept pets, draft a pet rules addendum and attach it to your lease. Please consider the needs of the pet. I have seen pet rules that require large dogs to be kept permanently tethered in the back yard on an eight-foot chain. Other inhumane rules require that a dog must be permanently kept in a basement or on a back porch. If you feel so little for the lives of animals, totally exclude them from your rental properties. Moreover, any pet owner who accepts such cruel restrictions does not qualify (in my opinion) as a responsible person or a responsible pet owner.

> **Develop your rules about pets to meet the needs of tenants and the pets.**

Security Deposits

Collect a security deposit from all of your tenants and cover these issues in your lease:

1. Amount of the deposit
2. When payable
3. Rate of interest, if any
4. Under what conditions tenants will forfeit all or part of their deposit
5. When the deposit will be refunded if tenants satisfy all terms of the lease

Amount and When Payable   In terms of amount, I favor high security deposits plus first and last month's rent—*always* payable in advance. (This lesson I learned the hard way.) You undoubtedly will get prospects who want to pay their deposit piecemeal over one to three months. Yield to this request and you invite trouble. (Ditto for postdated checks.)

Interest   Some local and state laws require owners to pay at least some minimum rate of interest to their tenants. If this law applies in your area, make sure your tenants know they'll be receiving interest. In fact, I recommend paying interest to tenants even if the law doesn't require it. Today, many tenants get upset if you insist on a deposit (especially a large one), yet refuse to pass along its earnings to them.

Forfeiture   At the time tenants first sign their lease, make sure they understand that their security deposit does not limit their liability for rent or damages. In addition, clearly explain to the tenants the level of care (cleanliness, damages) they must meet to get their full security deposit returned to them. Also, explain how you will calculate any amounts that you might have to subtract from their deposits (or under what conditions you will try to collect additional money from them.) Security deposits have become a large source of dispute between owners and tenants. Take special care to explain your deposit policies (and make sure you always comply with the law).

Deposit Return   As a courtesy to your tenants, return their deposits with interest as soon as you know the correct amount. If possible, the

Return deposits promptly.

best time is at the end of the final walkthrough. You pay. The tenants accept. You shake hands with them and wish them well in their new home.

Yard Care

When you rent out a house or duplex, you probably will want the tenants to care for the yard. But don't just say, "tenants are responsible for yard care." I once made this mistake with otherwise excellent tenants. To these tenants, "yard care" meant cutting the grass. To me it meant watering the lawn when needed, tending the flowers and shrubs, and trimming the hedges to maintain them at their existing height of four feet.

Because the house was located in Florida and I was living in the San Francisco Bay Area, my visits to the property were not frequent. When after two years I did return, the hedges had grown wildly to a height of seven or eight feet, many flowers and shrubs were dead, and the lawn had scattered brown spots.

Learn from my mistake. If you want your tenants to care for the yard, spell out exactly what care and condition you want them to maintain.

Parking, Number, and Type of Vehicles

Some tenants believe that if they can't find parking in a driveway or on the street, it's OK to park in the front yard. Or they may persist in blocking their neighbors' driveways. Or they leave unsightly junk (inoperable) cars to accumulate around the property. RVs, boats, and trailers also can create aesthetic and parking problems.

Don't let tenant cars create parking problems.

To head off this kind of trouble, place a "parking clause" in your leases. List the number and types of permitted vehicles. Then designate the *only* places where they may be parked properly. You also may want to restrict the backyard (or frontyard) mechanic who disassembles his car and leaves the parts scattered about for days, weeks, or even months.

Repairs

Increasingly, owners of rental properties are shifting at least some costs of repair onto their tenants. Stopped-up toilets and broken garbage disposals seldom occur without tenant abuse. As a minimum, you may want to charge your tenants, say, a $50 repair fee for each time a repair becomes necessary. Some owners even make tenants fully responsible for certain types of repairs—unless the service provider establishes that the tenants were not to blame. Overall, your repair policy should encourage your tenants to care for the property as well as reduce your out-of-pocket costs for unscheduled maintenance and replacement.

Appliances   Some owners tell their tenants that they may use the appliances currently in the property, but that the owner will not pay for repairs or replacement if the appliances fail to work right. If the tenants don't agree to accept the appliances on those terms, the owner then removes them and the tenants provide and maintain their own appliances.

Which Approach Is Best?   As with all lease clauses, no one approach to repairs works best in all situations. It depends on the types of tenants and properties you're dealing with. Undoubtedly, some people will show little care for your property. Yet at the same time, they expect you to jump into action whenever their abuse or neglect creates a problem. These are the people at whom you want to aim your tenant repair clauses. (Of course, ideally you want to avoid these kinds of tenants.)

> **At best, your repair policy encourages care and reduces costs.**

Neat and Clean

> **Roaches do not like to live in clean apartments and houses.**

Regardless of whether you are renting out houses or apartments, your lease should set standards of neatness and cleanliness. Proper disposal of trash and garbage are bare minimums. When tenant neglect invites roaches, ants, or fleas into the property, the tenant should pay the exterminator—not you.

Other do's and don'ts may address unwashed dishes; disposal of used motor oil, broken furniture, or appliances; bicycle storage; materials awaiting pickup for recycling; and vehicles that drip motor oil or transmission fluid.

Rules and Regulations

Especially for apartment buildings—or for rental units in co-ops or condominium projects—prepare a list of rules and regulations that tenants are expected to follow. Make sure your lease incorporates all of these rules (usually by addendum). Also, note within your lease that you (or the homeowners' association) reserve the right to reasonably amend or modify the listed rules.

Wear and Tear

So-called standard leases often state that your tenants are responsible for all damages *except* normal wear and tear. I would never use such a clause. It invites tenant neglect and abuse. Many tenants believe that soiled carpets, cracked plaster, broken screens, and numerous other damages reflect nothing more than "normal wear and tear."

> **Avoid a "wear and tear" clause.**

I disagree. If a tenant properly cares for a property, it will not suffer any noticeable wear and tear during a tenancy of one year or less. For such short-term periods of residence, tenants should leave the property in the same condition in which they accepted it. Eliminating the "wear and tear" clause will save you money and argument.

Lawful Use of Premises

As a matter of good business practice, and as a good-neighbor policy, your lease should require tenants to abide by all applicable laws, ordinances, and regulations. This clause may help you to remedy undesirable behavior that you didn't think to put in your lease. Especially enforce a zero-tolerance rule against illegal drugs or other offenses that can result in asset forfeiture.

Notice

To help reduce rent loss during turnover, require tenants to give you advance notice of the exact date they plan to move. Then you can begin to publicize the unit's upcoming availability. Ideally, you'll find a new tenant who will move in within a day or two after the previous tenants have moved out.

Most owners require 30 days' *written* notice. But if you're operating in a weak or seasonal rental market, you might ask for 45 or 60 days' notice. Or if you expect immediate demand for your rental property, you could reduce your advance notice to, say, 15 days. In other words, tie your written notice requirement to the length of time you believe necessary to locate a new, strongly qualified tenant.

Nonwaivers

For reasons of courtesy or practicality, you may, on occasion, permit tenants to temporarily breach a lease clause or house rule. To prevent tenants from stretching this courtesy beyond your intent, your lease can include a "nonwaiver clause." In this clause, you make clear that your kindness today in no way waives your right to enforce the letter of the lease tomorrow.

> **Don't let exceptions become the rule.**

Breach of Lease (or House Rules)

In a breach-of-lease clause, you reinforce your right to terminate the lease of tenants who breach *any* lease requirement or house rule. Without this clause, tenants may sometimes believe that if you accept the rent, you waive your enforcement of other tenant violations. Together, the nonwaiver and breach-of-lease clauses impress on tenants their obligation to comply 100 percent—or suffer the consequences of eviction.

No Representations (Full Agreement)

On occasion tenants may try to get out of their lease obligations by claiming you misled them with false promises. They could claim that you

> **Don't permit your tenant to accuse you of making false promises.**

got them to sign their lease by promising to completely paint and recarpet their unit. You know the tenants are lying, but a judge may not. To the judge, it's your word against theirs.

To prevent this charade, include a clause stating that the lease and its addendums covers the full extent of the rental agreement. This clause could also state that the tenants have not relied on any oral or written representations or promises that are not explicitly written into the lease.

Arbitration or Mediation

In many cities, the legal process is too slow, expensive, complex, and cumbersome to effect timely and affordable justice. As a result, some property owners write an arbitration (or mediation) clause in their leases. This clause steers unresolved owner-tenant disputes away from the courthouse and into a more informal hearing.

Before you adopt such a clause for your leases, investigate how well arbitration (mediation) works in your area. Learn whether your local courts show any noticeable bias for or against property owners. Arbitration and mediation tend to work best for investors faced with courts that generally side with tenants. (Unfortunately, some pro-tenant judges—at the urging of lawyers who fear a loss of business—refuse to enforce lease arbitration clauses.)

Attorney Fees (Who Pays?)

"Standard" preprinted leases often include an "attorney fees" clause that strongly favors property owners. In cases where you prevail in court, this clause requires losing tenants to pay your "reasonable" attorney and court costs. In contrast, when your tenants prevail, the clause (through its silence) leaves attorney fees and costs on the shoulders of each party who incurred them.

Those courts that still honor the principle that "judges shall not rewrite lawful contracts" will generally enforce this one-sided attorney fees clause. These courts reason that any tenant who wanted to modify

> **Some judges won't enforce a landlord's one-sided attorney fees clause.**

or eliminate this clause was free to negotiate the point prior to signing the lease.

On the other hand, so-called activist judges may use this clause to declare you liable for a winning tenant's attorney fees and costs. These judges hold that "what's good for the goose is good for the gander." These judges often lean toward the left-wing mindset of "powerful greedy landlords" versus "powerless victimized tenants." They see it as their duty to upset this supposed imbalance of power by placing their thumb on the scales of justice in favor of tenants.

So, do not place any attorney fees clause in your leases until you explore its practical and legal implications in your locale. Learn from the experiences of other real estate investors.

Written Notice to Remedy

A "written notice to remedy" requires an owner (or tenant) to give written notice prior to taking legal action to enforce a lease provision that the tenant (or owner) is currently breaching. From your perspective, written notice can help you in two ways: (1) When you wish to evict a tenant for cause, previous written notices lay a paper trail that supports your case; and (2) if in defense of an eviction (or suit for rent) a tenant falsely claims, "We didn't have any heat for most of January," you can force the tenants to prove that they sent you written notice of this problem. Because their claim lacks truth, their defense fails.

Landlording: Pros and Cons

From the preceding collection of lease clauses, you might say, "Forget it! Landlording involves too many potential headaches and risks." But imagine reading a list of laws, regulations, accidents, breakdowns, repairs, lawsuits, hassles, and expenses that you face when driving a car. By focusing only on the risks of driving, you might put your car in a garage and leave it there permanently.

> **Only possibilities to prevent, not probabilities to fear.**

When I point out potential sources of trouble, I don't mean to scare you away from owning income properties; rather, I want to present possibilities for your concern. It is the naive and unknowing investors who most often experience landlording difficulties.

Think of these concerns as possibilities to prepare for and guard against, not as probabilities certain to make your life a constant source of aggravation. They won't—unless you let them. Indeed, to own a smooth, trouble-free investment, simply follow the 12 secrets of successful landlording.

CHAPTER 18

The 12 Secrets of
Successful Landlording

You've undoubtedly heard the horror stories about managing rental properties. According to popular lore—mostly propagated by people who have never owned properties—managing rentals will require you to answer 2:00 A.M. phone calls from irate tenants, fix leaky plumbing on Saturday mornings, and chase after deadbeats.

You may have even seen the movie *Pacific Heights*. In that rental-property horror film, Michael Keaton plays a demented tenant who viciously torments his landlords (a naive young couple played by Melanie Griffith and Matthew Modine). In the end, the couple triumphs, but Keaton's character puts them through so much grief that they begin to question their own sanity (see Box 18.1).

The Good News

The good news is that neither popular lore nor *Pacific Heights* paints an accurate picture of landlording—which I prefer to redefine as "providing homes for good people." Think of any commonplace activity from jogging to taking a flight on an airline. At times, bad things do happen. But the benefits far outweigh the risks. The same is true of landlording.

1. They failed to obtain a prepurchase property inspection.
2. They failed to reasonably anticipate repair and renovation expenses.
3. They stretched so far to buy that they exhausted all of their cash and credit.
4. They believed their tenant's fish story.
5. They permitted their tenant to bring in an unapproved "guest."
6. They failed to get the cash before their tenant took possession of their rental unit.
7. They did not understand San Francisco's onerous tenants' rights laws.
8. They relied on the legal system to promote justice.
9. They failed to immediately consult a lawyer when their legal situation went awry.
10. They used (illegal) self-help tactics to encourage the tenant to move.

The good news: Did these beginning investors do anything right? Absolutely—they bought real estate. Had they continued to own that Pacific Heights property, they could sell it today for a price $2 million higher than what they paid for it in 1991 (when the movie was filmed).

Box 18.1 The *Pacific Heights* Investors Violated Almost Every Rule of Successful Landlording

> **Your management system can give you wealth without worry.**

Yet even if the horror stories did reflect everyday experience, the great wealth-building power of properties would more than compensate you for the aggravation.

Fortunately, owning rentals need not cause you hassles and headaches. To gain the benefits of property ownership without work and worry, you can either hire a property manager or develop a first-class system of self-management.

Hired Management versus Self-Management

More than likely, you think the task of property management includes cleaning the rental unit, advertising vacancies, showing vacancies to prospects, collecting rents, handling yard work, making repairs, and numerous other chores.

While it's true that someone does need to keep the routine rental operations running smoothly, that someone does not need to be you.

Employ a Caretaker or Property Management Company

You can delegate to either a caretaker or a property management company whatever duties you choose to avoid. As a true *manager* you're responsible for supervising the work of others, not doing everything yourself. As the leadership consultant, Phil Van Hooser, says, "A good manager is not someone who can do the work of 10 people. It's someone who can get 10 people to work."

A good manager manages.

The best owner-manager is the person who knows what needs to be done and then directs the performance of others. When delegating everyday activities, I prefer to work with caretakers.

What Is a Caretaker? A property caretaker looks after as many details of a rental property's operations as you wish to delegate. My caretakers have done everything from renting apartments to supervising tradespeople to dealing with routine maintenance.

Yet, even though my caretakers typically look after details, I handle market strategy, major improvements, and all policies and procedures. In other words, I *manage* my properties, but rarely get involved in the day-to-day issues.

Over the years, I have found two types of caretakers work best:

A qualified tenant. A well-qualified tenant who knows basic property maintenance and can deal effectively with people makes a good caretaker. Generally, I provide my caretakers free (or partial) rent plus an hourly fee for special jobs (repairs, improvements) that fall outside their normal scope of their responsibilities. (No firm rules apply here because I vary the responsibilities according to the competencies and time commitment of each specific caretaker that I have hired.)

A jack-of-all-trades. Another type of caretaker that I prefer is the retired or semiretired jack-of-all-trades. In my experience, older people tend to show a strong work ethic and good sense of personal responsibility. They also tend to know more about how to remedy specific repair problems.

Again, the scope of our work agreement determines the amount of base pay. On average, I've found that $12 to $16 an hour will get me a good person for the job. You might pay more or less. If you choose the caretaker approach to handling everyday operations, you'll just have to test the waters.

(I might add that I have never advertised for "help wanted." To find good candidates, I depend on referrals and informal job discussions, not formal applications for employment.)

Property Management Companies If you want to passively own your investments, you can hire a property management company. Typically, these companies manage hundreds of rental units for dozens of different property owners and offer four benefits:

- ◆ They talk with hundreds of tenants each month and (if they choose to) can develop excellent knowledge of the rental property market.
- ◆ Because of their broad experience, they may have developed well-tested policies and procedures that cover everything from repairs to tenant selection to rent collection to fair housing compliance.
- ◆ They may be the first to know when one of their clients plans to sell a property and can give you heads-up notice.
- ◆ By managing all rental activities, your management company can minimize the time and effort you devote to your properties.

For some passive investors, property management firms offer a needed and desired service. However, using these services also may impose two severe drawbacks:

- ◆ No company that manages multiple rental units for multiple owners will design a truly optimal rental strategy for your property. Property management firms develop policies and procedures to advance their own profits and economies of scale. Your investments won't receive special treatment.

◆ As a rule, property management firms not only charge a monthly fee (6 to 10 percent of all rent collections), but may also assess extra fees for tasks such as renting a vacant apartment (one-half month's rent, for example), carrying out an eviction, and contracting for repairs or improvements. In total, these costs can easily turn a property with positive cash flow into a cash drain.

Investors who rely on property management firms seldom come close to maximizing their profits. They can, though, take life easy.

Self-Management

As a beginning investor, I encourage you to actually self-manage your properties. When you build up your portfolio of rentals, you can then gradually turn over more and more of the day-to-day activities. Overall, self-management offers you these advantages:

◆ *You will save money.* You will eliminate the costs that you would otherwise pay to a management company, and by self-contracting your own repair work (or by doing it yourself) you will spend less.

◆ *Your vacant units will rent faster.* Whenever I see a long-term vacancy, 80 percent of the time that property is being "professionally" managed. Management firms seldom work diligently to fill vacancies. They're content to put up a sign, maybe run an ad, and merely wait for a rental prospect to show up. (As you will soon see, you can do much better than that.)

◆ *You will learn firsthand how to manage a property.* This knowledge will serve you well even if at some point you choose to delegate some or all of this work. Although I do not now get involved in the day-to-day work of property operations, the knowledge and experience I gained from my early do-it-myself years is still paying off. If you've never done it yourself, how will you be able to design (or critique) the rental policies and procedures of your property manager?

◆ *You will learn about the market.* When you personally talk with prospective renters, look at competing properties, and monitor vacancies and rent levels, you will build a valuable base of market information. With that market knowledge, you can choose the most profitable target market of tenants and then adapt your property, leases, and rental rates to display a competitive advantage.

For beginning investors, the benefits of self-management stand so far above your alternatives that even Robert Griswald, author of *Property Management for Dummies* (and owner of a large property management firm), advises,

> If you have the right traits for managing property, and if you have the time and live in the vicinity of your property(ies), you should definitely do it yourself. (New York: John Wiley & Sons, 2002, p. 14)

No matter which of these management choices you decide to adopt, you can still profit by learning the 12 secrets of successful landlording (see Box 18.2).

1.	Before You Buy, Verify, Verify, Verify
2.	Prepare the Property for Rental
3.	Craft a Winning Value Proposition
4.	Attract Topflight Tenants
5.	Create a Flawless Move-In
6.	Retain Topflight Residents
7.	When the Market Supports It, Raise Rents
8.	Anticipate and Prepare for Special Problems
9.	Maintain the Property
10.	Process Move-Outs Smoothly
11.	Persistently Find Ways to Increase Your Cash Flow
12.	Keep Trading Up

Box 18.2   The 12 Secrets of Successful Landlording

Before You Buy, Verify, Verify, Verify

Good management begins before you actually close on your first invest-ment. You want to make sure you fully understand the nature of the beast you are buying. You want no voracious alligators that will chew up your available cash and credit within the first few months of ownership.
At a minimum your prepurchase due diligence should include:

Property Inspection

Obtain a professional report on the condition of the property as well as reliable cost estimates for repairs and improvements.

People Inspection

Talk with the property owner's current (and past, if possible) tenants, neighbors, contractors, repair people, and suppliers. Search for inside in-formation that might signal potential problems (e.g., neighborhood noise or crime, tenant dissatisfaction, persistent trouble with plumbing, wiring, or roof leaks).

List of Personal Property

Many property sales include some appliances, window coverings, stor-age sheds, and other personal property. Secure an itemized list of these items. Verify the list with current tenants.

Tenant Rent Roll and Files

You want the names, telephone numbers, and leases for all residents of the property.

Verify Security Deposits

At closing, the seller should turn over all security deposits to you. Make sure you receive an accurate accounting. Verify the amounts with tenants. Remember, you are the person who will return these deposits when the tenants move out.

Licenses, Permits, Zoning, Building Regulations, Occupancy Codes

Because all kinds of laws apply to rental properties, find out whether the property currently complies with these laws (or, if not, what you will need to do to bring it into compliance).

Copies of Warranties and Service Contracts

If the roof, water heaters, appliances, HVAC, or other components of the property are guaranteed in some way, get copies of the warranties or service agreements (e.g., pest control and damage repair). Notify the service providers and pay transfer fees.

Arrange for Insurance Coverage

In some areas of the country, property insurance rates have shot up and some coverages have become more difficult to obtain (e.g., mold, hurricane, earthquake). Before you commit to closing, go over rates and coverages in detail with an experienced insurance pro (not an office clerk).

Prepare the Property for Rental

If tenants now live in the property you're buying, you will need to comply with their existing rental agreements until the terms of their leases end. Nevertheless, to plan for imminent vacancies (and perhaps a market repositioning of the property), you will need to get the property ready in the following ways:

Choose a Segment of Tenants

Remember, generic properties attract average tenants who pay so-called market rents. Targeted properties attract topflight tenants and yield more profits (that result from some combination of higher rents, lower operating expenses, lower turnover, and quicker rent up). So survey the market and decide the segment of tenants (Section 8, college students, seniors, families, young professionals, empty nesters, other) you wish to appeal to.

You are free to develop a market strategy, but you can't turn away any member of a protected class for reasons related to any protected characteristics such as race, religion, ethnicity, children, and so forth.

Clean and Paint

Regardless of which market segment you plan to appeal to, clean, paint, and sharpen the appearance of the property. Both the interior and exterior of the property should appear well kept and attractive. Never try to rent out a unit that fails the white glove test. Unless you're enjoying a very low vacancy rental market, dirty units will only attract those tenants to whom no sane owner would wish to rent.

> **Apply the white-glove test.**

Everything Must Work

Verify that the appliances, electrical outlets, and HVAC operate as they should. All windows should open and close easily. Repair or replace broken locks, doors, windows, and screens. Remedy any condition of the property that signals a state of disrepair.

Craft a Winning Value Proposition

When tenants compare your rental unit to the units offered by other property owners, they don't just look at its cleanliness and state of repair. They also look for a variety of other items that can lift a property above its competitors. They want a property that offers them the best total value proposition. For example, your tenants might prefer any of the following:

Owner Demeanor

Do you (or your rental agent) come across as a pleasant person? To achieve this demeanor, play down the authoritarian "do's and don'ts." Play up your "please the customer" attitude.

Pets, Furniture, Appliances

Can you better appeal to your target market if you accept pets or provide the units with furnishings, furniture, window blinds, or appliances?

Hot-Button Features

What desirable features can you provide that other properties typically lack? Views, storage, parking, study area, open floor plan, roommate-friendly floor plan, soundproof walls, great kitchens and bathrooms? Learn your tenants' hot buttons. Then offer those benefits that will wow your prospects.

Lease Terms and Conditions

Can you craft your lease to suit tenant preferences (while still offering you legal protection against defaults)? What lease period will seem most attractive—weekly, month-to-month, annual, longer? How will you handle repairs?

Security Deposits

Many cash-strapped tenants would prefer lower deposits. Can you figure out a way to reduce the security deposit without increasing your risks (cosignor, lien against tenant's car, phased payment, automatic transfer of funds)? On the other hand, some tenants are quite willing to pay a high security deposit in exchange for a top-quality property and perhaps a favorably priced unit.

Rental Rate

Learn the features, lease terms, and rent levels of competing properties. Learn tenant likes and dislikes. Then design and price your units to give your target market their best value—yet still provide you a good profit.

Attract Topflight Tenants

This principle of superior management requires you to perform two tasks. First, market the property effectively, and second, strictly screen your rental applicants.

Get the Word Out

Most owners seldom think beyond hanging out a "for rent" sign and running a classified ad. Savvy landlords try to think of inexpensive ways to quickly and directly reach their target audience. These techniques might include networking, referrals from current or past tenants, info flyers, brochures, bird dogs, employer bulletin boards, newsletters, or a college housing office.

> **Reduce ad costs through referrals and word of mouth.**

First, ask yourself, where do the types of tenants I would like to attract currently live, work, shop, play, worship, or go to school? Once you've thought closely about where your desired tenant might be reached, getting the word out about your great homes for rent will be easy.

What to Say

Your sales message should go way beyond the commonplace listing of basic features. It should include a benefit headline followed by the hot-button features that will pique the attention, desire, and action of your target market (see Box 18.3).

Property manager and author, Robert Griswald, tells about one of the lessons he learned about marketing rentals:

I once had a rental property located near a major university. The property had several vacancies in the 2-bedroom/1-bath units. Because I was wary of renting to large numbers of undergraduate students, my marketing plan was to attract university faculty or graduate students who I thought would have a roommate and be perfect for the 2-bedroom unit. Although many prospective tenants looked at the units, our actual rentals were very slow and our 2-bedroom vacancies remained unacceptable. Clearly, I was trying to define and force the rental market and prospective renters to adapt to my perception of their needs.

When it became obvious that my rental efforts were not having much success, I began to carefully review the comments of prospective tenants and actually listen to their needs. What I found was that there was a strong market for faculty and graduate students, but that they preferred to live alone. The WIFM (what's in it for me) from the perspective of the targeted faculty and graduate students was the desire for a quiet place to work or study without roommates. With this new perspective on the needs of our prospective tenants, I quickly realized that I could market these very same 2-bedroom/1-bath units to this new target market.

Armed with this knowledge, I revised my marketing efforts and changed my advertising in the college newspaper to read, "1 bedroom plus den." This change led to an increased interest in the property as well as a greater occupancy percentage. Just by changing the way the units were advertised, I found that I was able to reach my original target market of faculty and graduate students who wanted to live off campus.

Remember: Look at your rental property from the perspective of the most likely tenants. Then promote and accentuate the features of your rental property that will be of greatest interest to the market.

Reprinted with permission from Robert Griswald, *Property Management for Dummies* (New York: John Wiley & Sons, 2001), p. 70.

Box 18.3   Focus Your Ad on the Benefits Your Tenants Want

Don't Show the Property, Sell It

Do not assume that your prospective tenants will immediately recognize all of the competitive advantages your property offers. Just as with your printed sales message, your conversations with tenants should emphasize features and benefits. Explain why your units (and your lease) offer prospects their best value.

Thoroughly Screen All Tenants

Before any tenant moves into one of your units, verify that person's credit score, credit record, rental history, current and past employment, current and past residences, and personal photo identification. To get credit information, you can either ask the prospective tenants to run their own report at myfico.com and provide a copy to you, or you can subscribe to this service as provided by a local credit bureau. You can obtain the other necessary data from the rental application form.

Payment of Rent and Security Deposit

Never permit anyone to move into your units without allowing enough time for their rent and security deposit checks to clear. If you can't get the checks cleared prior to move-in, ask the tenants to pay you with a cashier's check drawn on a local bank.

Never Accept Fish Stories

As a property owner, you may hear your share of fish stories as to why the tenant cannot comply with your request for background information and verified payment of funds. Nine times out of ten, you want that fishy tenant to get away. (Review Box 18.1. In the *Pacific Heights* movie, Michael Keaton always reeled off some fish story as to why he could not—or did not—comply with the landlord's request for references or payment.)

> **Let your fishy tenants get away.**

Do not let your sympathy (or need for money) lead you into accepting a tenant who begins out with excuses that beg forbearance. If you do, I guarantee that those initial excuses won't be the last ones you hear from that tenant.

Learn and Comply with All Fair Housing Laws

As an owner of rental properties, your advertising and tenant selection process is governed by federal, state, and local law. To learn these rules and regulations, stop by your community's fair housing agency. Talk with the staff and pick up their brochures. Also, learn how the Americans with Disabilities Act (ADA) might govern your rental policies and property features (companion animal, parking, entryway access, etc.).

Maintain a Waiting List

If you strategically manage your properties, you will never want for tenants. Your advertising or word-of-mouth referrals will turn up more willing prospects than you can handle at any one time. Keep these surplus prospects on your radar screen. Create and maintain a waiting list. With an active waiting list, your vacancies will fall to nearly zero.

Create a Flawless Move-In

Aim your move-in policies and procedures toward satisfying these goals:

- Establish cordial relations that will smooth the tension that frequently characterizes a landlord-tenant relationship.
- Make sure you and your tenants see eye to eye on all rules that will govern tenant conduct, property upkeep, and unit occupancy (e.g., parking, guests, alterations, cleanliness, tenant insurance, pets, names and number of residents).
- Put the property in make-ready condition.

Cordial Relations

As noted, your property make-ready should confirm the cleanliness of the unit as well as the working condition of all operable components of

> **Provide your new tenants a "welcome home" gift.**

the unit. Make sure the tenants will enjoy their move-in week without need of complaint. As a special touch, give your new tenants a welcome basket of flowers, fruits, beverages, and snacks. If the tenants are new to the neighborhood, provide them a map and a list of nearby shops, stores, schools, services, and restaurants.

Rules and Regulations

Do not simply hand a list of house rules to your tenants. Go through each item. Explain why you believe the rule is important and how it contributes to tenant welfare, property appearance, or upkeep. Ask the tenant to sign a copy of the rules and put it in your files with the lease, rental application, and background reports.

Remind the tenant in a friendly way that the rental agreement incorporates the rules. A breach of the rules means a breach of the lease and thus triggers whatever remedies your lease provides.

Verify Move-in Condition

At the time your tenants move into the property, walk through with them. If you have performed your make-ready, you should find no broken windows, soiled carpets, or dirty appliances. Nevertheless, if you do find any damages that remain unrepaired, note them on your move-in checklist. Once the tenants are satisfied that they have discovered (and you have listed) every flaw, ask the tenants to sign the list to certify the move-in condition of the property.

> **On move-in day, capture a video record of your unit's condition.**

You might also videotape the unit on move-in day. If a dispute should arise later, a picture may be worth more than a thousand words.

Retain Topflight Residents

Now that you've filled your rental units with good tenants, what can you do to retain them as long as possible? Fortunately, you can achieve that goal pretty easily.

Keep Tenants Informed

Don't let tenants come home to find a backhoe noisily digging up the parking lot or a pest control man spraying in their apartment. Notify and explain to tenants when anything out of the ordinary is about to happen on or within the property. Tenants don't like it when you thoughtlessly disrupt their lives or invade their privacy.

Develop a Plan of Preventive Maintenance

Emergency repairs not only cost you big dollars, they upset residents. No tenant likes a furnace that won't throw out heat, a roof that leaks, or a

> **Anticipate and prevent repair problems.**

sink that won't quickly drain. You can eliminate most of these types of problems by executing a program of preventive maintenance. Don't wait for things to go wrong and then react. Instead, anticipate what can go wrong and then prevent (or at least minimize the probabilities).

Expect the Unexpected

Even the best preventive maintenance programs won't prevent every appliance malfunction or HVAC breakdown. So set up a procedure for dealing with these types of problems before they occur.

Make arrangements with reliable and trustworthy service providers. Give their telephone numbers to your tenants with instructions of when and under what conditions they should call.

For ordinary, non-emergency repairs, give your tenants a telephone number that's hooked up to your voice message machine. When necessary, ask your tenants to call and state their problem. Then acknowledge their request within 24 hours. If warranted, repair within 72 hours (less is even better). Nonresponsive landlords rank as one of the top three tenant complaints. Make repairs courteously and quickly and your tenants will sing your praises to their friends (and your future residents).

Enforce House Rules Strictly and Fairly

Topflight residents want you to enforce house rules consistently and without favor (or prejudice) among all tenants. Don't let those few bad apples spoil the entire barrel. Whether the rules pertain to parking, noise, unauthorized residents (long-term "guests"), or mishandling of trash and garbage, you must not let violators go unnoticed (and unpunished).

If you do, you will soon find that your good residents will move out and you will only be able to replace them with lower-quality residents. Draft rules for the benefit of all. Then enforce them against everyone equally.

When the Market Supports It, Raise Rents

Since I've already gone over the topic of rent collections and late fees in Chapter 17, I won't repeat that discussion here. However, there's still the topic of how you should handle rent increases.

Whenever you raise rents, you run the risk of losing a good tenant. Nevertheless, low rents depress your cash flows and diminish the value of your property. When you know the market will support higher rents (i.e., when you know topflight tenants are willing to pay you more than you're currently charging), go for it. Raise the rents.

Verify Market Support

Remember, I said initiate a rent increase *if* the market will support it. Some owners try to increase their rents even when the rental market softens and numerous large-scale complexes are offering move-in concessions such as two months' free rent or an all-expense-paid trip to Hawaii. In the face of strong competition, unjustifiable attempts to increase rents merely prolong vacancy periods, promote unit turnover, and invite tenant complaints.

Soften the Blow with Communication

When you do raise rents, provide evidence to justify the increases. Give your tenants the results of your market survey of competing properties. Let them know you've registered 16 names on your waiting list. Show them how your property taxes, property insurance, and maintenance expenses climbed 12 percent this past year.

When possible, phase in your rent increases frequently and gradually. A 10 percent increase all at one time will chase out more tenants than, say, a 4 percent increase levied each 6 months over a period of 18 months.

Do Something in Return

You can also dampen tenant grumbling and nonrenewals if you do something for them in return for that rent increase. How about adding covered parking, installing new carpets or appliances, installing ceiling fans, or putting in a new security system? Naturally, you don't want to wipe out the money you will gain from the rent increase. But you will create better tenant relations if you at least enhance the desirability of the property in some way the tenants will appreciate.

Anticipate and Prepare for Special Problems

On rare occasions, even the best selected residents may run into difficulty. Divorce, accident, ill health, unemployment, and bankruptcy represent several of the more common problems that tenants may encounter. If any of these setbacks affect your tenants' ability to pay their rent, what do you do?

Show Understanding and Forbearance? Be Careful

In my early years as a landlord, I was a soft touch for sob stories—real and fictional. Several times, with previously good-paying tenants, I offered forbearance. In every case, the tenants eventually moved out and never paid the money they owed me.

That's why my experience warns me to collect the rent every time, on time. Otherwise, you should request (or legally compel) the tenants to move. If your tenants need financial assistance, refer them to a charity or social services agency. Forbearance seldom pays off with a win-win solution.

(This same advice holds for tenants who persistently break the rules. If the rule is wrong, change it. If it serves a valid purpose, enforce it. Forbearance forecasts regret.)

Negotiate a Voluntary Move-Out

When your problem tenant pleads or threatens, but doesn't move out, you might try to negotiate a voluntary settlement rather than get involved with the costly, frustrating, and often ineffective court system.

To entice the tenants to leave, you'll generally have to forgive some of the monies they owe you. In some instances (although I never have done this), owners will even agree to pay the tenant to move. No doubt, in some circumstances, it's better to get rid of a tenant and accept a small loss than to drag out a bitter conflict and possibly lose thousands in rent collections and attorney fees.

If You Must Evict, Do It Lawfully

States and cities set the legal procedure that property owners must follow to terminate a lease and evict a tenant. This procedure normally covers (1) lawful grounds, (2) written notice, (3) time to cure or remedy the breach, (4) the time period before a hearing (or trial), (5) allowable tenant defenses, and (6) the number of days the tenants have to move after the judge issues the order to kick them out.

Learn this legal procedure as it applies in your area. Then follow it precisely. Failure to dot all of your i's and cross all of your t's can get your case thrown out. You must then go back and start the process again. Never threaten or assault a tenant; change door locks; turn off the tenant's water, heat, or electricity; or confiscate a tenant's personal property. Follow lawful procedure. Illegal self-help can expose you to numerous types of personal injury lawsuits and criminal charges.

> **Never use illegal self-help tactics to evict a tenant.**

Maintain the Property

Let me repeat: To attract and retain topflight tenants, minimize complaints, and enhance the value of your property, carefully maintain your grounds and your buildings. In addition to preventive and corrective maintenance and repairs, you will schedule three other types of maintenance programs:

- ◆ *Custodial maintenance.* Assign someone the tasks of yard care, picking up litter, and washing windows. Keep your property neat and clean.
- ◆ *Cosmetic maintenance.* Periodically inspect the grounds, common areas, and rental units to freshen up their cosmetic appearance. Don't ignore peeling paint, carpet stains, countertop burns, and other types of wear and tear. Without consistent care, a property will soon appear run-down.
- ◆ *Safety and security.* Always keep your eyes open to spot problems of safety or security. Quickly repair broken stairs, lighting, locks, window latches, or doors. Make sure all smoke alarms work. Ask your tenants to call you immediately should they discover any potential threats to safety or security.

Process Move-Outs Smoothly

Alas, all good things must end. At some point, you will see your tenants move on. When that time comes, make sure that your move-out process includes the following steps.

Require Written Notice

Your lease should require your tenants to give you formal, written notice (typically 30 days, more or less) of their specific move-out date. This notice will give you time to get the word out to topflight prospects that the area's best landlord (you!) will soon have a unit available for some lucky tenant. Early notice will also give you time to line up and schedule contractors or tradespeople to make improvements and repairs to the unit.

Schedule a Final Walkthrough

Do not under any circumstances postpone your damage inspection of the unit until after the tenant has moved away. Always schedule a final walkthrough of the unit on the same day your tenants are loading up their moving van. Compare the unit's condition to your move-in checklist, photos, or video.

> **Settle damage claims the day the tenants move out.**

At that time, make every effort to settle any damage claims that you think the tenant should pay. If you've treated the tenants fairly throughout the time they've lived in your building, you usually can settle up without controversy.

Owners who run into move-out problems generally have made one or more of these errors:

♦ They have failed to maintain the property and try to stick the tenant with costs that were properly the obligation of the owner.

♦ They have not monitored the condition of the unit throughout the tenancy, and then during the final walk-through, allege all kinds of expensive damages.

♦ They try to charge tenants far more for cleaning or repairs than the owners will actually have to pay to correct the problem.

With infrequent exception, I have found that when I treat my tenants with respect and consideration throughout their tenancy, when I document their damages, and when I don't try to overcharge them, they readily honor their responsibility to cover the reasonable costs of repair.

Persistently Find Ways to Increase Your Cash Flow

Do you know the word *kaizen?* Tony Robbins popularized this Japanese term, signifying "continuous improvement." It means that you should persistently search for ways to improve. Few of us ever perform at the top of our game. Much of the time we get lazy. We turn off our creative impulses. We fail to see obvious opportunities. We achieve much less than we're capable of achieving.

Remember the Value Formula

Remember, every net $1,000 you add to your annual rent collections boosts the value of your property by at least $10,000 to $12,000. Every net $1,000 you eliminate from your operating expenses boosts the value of your property by $10,000 to $12,000.

$$V = \frac{\text{NOI (Rent collections less expenses)}}{\text{R (Cap rate)}}$$

Reread Chapters 13 and 14 at least once every several months. Keep all of your possibilities for improved cash flows clearly in view. Even if you're operating your properties today at peak performance, markets change.

> **Stay up to date with changes (opportunities) in the market.**

Over any six-month period, your competition can change. Your tenant segment may change their preferences. You might even discover new, more profitable tenant segments to serve. The most successful investors persistently adapt and refine their market strategies and management policies.

Regularly Refinance Your Properties

Because (in the early years of property ownership) mortgage interest costs eat up more of your rent collections than any other expense, stay in touch with several savvy mortgage brokers. Tell them about the costs and terms of your current financing. Tell them how long you plan to own the property.

Then ask these loan reps to notify you whenever a refinance might make you money. Slice your mortgage payments by, say, $500 a month and you add $6,000 a year to your cash flows.

Keep Trading Up

In his classic book, *How I Turned $1,000 into a Million in Real Estate in My Spare Time* (New York: Simon and Schuster, 1958), William Nickerson first bought a $10,000 property. After creating value with that property, Nickerson then traded up to a $40,000 property. He repeated his process of creating value and next traded up to a $150,000 multiunit apartment complex. After just 16 years, through the continuous process of creating value and trading up, Nickerson owned millions of dollars in properties.

Although today's prices in most areas of the country dwarf those of Nickerson's day, the technique of creating value and trading up still works. I've used it. Most of the professional investors I know have used it. Likewise, you can use it.

Creating value and trading up offers you the safest and surest path to building wealth in real estate. If you get started now, experience proves that within 16 years (or less) you, too, will enjoy a multimillion-dollar net worth. I wish you good luck and good fortune. Call me and let me know how you're doing at (800) 942-9304, extension 20691, or e-mail garye@stoprentingnow.com.

INTERNET APPENDIX

Throughout this book, I have referred you to a variety of websites that complement or expand upon the topics covered. For your convenience, I have listed below these and other websites by category.

City and Neighborhood Data

www.census.gov
http://stats.bls.gov
http://usacitylink.com
www.virtualrelocation.com
http://verticals.yahoo.com/cities
http://venus.census.gov
www.ojp.usdoj.gov.bjs
www.crime.org

Comp Sales

www.dataquick.com
www.propertyview.com
www.latimes.com
www.domania.com
www.iown.com
www.ocpa.gov

Credit Information

www.econsumer.equifax.com
www.experian.com
www.transunion.com
www.creditscoring.com
www.creditaccuracy.com
www.myfico.com
www.qspace.com
www.credit411.com
www.ftc.gov
www.creditinfocenter.com
www.fairisaac.com

Financial Calculators and Spreadsheets

www.loan-wolf.com
www.moneyweb.com
www.mortgagewizard.com
www.mortgage-minder.com
www.hsh.com

Foreclosures and Repos

www.brucebates.com
www.bankhomes.net
www.4close.com
www.all-foreclosure.com
www.homesteps.com
www.hud.gov
www.va.gov
www.bankreo.com
www.treas.gov
www.premierereo.com
www.fanniemae.com
www.bankofamerica.com

Home Improvement

www.hometime.com
www.michaelholigan.com

www.askbuild.com
www.hardware.com
www.bhglive.com
www.housenet.com

Home Inspection

www.ashi.com
www.creia.com

Homes for Sale

www.realtor.com
www.homeseekers.com
www.homeadvisor.com
www.cyberhomes.com
www.homes.com
www.bamboo.com
www.ipix.com
www.owners.com
www.efsbo.com
www.buyowner.com
www.fsbo.com
www.realfind.com

Insurance Information

www.cpcu.com
www.statefarm.com

Law Information

www.lectlaw.com
www.lexis.com
www.lawstar.net
www.nolo.com

Mortgage Applications

www.interest.com
www.mortgage101.com

www.mortgagequotes.com
http://mortgage.quicken.com
www.lendingtree.com
www.fhatoday.com
www.loanweb.com
www.mortgageauction.com
www.clnet.com
www.eloan.com
www.iown.com

Mortgage Information

www.loan-wolf.com
www.mortgageprofessor.com
www.hsh.com

Mortgage Providers (Underwriters)

www.fanniemae.com
www.homesteps.com
www.va.gov
www.hud.gov

Real Estate Information

www.inman.com/bruss
www.ired.com
www.stoprentingnow.com
www.ourfamilyplace.com
www.realtor.com
www.johntreed.com
www.arello.org

School Data

www.2001beyond.com
www.schoolmatch.com
www.schoolreport.com

With hundreds of thousands of websites related to real estate and mortgages, the above list only samples some of the most popular sites.

Nevertheless, if you've got the time and the will to sort through the data overload that the web now offers, you can certainly make a more informed investing and borrowing decision.

Still, beware. Many sites do not provide accurate data, nor does the data necessarily relate to your specific need. For example, neighborhood data and school data are plagued with inconsistencies, omissions, errors, and ill-defined measures. Don't accept web-based data as the last word. Check and verify all information. The web does not reduce your need to "walk and talk" the neighborhood; visit schools, shops, parks other facilities; physically view comparable sales; and drive areas you might like to search out "for sale" signs.

On a final note, I will admit that real estate investing can seem challenging at times. But persevere. You'll never regret owning. In the meantime, should you have questions about your investing, give me a call at (800) 942-9304 (X-20691) or e-mail me at garye@stoprentingnow.com. If you e-mail me, though, please include your address and phone number. I will respond one way or another.

Once again, I wish you the best and know that you can profit from the successes (and mistakes) of the thousands of people who in some way have contributed to the contents of this book. Good luck and good fortune.

INDEX